THE ENLIGHTENMENT

THE ENLIGHTENMENT

HISTORY OF AN IDEA

Vincenzo Ferrone

With a new afterword by the author
Translated by Elisabetta Tarantino

PRINCETON UNIVERSITY PRESS

PRINCETON AND OXFORD

The Library of Congress has cataloged the cloth edition as follows:

Ferrone, Vincenzo.
[Lezioni illuministiche]
The enlightenment : history of an idea / Vincenzo Ferrone;
translated by Elisabetta Tarantino.
pages cm
Includes index.
ISBN 978-0-691-16145-7 (hardcover : alk. paper)
1. Enlightenment. 2. Enlightenment—Historiography. I. Title.
B802.F4713 2015
001.09'033—dc23
2014015233

British Library Cataloging-in-Publication Data is available

The translation of this work has been funded by SEPS
Segretariato Europeo per le Pubblicazioni Scientifiche

Via Val d'Aposa 7—40123 Bologna—Italy
seps@seps.it—www.seps.it

This book has been composed in Minion Pro and ITC Avant Garde Gothic
Printed on acid-free paper. ∞

Printed in the United States of America

3 5 7 9 10 8 6 4 2

CONTENTS

IIIIIIIIIIIIIIIIIIIIIIIIII

INTRODUCTION

||||||||||||||||||||||||||

Living the Enlightenment

PARAPHRASING THE GREAT Karl Marx in the *Manifesto of the Communist Party*, one might say that a specter is haunting Europe: it is the specter of the Enlightenment. It looks sad and emaciated, and, though laden with honors, bears the scars of many a lost battle. However, it is undaunted and has not lost its satirical grin. In fact it has donned new clothes and continues to haunt the dreams of those who believe that the enigma of life is all encompassed within the design of a shadowy and mysterious god, rather than in the dramatic recognition of the human being's freedom and responsibility.

After the fall of the Berlin Wall in 1989, some thought that it was time to liquidate what was left of the heritage of the Enlightenment. Surely they could now, finally, lay to rest that ambitious and troublesome cultural revolution, a movement that in the course of the eighteenth century had overcome a thousand obstacles to overthrow the seemingly immutable tenets of *Ancien Régime* Europe. One could at last put paid to the fanciful Enlightenment notion of the emancipation of man through man, i.e., to the idea that human beings could become enfranchised by their own forces alone, including the deployment of knowledge old and new that had been facilitated by the emergence of new social groups armed with a formidable weapon: critical thought.

Sapere aude—dare to know. Come of age. Do not be afraid to think with your own head. Leave aside all ancient *auctoritates* and the viscous conditioning of tradition. Thus wrote the normally self-controlled Immanuel Kant in a moment of rare enthusiasm in 1784, citing the Enlightenment motto. However in our day, under the disguise of modern liberals, some eminent reactionaries have even entertained the dream that it might be possible to restore all the *Ancien Régime*'s reassuring certainties without firing a single shot. They would all come flooding back: God's rights (and therefore those of ecclesiastical hierarchies), inequality's prescriptive and natural character, legal sanction for the rights of the few, the primacy of duties over rights, the clash of communities and ethnicities against any cosmopolitan or universalistic mirage.

In fact, even though pain and injustice still persist and any hope of emancipation seems lost, if one peers closely into the dark clouds of our times a different picture begins to emerge. Those same epochal events of 1989 have had a liberating effect on the old and now sterile interpretative paradigms and imaginary philosophies of history that harsh reality has refuted. The storm raised by those events let through some faint rays of sunshine. The events themselves were positively marked by the end of ruthless communist dictatorships and by a toppling of the violent myth of class struggle, which had been conceived as a necessary tool through which to achieve the various stages of an imaginary material progress that gave no purchase to liberty and the rights of man. Now, that storm has rekindled our hope in a better future, moving us beyond countless illusions and recurring disappointments, it has given rise to new studies everywhere, and to the need for new inquiries into the Enlightenment. Today questions are posed that have never yet been asked about that profound cultural revolution, which sought to emancipate and enfranchise man, and whose width of horizon and long-term effects can be compared only to those of the rise of Christianity and its dissemination across the Western world.

We have finally started to untie the crucial knot constituted by the hoary old question of the link between the Enlightenment and the French Revolution—which had been a dogma and the beating heart of European historical consciousness until now. We are seeing the beginning of a new period in historiography under the banner of discontinuity. Historians are now free from the teleological bond, and from the multifarious ideological conditioning imposed by a powerful paradigm that had long coupled the ultimate meaning of the experience of the Enlightenment to the French Revolution in a deterministic and organic way. The Enlightenment, as a result, had been identified with the unstoppable dynamic of revolution that infected Western society, leading one to forget that the original impetus of the Enlightenment was towards reform, and obscuring the ways in which its specific forms and contents constantly oscillated between utopia and reform. This new historiographical period now faces the task of giving back dignity and an autonomy of meanings to the world of the Enlightenment *iuxta propria principia*. Contrary to the belief of historians of ideas, whose every reading is geared towards the final revolutionary outcome, that complex cultural system was made up of more than the circulation of subversive ideas within a circumscribed and elitist intellectual movement. It consisted also and primarily in the rise of a new civilization that was strongly rooted in society, as new research has clearly begun to show. The picture has started to emerge of an original culture that boasted a wide and solid diffusion and a thoroughly critical spirit, a culture that consisted in the production and consumption of new representations, institutions, values, practices, languages, and styles of thought: a new and polemically alternative way of thinking and of living everyday reality under the *Ancien Régime*. Hence the absolute centrality of the expression *living the Enlightenment*. The focus here is on a life experience, a brand new and original way of inhabiting the world by thinking and practicing in new and dramatically different terms the relationship between nature and culture, between being and having to be, between the challenges posed by the historical context and the range of possible responses to those challenges. This picture puts man firmly at its center, with his capabilities and his limitations, his growing and ever more tragic and acute awareness of his dramatic finitude, his need to constantly redefine the very foundations of the religious question, of social, political, and economic order, so as to give rise to what we now see as our modern civil society, a kind of society without which, at the time, no program of emancipation could be put into practice.

As early as the 1760s, a famous Enlightenment manifesto prefaced by Diderot to Boulanger's works quite rightly and proudly described the attempt that was then taking place to forge a new cultural identity in the Western world by changing the very course of history and making history with one's own hands: "One has talked of a *savage Europe*, a *pagan Europe*, a *Christian Europe*, and worse could be said still. But the time has finally come to talk about a *Europe of reason*."[1] This accurately summarized the work of those who were about to set their republican spirit against the despotic absolutism of the princes, against ancient forms of domination, against the social and economic system of the guilds, and the intolerance of authority and religion towards the rights of man.

Redefining the traditional chronology and geography of the Enlightenment in the Western world was indispensable to a new cultural history of eighteenth-century European society, and for this the so-called "late Enlightenment" has proved a crucial period, especially the last quarter of the century, and especially the years between the American and the French Revolutions of 1776 and 1789, respectively.

It is necessary to gain an understanding of that period in order to bring into focus the original and fundamental traits of that world of the Enlightenment, whose legacy would provoke in later generations the incandescent polemics and struggles that constitute one of the most important questions analyzed in this book. In those years, far from being restricted to a few persecuted intellectuals in love with abstract ideas, the Enlightenment in fact triumphed in all quarters, becoming the hegemonic culture of European élites: a resounding phenomenon *à la mode* with massive political and social impact over both supporters and adversaries. The language of the Enlightenment was adopted by both its friends and its enemies. Its ideas, values, and cultural practices affected academies, masonic lodges, social gatherings, university clubs, reading societies, even court politics. From St Petersburg to Philadelphia, from London to Naples, and from Paris to Berlin, in the provinces as well as in big capital cities, the culture of the Enlightenment placed the new language of the rights of man once and for all at the center of its republican conception of politics, a conception that was understood to require ever-wider participation in the government of the commonwealth. The Enlightenment saw to the constitutionalization of that language in written documents and its final transformation into *droits politiques*, as Condorcet would put it. It fostered the establishment of modern public opinion, the transformation of printing into the publishing industry, and the rise of new forms of political and social communication.

It was not only philosophers, scientists, sovereigns, and politicians of every rank, then, who experienced the Enlightenment and came to grips with a new style of thinking and new cultural practices. Painters, musicians, literary figures, and artists of every stature were affected. It is no surprise therefore that every European gazette reported with enthusiasm and admiration Voltaire's coronation in March 1778 at the *Comédie française* in Paris. Apart from rather belatedly and highly symbolically recognizing the importance of the famous figure himself and of the generation that had created the *Encyclopédie*, that accolade, granted by the *Ancien Régime,* also represented a clear passing of the mantle to a younger generation, that of Raynal and Condorcet, Filangieri and Pagano, Alfieri, Jefferson, Jovellanos, Goya, David, Lessing, Goethe, Beaumarchais, Mozart, and many others. In the decade before the great Revolution, while they were still very young men, these figures experimented with putting effectively into practice that peculiar and demanding Enlightenment humanism that had taken shape at the start of the century in polemical opposition to ancient Christian humanism.

In their paintings, music, novels, juridical and economic treatises, and plays, as well as, in some cases, in their direct engagement in civil and political matters, there is no sign of that abstract "enthronement of man" or of the individual subject that characterized the Enlightenment's epistemological project in Foucault's famous image. There is no hackneyed rehearsal, no working to an early death of ideas produced in the first half of the century and at the time of the *Encyclopédie*. There was, on the contrary, something that was totally new and original to these later decades of the Enlightenment: namely, a conscious

and passionate creative effort aimed at bringing about a fairer and more equitable society, made by man for man, an attempt to put into practice individual
rights, giving political space to what was the truly revolutionary discovery of
the natural right of man to pursue happiness as the ethical foundation for a
new universal morality. These men were faced with the crisis of the *Ancien Régime*. And the Regime was creaking in every one of its ancient joints under the
weight of huge economic changes, of the marked increase in commerce, and of
the first significant stages in a process of globalization that had begun with the
Seven Years' War (1756–1763)—the first real world war, the war that gave rise
to colonialism and modern empires.

Without a doubt, the defining characteristic of the late Enlightenment—and
the most positive aspect of its legacy to the Western world today—is the creation of a distinctive language of the rights of man, and the use of that language
as an instrument in its struggles, with an attendant politicization of intellectual life in all its aspects. However, subsequent positions immediately came up
against the bitter reality of those years. Conflicts were unavoidable, and this
specific period of the Enlightenment came to be characterized as deeply experimental and problematic, a time of inevitable contradictions, of greatness,
and misery. One might say that the late Enlightenment was not at all a part of
the historical construct we now identify as *modernity*, using the term to confer
a sense of something completed and definitive. It was, rather, the *laboratory of
modernity*. Although a lot of work still needs to be done in reconstructing this
fundamental historical phase, one could perhaps cite briefly some of the difficulties that have been encountered and the solutions that have been suggested.
This will perhaps give an idea of why the term "laboratory" is so appropriate.

How could one give the "rights of man" real credibility and impact in the
face of the exponential growth of the modern trade slave in the second half of
the eighteenth century? We should never forget that those subjective "rights"
could only lay claim to that name if a series of qualities and requirements were
also present, conditions that only a centuries-long process of stratification had
made possible: such rights had to be 1) *naturally inherent* in human beings as
such; 2) *equal* for all individuals, with no distinction of birth, census, national-
ity, religion, gender, or skin color; 3) *universal*, that is to say valid everywhere,
in every corner of the world; 4) *inalienable and imprescriptible* before the power
of any political or religious institution. One could scarcely imagine a greater
challenge to the political action and coherence of those European citizens who
were working with passion and intellectual honesty to spread the new political
language than the deportation of millions of African slaves mostly towards the
United States of America, the self-styled homeland of rights and freedom. It
was precisely thanks to an emphasis on the principle of inalienability that a few

scattered and ultimately harmless references to subjective rights in the state of nature, which in previous centuries had already been investigated by legal experts from the school of natural law, had been transformed by Enlightenment culture into a powerful political language capable of overthrowing the *Ancien Régime*. Now, for the first time, that culture came into conflict with the crude economic interests of both individuals and the colonial powers. A politics of values voiced by reformist thinkers ran up against reality and the politics of self-interest championed by the forces of conservatism.

On the other hand, contradictory signals were given by the rapid progress throughout the eighteenth century in the "human sciences," the crowning glory of a humanism that was determined to place the scientific revolution at the service of mankind, rather than vice versa as some late positivist ideas would later seem to imply. The discovery of the historical world, the rethinking of history from its foundations up, and its study from the point of view of the Enlightenment seemed to demonstrate that man's destiny was on this earth and consisted in liberty, and to establish also the ethical postulates of equality and of the existence of human rights as an effective foundation for a new universal and rational morality that had as its aim the happiness and well being of nations. At the same time, however, disciplines such as physiology and comparative anatomy, the rigorous scientific study of the human being, instead focused on the peculiarities and differences that distinguished individuals and species one from another, a mode of thought that more or less consciously supported early racist views. In the last quarter of the eighteenth century profound transformations affected even the great question of the Western world's religious identity, a question that arose following the definitive collapse of the *Respublica christiana* in the sixteenth century and then came to a boil at the beginning of the eighteenth century when the Enlightenment proposed its answers.

For instance, it was one thing for a circumscribed group of intellectuals to discuss atheism, as had happened up to now, quite another to arrange for its popular diffusion and propaganda via a publishing campaign like that attempted without great success by adherents of the Radical Enlightenment. It was one thing for the different Christian denominations and the great revealed religions to be split by bloody and incomprehensible theological controversies. It was another matter entirely to posit point blank the idea of establishing a new universal and natural religion common to all the peoples in the world, a religion that was rational—devoid of dogmas, churches, hierarchies, and priests—and that would take hold first among the élites and then among the rest of the population. This implied the existence of a God who was very far away and frankly uninterested in human events, and whose sole function was that of granting the ultimate guarantee for man's freedom and responsibility and none whatsoever for the authority of any Church.

Late Enlightenment humanism profited greatly from the solutions arrived at by Italian and French *libertins* in the sixteenth and seventeenth centuries, by Dutch and English freethinkers, and by Voltaire and Rousseau. However, it also went further. It did not just step up the fight against the *Infâme*, that is to say against the betrayal of the authentic Gospel message of love and charity, a betrayal perpetrated by historically realized Christianity and by the inquisitorial violence exercised by a Church that invoked the Donation of Constantine, and one corrupted by the exercise of power, as well as by Luther and Calvin's fanaticism and intolerance. Through novels, paintings, plays, and musical works, Enlightenment humanism also took it upon itself to penetrate the drama of the human condition, the implacable presence of evil, and the need to live a religious experience in some way so as to give meaning to human existence. The struggle for tolerance and the individual's right to freedom derived vital momentum precisely from those first crude analyses of the human being's dignity and potentialities, of man's limitations and finitude as well as his iniquity and will for power. A clear-cut separation between politics and religion and between Church and State had been advocated by Locke and Voltaire, who in their writings provocatively reintroduced the evangelical maxim, "Render unto Caesar the things that are Caesar's, and unto God the things that are God's." That separation finally became a matter tenet of constitutional order, passionately supported by jurists such as Filangieri, politicians like Jefferson, and such literary figures as Lessing. Rousseau's stipulation that religious sentiment belonged within one's heart, while the public sphere should be given over to the construction of a new civic Christian religion that was tolerant and unflinching in its sacralization of the principle of sociability and of human rights, became the primary task of Masonic Lodges and of admirers of Spinoza's pantheism and his sacralization of nature.

In the late Enlightenment, this new humanism, bent on finding on earth the best conditions likely to safeguard the individual's natural right to the pursuit of happiness, also began to address in concrete terms the problem of social rights. It examined the question of how to guarantee work and education, and how to safeguard everyone's right to live in the face of ever stronger attacks launched against the corporative system in the name of freedom by the same Enlightenment circles, attacks that provided early signs of the rise of what we now call the market economy. Despite those first few difficult and contradictory solutions, which saw different sets of rights opposed to one another, the late Enlightenment was nevertheless a real and still unexplored laboratory of modernity. In fact, it bequeathed to later centuries something extremely important: values, ideals, cultural practices, languages and representations that—as we stressed at the beginning of this introduction—still bother those who nowadays dream of an impossible return to the logics of the *Ancien Régime*.

Those values consist in the construction of a universal morality founded on recognizing the common identity of all human beings, on equal rights, on the diffusion of a spirit of tolerance, on a non-arrogant use of reason as an instrument to ensure peaceful relationships among human beings and to keep at bay those terrible monsters created by our own mind that were so admirably illustrated by the great Goya. They also issue a solemn warning to all religions never to forget the centrality and dignity of man, or to transform him into a mere cog in God's design. These values remain important components of a possible life program and of the meaning of existence for all men of good will.

This book was written in part to defend this noble legacy against recurring attacks from the enemies of the Enlightenment, in the awareness that the search for historical truth can and must still have a public function. It consists in the first two lectures I read at the Collège de France in 2005 as part of a course entitled *Les Lumières dans l'Europe d'Ancien Régime entre histoire et historiographie*. Two other lectures, on the rights of man and Vittorio Alfieri's political and intellectual experiences, are to be published separately.[3] In the chapters of this book I have sought to rethink the historical experience of the Enlightenment as a whole, from different points of view, keeping well in mind its irreducible vitality and the ever more urgent need to clarify its authentic meaning in face of the repeated attempts to manipulate and obfuscate it that have taken place in the course of the centuries down to our own time. The opportunity I was generously given by my Parisian colleagues seemed to propel me specifically in that direction.

Because of the Collège's history and the nature of its audience, which is not made up exclusively of eminent colleagues and specialists, its invited scholars are required not only to present the results of their research, but, if possible, also to verify the applicability of those results to the contemporary public sphere. To that effect, I thought it would be useful to compare and even polemically contrast the point of view of the historian and that of the philosopher in the genesis and the very manner of their thinking about the Enlightenment. This would, I hoped, allow me to clearly distinguish research hypotheses from ideologically biased positions and from those results that are now generally accepted by the scholarly community. The decision to adopt this way of proceeding matured slowly in the course of my thirty years' work on this subject. Its first glimmerings appeared as far back as my early formation at the University of Turin Faculty of Letters.

Ever since that distant day in July 1977 when I handed in my dissertation on a French eighteenth-century topic to Franco Venturi just before my oral examination, I realized that there was something singular in the way he viewed the Enlightenment, something that deserved to be investigated further. As he welcomed me smiling on his doorstep, without ceremony because "that's how we do things among Enlightenment people"—those were his very words, which I shall never forget—that great scholar enrolled me without further ado into the eternal Enlightenment party. Little did he know that he was in fact opening up for me a huge epistemological problem. Did it really make sense to allow past and present to merge in that way, with only apparent irony, as though there was indeed a perennial philosophy of the Enlightenment? Behind that kind of "lay baptism" there must be something more than a whimsical attitude and the recognition of the persistence of a glorious legacy from the past. It was a long time before I came across a first answer to that question. I was working on Benedetto Croce and the formation of Italian historical consciousness in the twentieth century. In his 1938 book *La storia come pensiero e come azione*, Croce, oscillating as usual between Kant and Hegel, concisely defined the Enlightenment as an ideal and eternal category of the spirit, a type of abstract rationalism that "is on the one hand a perpetual form of the human spirit and one of its necessary arms, and on the other has given its name to a very vigorous and productive epoch of European life."[2] One could not have hoped for a better definition of what in the following pages I call *the paradigm of the Centaur*; that is to say of the way in which philosophers in thinking of the Enlightenment mix together history and philosophy. Although he had little time for literary scholars and philosophers and proudly claimed for himself the title of historian, Venturi remained ever fascinated by Croce's remark. And he was not alone. Much of the current debate seems unable to break the spell of the Centaur—and not only in Italy.

This is why the first essay presented here spends quite a lot of effort on examining this paradigm's genealogy and its huge relevance to historians' research hypotheses, as well as on tracing how scholars have progressively focused on the Enlightenment as the leading philosophical issue of modernity, a key in their search for the ultimate foundation of man's very nature, i.e., of the subject. I then examine the most important and cogent solutions to the problem put forward in Europe, following developments up to the current unexpected metamorphoses of this issue, as it turns from a philosophical into a theological matter. Here the focus is on the analyses offered by eminent Catholic scholars, and especially by Joseph Ratzinger. Those analyses followed from the process of deconstruction of the Enlightenment carried out by so-called postmodern philosophers, and above all from the radical changes in the historical context caused by totalitarianism, the Holocaust, and the Second Vatican Council's so-called "anthropological turn."

The second of the essays in this volume takes issue with those public figures who take into consideration only the philosophical reading of the Enlightenment, thus leaving the door open to misleading interpretations of an ideological and political nature that go far astray of the historical truth. Accordingly, I have attempted to take stock of our current knowledge of the historical phenomenon of the Enlightenment as a cultural revolution within the *Ancien Régime*. This analysis of the state of the question was conducted in a critical spirit and with an awareness that new generations of historians must finally see through easy teleological shortcuts and abandon political myths, such as those of a link between the Enlightenment and the French Revolution, or the myths of an imaginary organic tie between the Enlightenment's way of conceiving science as solely the servant of man and the positivist era, an era that was in fact characterized by entirely different positions from those of the Enlightenment. Above all, our new generations should finally renounce those historiographical nationalisms, based as they are on ideologies that have caused so much grief in the last century. The new united Europe that is on the rise badly needs to find again its authentic roots within eighteenth-century cosmopolitanism, tolerance, liberty and, more generally, within that notion of the rights of man that Enlightenment culture promoted as the proper political language of the modern and as a legitimate existential aspiration for all people of the earth.

ACKNOWLEDGMENTS

From the early years of my long journey through the world of the Enlightenment I have been fortunate in being able to count on the expertise and patient friendship of Raffaele Ajello, Elvira Chiosi, Massimo Firpo, Luciano Guerci and Marisa Perna. I should like to extend to them my most sincere and warmest thanks. I have also benefited from the hospitality and the rich library holdings of institutions such as the Fondazione Einaudi and the Fondazione Firpo in Turin, the Ecole Normale Supérieure in Paris, and Princeton's Institute for Advanced Study, where in 2004 I enjoyed Jonathan Israel's unstinting hospitality. All of these institutions contributed much to the intellectual development and to the results of the research presented in this volume. Finally, I am grateful to Giuseppe Rutto, Franco Motta, and Gerardo Tocchini for their kind help in the final revision of this text.

This book is dedicated to three teachers and very dear friends to whom I am most deeply indebted as a historian and as a scholar of the Enlightenment: Margaret Candee Jacob, Daniel Roche, and Giuseppe Ricuperati.

V. F.
Bonzo, Graian Alps
August 2009

PART I

|||||||||||||||||||||||

THE PHILOSOPHERS' ENLIGHTENMENT

Thinking the Centaur

1

IIIIIIIIIIIIIIIIIIIIIIIII

HISTORIANS AND PHILOSOPHERS

The Peculiarity of the Enlightenment
as Historical Category

WHAT DO WE KNOW about the Enlightenment? Quite a lot, it would seem. The number of studies on this subject from every part of the world is extensive and growing constantly.[1] In the twentieth century a lot of effort was devoted to the analysis of an "Enlightenment question," which proved pivotal in the study of the rise of modern European civilization. On the plus side, this produced new insights, highlighted several sensitive points, brought to the fore neglected or even hitherto unknown personages and facts. But there was a downside. These studies often failed to break free of past schemes and modes of analysis, which were informed by ideological prejudice or by so blatant an apologetic intent that they were capable only of rehearsing well-known themes. Cultural and political battles of an exceptionally intense and passionate character have been fought over the last few centuries for and against the Enlightenment. Our new-born century therefore has the difficult task of rethinking the Enlightenment: this involves investigating its meaning and the many historical forms that it has taken in Western civilization, summing up and reviewing current knowledge, and separating the old from the new, all the while keeping to a minimum the prejudices and spurious influences that constantly tend to contaminate our search for truth and frustrate efforts at gaining a scientific understanding of the past.

One way of achieving these goals might be to investigate both the profound differences and the important points of contact and reciprocal influences between the views of the Enlightenment held by philosophers and those held by historians. This could in fact prove the precious red thread that will help solve many a problem and aid a new generation of historiographers in bringing about the renewal of their discipline that is nothing less than their duty. The starting point has to be an awareness of the double nature of this eighteenth-century epistemological paradigm, caught between history and philosophy, which in turn leads to a discussion of its unique historiographical character.

The Enlightenment, a kind of conceptual Centaur,[2] is unlike any other traditional historical category, different, for example, from humanism, the Renaissance, the Baroque, and Romanticism, which are defined by their philosophical origin to a much lesser extent.[3] The Enlightenment expressly defines itself on a critical and philosophical level. It was, in fact, the first cultural phenomenon expressly recognized by its contemporaries through the name that it gave itself. At the same time, by this very act of self-identification, the Enlightenment also revolutionized contemporary notions of universal history and of historical time, effectively giving rise to the modern Western consciousness of time and launching a debate that still engages us today because it coincides to a large extent with the ongoing investigation into what constitutes modernity.[4] Given the complexity of the issues at stake, let us take one thing at a time.

To call Hegel the "father of the Enlightenment" may seem surprising and even paradoxical, but it appears less so if we consider the history of philosophical thought and the dominant influence of Hegel's interpretation on the way in which many European thinkers see the Enlightenment, i.e., within a dialectical system, as thinking reality, a simultaneously logical and historical category of the phenomenology of spirit. And yet, setting aside the specific case of Hegel and his importance for historical research, to which we shall return later, it was undoubtedly philosophers who first taught historians to think of the Enlightenment as a specific concept and category within the study of the rise of modernity. Thus a gauntlet was thrown down. It was claimed that no effective discussion of the historical dimension of this subject could proceed without both a clear, precise, and theoretically well-founded idea of the nature of the Enlightenment, and an awareness as well of the fact that historical events are not possible and therefore not thinkable without linguistic acts.[5]

In fact, this peculiarity of the Enlightenment as a category in the history of Western culture becomes especially obvious when we consider the way in which eighteenth-century thinkers like Montesquieu, Voltaire, Hume, Gibbon, and many others redefined universal history and the very idea of historical knowledge through the introduction of the radically new concept of a secularized "historical time." That concept was based on the distinction—cultural and, even more, anthropological—between past and future, experience and expectation.

No one really subscribes any longer to the nineteenth-century condemnation of Enlightenment historiography as "anti-historical," a view born mostly out of political and ideological motives. Nowadays it would be difficult to refute Reinhart Koselleck's assertion, in the wake of Wilhelm Dilthey's famous rehabilitation of the Enlightenment,[6] that "[o]ur modern concept of history is the outcome of Enlightenment reflection on the growing complexity of 'history in general'," i.e., of history finally considered *per se*, history in the collective singular, an autonomous entity not linked to any object or subordinate to any subject.[7]

In the course of the eighteenth century a long and complicated process that had begun in the middle of the sixteenth century finally came to a head. It saw the emergence in people's consciousness of the idea that they were living in new times, times that were completely different from any previous epoch: a "modern" era, characterized both by its otherness from the past, which was now being critically reviewed, and by its ability to see the present as new in so far as it contained the seeds of the future. Many started to talk about modern history as a time when nothing was stable any more: the very term "modern" derived from *modus*, by which was meant concrete reality's constant state of flux, the accelerated transition of every thing.[8] Accordingly, in his *Essai sur les moeurs*, Voltaire wrote of a "histoire ancienne" that preceded the "histoire moderne," as well as of "temps modernes" and the "progrès de l'esprit humain," thus confirming the *importance* of certain formulae that had by then become current in historical discourse. In 1765 Voltaire also invented the phrase "philosophie de l'histoire," through which he interpreted historical events once and for all in a way that diverged radically from Christian tradition, i.e., from the tradition first developed by Augustine that was still being applied in its fundamentally religious sense by Bossuet in his 1681 *Discours sur l'histoire universelle*.[9] In other words, at the end of the eighteenth century, the Enlightenment opposed a brand new *philosophy of history* to a centuries-old *theology of history*, thus ringing the death knell for that reading of the future as a providential plan validated by prophecy that was one of the central tenets of Christian thought and one of the bases of the Church's cultural system.

This process had begun in the previous century, when the politics and logic of power of the absolutist state had first undermined the power of the Church over people's consciences and appropriated the right to make predictions about the future based on reason rather than faith, thus substituting prophecy with prognosis. In the wake of that shift, the vast historical scenarios built by the Enlightenment completed the secularization of that theologically based eschatological time that had been expounded with great subtlety by Augustine in his *City of God*, replacing it now with a time created by man and nations planning their earthly future. Time then became something more than mere chronological form encompassing all histories in their cyclical course: it turned into a dynamic force in its own right, acquiring a *historical quality* of its own. History was no longer *inside* time but *through* time.[10]

All this of course constituted a great epistemological revolution. Gone was the "naive realism" of the Ciceronian *historia magistra vitae*, of history as chronicle and a static collection of exempla, as a never-changing catalogue and *speculum vitae humanae* validated only through witness accounts. In came prospective models, the discovery of the point of view as a necessary cognitive element that plays an entirely legitimate and even decisive part in our modern concept of historical knowledge. The works of the Enlightenment were, in contrast, informed by specific ideological and philosophical stances, among them the idea of a stage-by-stage development of civilizations that enabled thinking about mankind's progress as a whole. Thanks to these works historians discovered that in order to capture history *per se* the epistemological process could not rely solely on source criticism, which, though it remained a fundamental element, "would no longer be so central as it was to antiquarian forms of erudition. Instead, historians needed to recognize philosophy's heuristic role and to accept the idea of history as constantly liable to rewriting, a *filia temporis* to be pursued both with critical and philological instruments and by formulating "points of view" and historical judgments that themselves would be subject to the influence of the times.[11]

The ultimate import of this revolution in Western thought was admirably synthesized by Goethe: "There remains no doubt these days that world history has from time to time to be rewritten." The same conviction was expressed by Hegel: "History's spiritual principle is the sum total of all possible perspectives."[12] It is within this intellectual context that our modern concept of the Enlightenment began to develop. This unique Centaur, with its double nature, both historical and philosophical, would soon become fundamental in the study of a modernity that had newly entered Western history and must now create its own self-consciousness and its own norm.[13]

2

||||||||||||||||||||||||

KANT: *WAS IST AUFKLÄRUNG?*

The Emancipation of Man through Man

IN 1784, KANT published a short essay putting forward an "Idea for a Universal History from a Cosmopolitan Point of View" in the journal *Berlinische Monatsschrift*. The article offered a good synthesis of the search for meaning or purpose in the historical process as carried out by Kant's contemporaries, and above all of the growing importance in that regard of a new cultural phenomenon that German scholars were beginning to call the *Aufklärung*.

In the essay Kant distinguished clearly between the traditional "work of practicing empirical historians," which consisted in a mere narrative of events (*Historie*), and the effort to draft instead an "[i]dea of world history, which is to some extent based upon an a priori principle" and is philosophical in kind (*Geschichte*).[1] The principle in question was embodied in a cosmopolitan perspective of the fundamental unity of mankind, which, despite all the vicissitudes it underwent, nonetheless showed a constant propensity towards "progress." Proof of this was to be sought within a view of universal history that wove together nature and morality, being and having to be, biological determinism, and the liberty of man. That evidence was provided both by the laws of nature as delineated by Bonnet, Haller, and Blumenbach in their research on the epigenesis and preformation of species, and by the real meaning behind the way in which the French Revolution had burst onto the European scene. Despite the Jacobean Terror and the many "atrocities" it engendered, that radical event remained for Kant an obvious historical sign of mankind's moral disposition to feel a positive kind of enthusiasm and to participate in the collective construction of a moral ideal tending towards progress and the good, and towards the defense of liberty and the rights of the individual: "For such a phenomenon in human history *is not to be forgotten*, because it has revealed a tendency and faculty in human nature for improvement."[2]

From his first essay on the idea of universal history from a cosmopolitan perspective onwards, Kant often mentioned the "enlightenment," attributing to it the function of the engine and fundamental condition for progress, without however giving a more precise definition of its contents. He simply highlighted the importance of the action exercised on mankind by this process of "continued enlightenment." That process determined the kind of moral behavior that was at the basis of a "universal civic society which administers law among men," a society that therefore puts in place constitutions and treaties capable of ensuring liberty, peace, security, and rights within and outside individual states. Although man in himself (being made of "crooked wood") at the individual level all too often remained enslaved to his own tendency to evil, the observation of nature showed instead that, as a species, mankind was capable of achieving the purpose of a "universal cosmopolitan condition" that could guarantee the rights of every human being on earth, without distinctions or favoritism.[3] And that was due precisely to the action of the Enlightenment. As Kant explained, nature "needs a perhaps unreckonable series of generations, each of which passes its own enlightenment to its successor in order finally to bring the seeds of enlightenment to that degree of development in our race which is completely suitable to nature's purpose."[4] Those seeds were indestructible. Universal history bore witness to the fact that, despite setbacks, wars, and all kinds of horrors, there remained a certain "plus," "a germ of enlightenment [. . .] left to be further developed by this overthrow" through which "a higher level was thus prepared."[5]

A few months later, in the same Berlin journal, Kant returned to this subject, which was by now at the center of an intense dispute, with another article, entitled "Beantwortung der Frage: Was ist Aufklärung?" (An Answer to the Question: What is Enlightenment) Here he described the Enlightenment as a precise modality of the exercise of reason, which was animated by a strong "spirit of freedom" and intimately connected with mankind's natural need for knowledge: a cultural practice, to use a modern phrase, able to guarantee "the progress of mankind toward improvement" through the "freedom to make public use of one's reason at every point." However, this attitude led to consequent actions, with grave and subversive consequences with respect to the *Ancien Régime*. Those consequences were not ignored by Kant, who however certainly did not stress them, for fear of causing too much alarm. They consisted, for instance, in the need to break with the primacy of tradition as moral guidance, to critique the very foundations of current existence, to fearlessly challenge the centuries-old domination of *auctoritates* of every kind and in every field, in order to assert man's right to the pursuit of happiness.

In Kant's concise depiction, the Enlightenment was nothing other than a great act of courage, a passionate invitation never to be afraid of emancipation. It represented

> . . . man's release from his self-incurred tutelage. Tutelage is man's inability to make use of his understanding without direction from another. Self-incurred is this tutelage when its cause lies not in lack of reason but in lack of resolution and courage to use it without direction from another. *Sapere aude!* "Have courage to use your own reason!"—that is the motto of enlightenment.[6]

Seen in this way, as both the right and duty of man's emancipation through man, the exercise and cultural practice of the Enlightenment could not be denied at any time or in any place in universal history. To deny was "to injure and trample on the rights of mankind," to hamper "the progress of mankind toward improvement." As Kant pointed out, "An age cannot bind itself and ordain to put the succeeding one into such a condition that it cannot extend its [. . .] knowledge." To that effect, he clearly explained what limitations were acceptable in the exercise of liberty. "The public use of one's reason must always be free, and it alone can bring about enlightenment among men." *Private* use, in the sense of the use of reason at work or in a public office, was a different matter. Obedience could legitimately be required of both clergymen and state officials, to quote just two examples, when they were exercising their ministry or carrying out their job. In those cases, it was acceptable to limit the subjects' liberty, expecting them to adhere to directives and regulations. However, those same subjects were absolutely free when they exercised their right/duty to criticize and used their reason publicly by expressing their opinion. No censorship was ever licit towards scholars, who were members of a virtual Republic of letters that was seen as an ideal life model for mankind as a whole. As Kant would stress, *Caesar non est supra grammaticos* (Caesar is not above the grammarians).

It would seem, then, that in the field of politics and legislation, or "lawgiving," the right to criticize had been accepted by rulers themselves, who now found it to their advantage "to treat men, who are now more than machines, in accordance with their dignity." The battle was still to be fought, on the other hand, where religion was concerned. In that arena the weight of tradition and of the past, intolerance, and the principle of authority still held sway, preventing the onset of that modern era which elsewhere was already aimed full-thrust into the future. Paul's peremptory invitation, in his *Letter to the Romans*, to believe in the words of Jesus if one wished to be saved contrasted powerfully with Horace's *sapere aude*, Kant's chosen motto for the Enlightenment. Kant expresses clearly his awareness of both the difficulty and the inevitability of a clash between faith in God and the Enlightenment's exercise of reason:

I have placed the main point of enlightenment [*Aufklärung*]—the escape of men from their self-incurred tutelage—chiefly in matters of religion because our rulers have no interest in playing the guardian with respect to the arts and sciences and also because religious incompetence is not only the most harmful but also the most degrading of all.[7]

It would be impossible to express better the gulf between the exhortation to believe and the directive to think with one's own head and hurry along the road towards emancipation.

At the end of his discussion, after finally attempting to clarify what he meant by "Enlightenment," Kant could not in any way escape the crucial question, Do we now live in an *enlightened age*? His answer to that question, so eagerly awaited by his contemporaries, was: No. The eighteenth century was simply "*an age of enlightenment*":

As things now stand, much is lacking which prevents men from being, or easily becoming, capable of correctly using their own reason in religious matters with assurance and free from outside direction. But, on the other hand, we have clear indications that the field has now been opened wherein men may freely deal with these things and that the obstacles to general enlightenment or the release from self-imposed tutelage are gradually being reduced. In this respect, this is the age of enlightenment, or the century of Frederick.[8]

In this passage Kant is then stressing that the Enlightenment was not a particular and unrepeatable historical era. The conditions for a free and public use of reason had already somehow occurred in the past and could occur again in the future. Neither was it a logical, historically determined thought category, since the forms of reason were always the same, and so were its potentialities and limitations. The Enlightenment was rather a specific condition in which reason was exercised. It was a historical condition that needed to be created, an extraordinary state of things and at the same time absolutely necessary to guarantee mankind's progress towards an ideal future enlightened age. This suggestive representation opened the way to a perspective that is still today quite widespread. It is the view of the Enlightenment as above all cultural practice, political myth, progressive ideology, a perennial philosophy of man as master of his own destiny, a utopia to be realized in each latest "neo-Enlightenment,"[9] and the emancipation of man through man. After all, this discussion was positioned as almost Kant's concluding reflection in an extraordinary overall rethinking of the individual, of his autonomy, and of the limits of his knowledge. This is why his ideas have been so powerful, influential, and persistent in time. After the astounding successes of Galileo and Newton's scientific revolution, and the resulting effects of emancipation on man's life, metaphysics had become in his eyes something very different from what it was in the past, in line with what Diderot, Rousseau, Filangieri and many others had insistently called for in their writings. In 1798 Kant wrote as a final synthesis, almost, of his entire work, the following clear statement:

> I have learned from the *Critique of Pure Reason* that philosophy is not a science of representations, concepts and Ideas, or a science of all the sciences, or anything else of this sort. It is rather a science of man, of his representations, thoughts and actions: it should present all the components of man both as he is and as he should be—that is, in terms both of his natural functions and of his relations of morality and freedom.[10]

3

||||||||||||||||||||||||

HEGEL

The Dialectics of the Enlightenment
as Modernity's Philosophical Issue

AS WE KNOW, KANT was not the only thinker who, at the end of the eighteenth century, posed questions on the nature of the Enlightenment in relation to universal history. A furious debate arose in the *Berlinische Monatsschrift* in which several famous authors took part.[1] A deluge of pamphlets and articles was unleashed, confirming the urgency and relevance of the question of the historical self-awareness of the modern age as achieved specifically through an investigation of the nature of the Enlightenment. It is not by chance that the Jesuits, always quick to understand the political consequences implicit in intellectual confrontations, invented for the occasion the category of a *katholische Aufklärung*, a Catholic Enlightenment that was polemically opposed to the *falsche Aufklärung*, or "false Enlightenment," of Kant's supporters.[2] And yet, however interesting, that debate soon faded and was forgotten, replaced by the far longer-lived and more controversial formulations on this topic put forward by Friedrich Hegel.

At the beginning of the nineteenth century, between the Napoleonic period and the age of Restoration, it was Hegel who laid the foundations of what we have called the philosophers' Enlightenment, which still largely dominates our discussions. He did so in the name of a concept of philosophy entirely different from that of Kant and other Enlightenment figures. He shifted the focus from the primacy of the subject, which was seen almost as though looking at itself in the mirror, to that of the spirit, the maker of reality. Hegel denied that man, in his autonomous finitude, could be at the center of theoretical interests. He placed the emphasis on the organic union of man and universe, within which eternal nature operates, rather than on an abstractly determined individual tending towards his own happiness. Whereas Kant had attempted to create a philosophy of reflection seen mainly as the "science of man," Hegel—true to his Lutheran education—saw philosophy instead in terms of the phenomenology of the spirit, i.e., as a new and original science that brought back to life the *Creator Spiritus* from the Johannine Christian tradition and the Trinitarian view of God, thus capturing knowledge in its becoming through the various stages of the spirit's dialectical self-realization in history. The common interest in the authentic meaning of the onset of the modern era in universal history, a topic that had fascinated the eighteenth century, became a crucial point in Hegel's philosophy. It was the philosophical issue *par excellence*, and it linked together, indissolubly, modernity's self-understanding and the Enlightenment's self-determination, understood in its profound nature as dialectical movement.[3]

Hegel did not in the least share the *Aufklärer's* disregard for the problems and costs of the modern, for the catastrophic discontinuities and fractures wrought by the new era in breaking with the past and its traditions. How could one, by a simple act of will, judge the past, erase it, and place the subject at center stage? Viewing the modern era as nothing other than a positive move in the inevitable course of progress seemed to him dangerous, and above all unilateral. He could not subscribe to the idea of a present that was totally open towards the future and indifferent to the terrible crises brought about by a rift with the past (which, among other things, gave rise to the very need for philosophy) or to a present indifferent to the spirit's estrangement and to its unhappy consciousness, both processes caused by the determination of the principle of subjectivity in its historical happening.

The French Revolution and the slaughters produced by the Napoleonic wars certainly left little room for an entirely serene view of reality and of the destiny of mankind. The life of the spirit, in all its aspects, could not be contained wholly within the principle of subjectivity that had forged the character of modernity. That much was obvious. From Descartes's *cogito ergo sum* to Kant's absolute self-consciousness, this principle had expressed itself in a variety of forms: individualism, an "atomistic subjectivity," a progressive disenchantment and objectivization of nature brought about by the scientific revolution, the free exercise of one's right to criticize as prelude to political action, and a new self-consciousness of becoming. In fact, Hegel knew perfectly well that the positive perception of progress ingrained in the modern era was increasingly accompanied by a general sense of crisis, and by a profound existential unease in those who witnessed with dismay how the demise of the *Ancien Régime* went hand in hand with the demolition of centuries-old customs and traditions. In opposition to Kant's philosophy, a philosophy founded on the reflection of the subject on itself and on the autonomy of reason with respect to reality, with all the attendant consequences in terms of breaks with the past and forms of estrangement in the present, Hegel propounded his own philosophy of unification and "conciliation." The latter is a key word in Hegel's science of the phenomenology of spirit, which is founded on two premises: the concept of the Absolute Spirit and that of "consciousness [that] has stepped out of the totality, that is, [. . .] the split into being and not-being, concept and being, finitude and infinity." The task of philosophy became then to unite these two premises, striving towards conciliation, which is seen not as an art of the mind, but rather as the mind reproducing the spirit's essence in its happening. That is to say, "to posit being in non-being, as becoming; to posit dichotomy in the Absolute, as its appearance; to posit the finite in the infinite, as life."[4]

Within this framework, dominated as it is by an entirely immanent standpoint and by a view of reason as the unity of the I and reality, the self-understanding of the real meaning of the Enlightenment within the phenomenology of spirit manifested itself as critique and dialectic of the Enlightenment itself; that is to say, in the precise identification of the Enlightenment as a stage and logical "moment" in the life of the spirit and, at the same time, as a decisive era in universal history. Hegel's phenomenology aimed at exposing knowledge in its becoming, at illustrating the various stages of the spirit's unfolding by examining moments, figures, degrees, and stages in the tormented dialectical course through which the spirit attained the status of pure knowledge, i.e., of Absolute Spirit "that knows itself as spirit." Furthermore, this new science of knowledge examined on each occasion one of the various forms assumed by the spirit (i.e., its ethical, cultural, moral, or religious form), as it enacted the mechanisms of consciousness, self-consciousness, and of both observing reason and acting reason. Thus, the Enlightenment broke onto the historical scene as a particular crisis phase, as the world of self-estranged spirit, a dramatic final phase in the progressive domination of culture viewed as the estrangement of the natural being.

Within the dialectical movement that saw the spirit's implacable and constant three-stage progression from in-itself to for-itself and in-and-for-itself, the Enlightenment embodied the logical figure of pure Insight (the absolute self), i.e., the final degree of the principle of subjectivity: abstract reason empty of all content, whose final development consists in becoming itself its own content. Highlighting a decisive point in his exposition, Hegel stresses how the Enlightenment "completes the alienation of Spirit in this realm, too, in which that Spirit takes refuge and where it is conscious of an unruffled peace." The Enlightenment achieves this by waging war against its opposite, the counterpart of "pure insight," i.e., "Faith as the alien realm of *essence* lying in the beyond." It persists in that war to the point of upsetting "the housekeeping of Spirit in the household of Faith by bringing into that household the tools and utensils of *this* world, a world which that Spirit cannot deny is its own, because its consciousness likewise belongs to it."[5]

The Enlightenment undertook a fierce and dramatic struggle against religious Faith, a fanatical "extirpation of error" carried out through the unmasking of superstitions and miracles, setting itself in opposition to popular beliefs, the clergy, and any kind of Revelation founded on tradition.[6] And in order to win that struggle its proponents did not hesitate to lie and to undervalue Faith's very reasons, since they believed it to be nothing more than a form of "error and prejudice" (333). The irreducible opposition between human law and divine law thus became one of many examples of the rifts and of the general crisis brought about by an implacable no-holds-barred "struggle," (ibid.) fought between two unilateral moments in the spirit's consciousness; i.e., Faith and the Enlightenment, each unable to become reconciled with the other. One need only say that pure Insight, that is to say the protagonism of the self-estranged subject, within the perspective of the "purposiveness" of reflexive reason (338–39), did not hesitate to reduce religion to an entirely earthly and universal category: it was a category that it had itself invented—that of Faith as "supremely useful" (343), nothing more than an object or commodity. Consequently, however, the same destiny awaited man, who went from being the world's great master and exploiter to being used himself. Hegel describes in some particularly evocative pages the final victory of the Enlightenment, whereby "heaven is transplanted to earth below" (355). However, precisely because of the logics inherent in the dialectic of a restless spirit that can never pause in its unstoppable race towards absolute knowledge, that state of things was liable to experience a rapid dialectical reversal as new moments and figures manifested, that were destined to expose the dark side of the principle of subjectivity and the conflicts caused by its ephemeral triumph.

Once victory has been achieved, with the attendant pollution of "its *spiritual* consciousness with mean thoughts of *sensuous* reality" (348), according to Hegel the "Enlightenment is caught up in the same internal conflict that it formerly experienced in connection with faith, and it divides itself into two parties" (350):[7] on one side are those who adhere to atheist materialism, on the other are the supporters of deism and of a civic and natural religion without any Churches, who are determined to own and use themselves that principle of faith to which they had previously been fiercely opposed. However, outside, in the background to that struggle, the spirit's estrangement persisted as an unresolved problem arising from the "blemish of an unsatisfied yearning" of the Enlightenment itself "as *action* and *movement*, in *going beyond* its individual self" (349). Hegel pointed out that the universal aspect that was common to both "parties" of the Enlightenment was "the pure Notion as *implicitly* existent, or *pure thought within itself.*" Both parties had in fact "arrived at the Notion found in Descartes's metaphysics, that being and thought are, *in themselves*, the same [. . .] that *thought* is *thinghood*, or *thinghood* is *thought*" (352).

This is why Insight was determined to transform pure thought into pure thing, and to objectify itself into the world of the Useful. It also explains why a "new shape of consciousness, *absolute freedom*" (356) appears on the scene: a new form that, after Faith's defeat, "ascends the throne of the world without any power being able to resist it" (357). "Spirit thus comes before us as *absolute freedom*. It is self-consciousness which grasps the fact that its certainty of itself is the essence of all the spiritual "masses," or spheres, of the real as well as of the supersensible world" (356). No wonder that its action, being totally unchecked and incapable of distinguishing between reality and thought, ends up programmatically producing "death" and "terror" (362) in its unstoppable and necessary determination, before coming to rest in a new phase of conciliation.

One might continue to follow in every detail the obscure and at times undecipherable course of the phenomenology of spirit in its complex logical and dialectical definition of the Enlightenment as a major philosophical issue. We might trace its contradictions, rifts and temporary conciliations, and experience that anguished sense of profound crisis caused by the spirit's resolution into the reality of the modern era, that emerges here and there in Hegel's words. However, we would then risk losing sight of the real objective of our discussion, which is to throw light on the genesis of the "Centaur" as a powerful and still-active paradigm and, at the same time, on the strength and persistence of the European anti-Enlightenment tradition, starting precisely from the latest developments of the critique and dialectic of the Enlightenment as described in the 1807 *Phenomenology*.

To that end, it may be more useful to turn to another work by Hegel, the famous *Vorlesungen über die Philosophie der Geschichte* (*The Philosophy of History*), published posthumously in 1837. In that text the German philosopher outlined with far greater clarity and effectiveness his complex representation of the Enlightenment from a historical and philosophical point of view, as the enthronement of thought, i.e., as the final and decisive stage of the modern era's unhappy self-estranged spirit. Here the principle of subjectivity that had been the basis of Kant's philosophy of reflection took it upon itself to shape reality, ruthlessly excluding all recourse to the authority principle, or to the example of the past and the force of tradition, and ended up by paying for it with the Revolution and the Reign of Terror. This was different from the result produced by the Lutheran Reformation, which had brought about "Modern Times" through its role as "the period of Spirit conscious that it is free, inasmuch as it wills the True, the Eternal—that which is in and for itself Universal."[8] That was a time when the discovery of individual consciousness and of the spiritual freedom of the self had harmonized with the message of Revelation in a claim for universal priesthood, thus concretely reconciling God and man, finite and infinite. By contrast, the Enlightenment had sought every answer, every content, exclusively within nature and man himself. This had produced fractures and dramatic lacerations, which became comprehensible only if one understood the fundamental dialectical relationship between the Enlightenment and the French Revolution, which was the third decisive historical moment of the modern era. "Thought is the grade to which Spirit has now advanced" (439), Hegel wrote, and further pointed out:

> These general conceptions, deduced from actual and present consciousness—the Laws of Nature and the substance of what is right and good—have received the name of *Reason*. The recognition of the validity of these laws was designated by the term [. . .] *Aufklärung* [. . . .] The absolute criterion—taking the place of all authority based on religious belief and positive laws of Right (especially political Right)—is the verdict passed by Spirit itself on the character of that which is to be believed and obeyed. (441)

In describing the Enlightenment's historical expression in the course of the eighteenth century, Hegel assigned extraordinary importance to the reforms introduced by individuals of cosmic-universal stature, such as Frederick II, and to the effects of the political theories of Rousseau and of the French *philosophes*. He also took into account the profound transformations wrought by the exercise of the principle of subjectivity and by the philosophy of reflection hinging upon the primacy of the subject that had been brought to its highest level by Kant. These transformations were analyzed in relation to their effects in redefining politics, morals, religion, and every form of knowledge. The historical world produced by the Enlightenment seemed to him to be completely different from the *Ancien Régime*—a definitive break with the past. The idea of a thinking State is due to the "jusnaturalism" of the Enlightenment:

> Right and Morality came to be looked upon as having their foundation in the actual present Will of man, whereas formerly it was referred only to the command of God enjoined *ab extra*, written in the Old and New Testament, or appearing in the form of particular Right in old parchments, as *privilegia*, or in international compacts. What the nations acknowledge as international Right was deduced empirically from observation (as in the work of Grotius); then the source of the existing civil and political law was looked for, after Cicero's fashion, in those instincts of men which Nature has planted in their hearts. (440–441)

With the Enlightenment, the subject's boundless freedom, which was the authentic founding principle of modernity, had reached its apex and had presented itself as being absolute. The will had become pure, omnipotent, "in and for itself." From Rousseau, for whom man is will and is free only insofar as he wishes what corresponds to his will, one had thus reached Kant's philosophy, whose analysis of practical reason reiterated once again that every content, whether in respect of liberty or will, lay within man himself. Hegel, as he wrote in every one of his works, never harbored the least doubt that the French Revolution had its genesis and its beginning in thought, i.e., in philosophy as "World Wisdom," or "Truth in its living form as exhibited in the affairs of the world" (446). For Hegel it was the complex meandering of this dialectic that held the secret of that momentous universal event that had changed the history of the world forever.

Unlike Kant, who saw in the French Revolution above all a "historical sign" of mankind's moral disposition to progress, Hegel considered it proof of the unilaterality and dangerousness of the self-estranged spirit as it acted through the subject's absolute freedom. To begin with, this freedom had been met with more or less general approval and optimistic expectations, including his own. The rise to power by a fully autonomous human thought was bound to be greeted with emotion and excitement by a world that had no inkling of the consequences that it would bring to bear. Hegel described this "first" in universal history as follows:

> Never since the sun had stood in the firmament and the planets revolved around him had it been perceived that man's existence centres in his head, i.e. in Thought, inspired by which he builds up the world of reality. Anaxagoras had been the first to say that *Nous* governs the World; but not until now had man advanced to the recognition of the principle that Thought ought to govern spiritual reality. This was accordingly a glorious mental dawn. All thinking beings shared in the jubilation of this epoch. Emotions of a lofty character stirred men's minds at that time; a spiritual enthusiasm thrilled through the world, as if the reconciliation between the Divine and the Secular was now first accomplished. (447)

However, no conciliation was imminent—quite the opposite, in fact. Subsequent tragic events made it clear that the thoughts produced by the culture of the Enlightenment, in their abstract quality and claim to truth, were destined to become increasingly fantastical and polemical towards all that exists. By an inexorable kind of revolution mechanics, which was implicit in the dialectical movement of historical processes, the subject's absolute freedom and boundless will, together with the rejection of traditions and religion, had turned into an ostentation of virtue, thus opening the door to suspicion and fear, followed by terror and bloodshed.

As a matter of fact, with these lectures that he read at the University of Berlin, in which he described how the Enlightenment's dialectical movement through history ultimately resulted in the tragedy of the Reign of Terror, Hegel more or less consciously added his own contribution to the already formidable arsenal of anti-Enlightenment arguments, according to a tradition still in operation today that was developing precisely in the years following the Congress of Vienna, thanks to the polemics raised by the followers of Romanticism.[9] In fact, this was nothing new. Hegel had done it before, when he had criticized the inadequacy of the knowledge value of modern science, and of Newtonian science in particular, for the purposes of the search for truth, and also when he had opposed cosmopolitism, the rights of man, the individual's atomization in the kind of civic society envisaged by the Enlightenment, and the philosophy of reflection.[10]

However, with his analysis of the dialectical processes behind the Reign of Terror, Hegel had gone further. He had divested Kant's subjective reason of its claims of emancipation, and revealed the existence within it of a precise and disturbing tendency towards domination, an inclination towards the distortion of reality and the subjugation of the individual. The same reasons that explained why the Revolution had happened in France rather than in the German States, confirmed for him the correctness of his view of philosophy as phenomenology of spirit and as drive towards conciliation.

In Germany, after Luther and the Reformation, there had been no revolutionary movements on a national scale, because the German world had already long before achieved its conciliation with reality through a "real" revolution: that is to say a revolution of a religious nature, rather than a social or political one. This had finally recreated in its consciousness that unity of finite and infinite, of religion and politics, that had characterized Christianity in its original state. And this for Hegel was not simply the only authentic universal religion (in whose concept of Christ, the God-made-man, the world had found peace and conciliation), but also a fundamental historical model for a unified spirit and an ethical state in which a community lived by its own free choice. Conversely, in the Catholic world, the crystallized Church-State dualism had led to the persistence of two powers and therefore two kinds of consciousness, one opposed to the other. This had undermined the social organism of peoples from the inside, which ultimately resulted in a conflict between Faith and pure Insight, thus setting up the conditions for a profound crisis that would be passed on to nineteenth-century Europe.

It was through Hegel that the Enlightenment became a fundamental universal category in the intellectual life of the Western world, permanently and indissolubly associated with the debate on modernity's critical self-understanding. However, as we have tried to demonstrate, this took place within an entirely original conceptualization and understanding of events, a view that was at one and the same time historical and philosophical in character: i.e., that strange and captivating paradigm of the Centaur that everyone was ultimately forced to reckon with, whether they were aware of it or not.

In his *Philosophy of History*, Hegel again aired this original view of history through his polemics against the methods of investigation applied by the powerful corporation of professional historians, which at this precise time was becoming an institution within German universities. Hegel's critique was directed against those who harbored the illusion that one could attain truth by simply adhering faithfully to philology and to the imagined objectivity of historical data, while feigning ignorance of the fact that one's thought is never "passive." A historiographer always "brings his categories with him and sees all of the phenomena presented to his mental vision exclusively through these media."[11] In contrast to the "original history" of Herodotus and Thucydides, which was founded on witness accounts, and to the Enlightenment's universal "reflective history," born of the spirit's critique and inquiry into the past, Hegel proposed a new kind of history, a "philosophical history" (1). This was a genre different from either Augustine's traditional "theology of history" or Voltaire's "philosophy of history." It saw history as modern theodicy; that is to say as a discipline capable of translating theology into philosophy, of showing the spirit's progress within the consciousness of liberty. Behind the study of the history of peoples there was then the conviction that everything "that has happened, and is happening every day, is not only not 'without God,' but is essentially His Work" (457).

Within this evocative framework, the Enlightenment appeared radically altered from Kant's earlier conception. According to the latter, which referred to a philosophical kind of history but one played out entirely within a cosmopolitan perspective, the Enlightenment was defined first and foremost as a specific modality of the exercise of reason on the part of man in the course of "enlightened" centuries in the past and, presumably, in the future. With Hegel it became nothing more than a specific era in universal history, essentially coinciding with the eighteenth century as it unfolded in Europe. It was an era characterized by specific and clear-cut features, and, in any case, an era now definitively consigned to the past by the action of one of the World Spirit's most important historical and logical laws, that of annulment or "sublation," whereby the spirit progressed inexorably in its becoming, moving from lower determinations to higher principles and concepts of itself, and ever-more evolved representations of its idea.

Thus the age after the Congress of Vienna that was marked by the rise of liberalism, by Romanticism, and by attempts to restore the Old Order had moved irremediably beyond the age of Voltaire. This meant that it was now the historians' task, as well as problem, to investigate and thoroughly understand the characteristics of that era, which had proved so decisive for universal history, starting with the self-evident connection between the Enlightenment and the Revolution, and between the growing passion for reform and its ultimate conclusion in terror. However, a far more complex question remained, and one more difficult to settle. How should the major philosophical issue of the Enlightenment be resolved; namely, the dilemma of man, who, starting from the finitude and autonomy of the subject, questions his destiny and the meaning of life?

Hegel formulated this issue in the clear terms of the "dialectical moment," linking it to the theme of the self-foundation and sublation of the crisis opened by modernity—a formulation that was based on the phenomenology of spirit and its concept of the sublation of subjectivity within the limits of the philosophy of the subject. Hegel's solution was based on judgments and choices linked to that particular historical moment. As such, it came to be seen as partial and inadequate in the course of time. Nevertheless, anyone who took up the challenge posed by this issue could not but make use of the arsenal of conceptual tools, and particularly of the overall frame of reference created by Hegel. Like it or not, the dialectical method as rule and paradigm shaping our philosophical representation and mental image of the Enlightenment has dominated the scene since Hegel, down to our own times—although this may today be more a matter of reading between the lines than of explicit expression. In fact, however, Hegel's success in this regard rested on solid bases. In contrast to the utopian and optimistic formulations expressed by Kant within the framework of the philosophy of reflection in his *Was ist Aufklärung?* Hegel provided a realistic depiction of the many shadows and contradictions that lurked behind the lights, among them a depiction of the way in which emancipatory reason had turned into its very opposite with the barbarity of the Reign of Terror, and of the dramatic and historical import of the wounds and the estrangement that the principle of subjectivity inflicted on the history of the Western world in the process of breaking with the past and its traditions.

Taking a long view of things, as indeed his goal of defining the Enlightenment from the starting point of the life of the Absolute Spirit required, Hegel had not only denounced the negative results of a project of liberation that centered exclusively on the autonomy of the individual and of a reason that was still wholly anchored to its subject. He had also pointed out the need for a new philosophy of conciliation capable of overcoming the crisis that had erupted with the onset of modernity in art and religion. No wonder, then, that the Enlightenment's dialectical movement has become the route necessarily taken by anyone who is interested in reflecting on the destiny of mankind from the starting point of the project of a new humanism formulated by Voltaire, Rousseau, Kant, Filangieri, Jefferson, and many others.

4

||||||||||||||||||||||||||

MARX AND NIETZSCHE

The Enlightenment from Bourgeois Ideology
to Will to Power

MARX WAS ONE of the first to travel along the road indicated by Hegel. He did so with great originality, at the same time however shifting into a negative key, perhaps even beyond his own intentions, the view of the Enlightenment and of its socialist and reformist offshoots subsequently held by a large part of the revolutionary Left in Europe. Marx based his analysis on the so-called materialist overthrow of Hegelian dialectical idealism, without abandoning what we have termed "the paradigm of the Centaur." Thus, he developed an entirely different form of Enlightenment dialectics, one that privileged social and economic analysis on a historical and philosophical level. The center of the dialectical mechanism shifted from thought and the concept of reflection to that of production and exchange, and from the question of self-consciousness to that of labor. Hegel's estrangement and unhappy consciousness, which needed to be healed and sublated, were transformed in Marx's analysis into the crucial theme of a human alienation that is the consequence of economic and productive expropriation carried out by the ruling class. This kind of alienation, too, was to be overcome by dialectic, in this case through the revolutionary overthrow of the current economic structure and the setting up of a daring new political system by the modern industrial proletariat.

Within the framework of this new historical and dialectical materialism, which aimed at solving the enigma of history (to use Marx's famous phrase) through the foundation of a communist society, the Enlightenment was examined from two dialectically linked perspectives. The first was structural, analyzing the Enlightenment as a decisive generative moment of modern European society, with its specific economic and social characteristics founded on the natural right to property and freedom of exchange, as against the previous feudal system and its guilds and corporations. The second perspective was a suprastructural one, which considered the Enlightenment as an ideology artfully created by the bourgeois class. The real historical product of the "political revolution" brought about by the *Aufklärung* was, in Marx's view, the birth of civil (or bourgeois) society (*bürgerliche Gesellschaft*) as a consequence of the French Revolution.[1] In this context one should not overestimate the impact of the failure constituted by the Reign of Terror, which had been a delusory and anachronistic attempt at reviving "the ancient, *realistic-democratic commonweal.*" As Marx wrote in *The Holy Family* (*Die heilige Familie*, 1844–1845):

> After the fall of Robespierre, the *political* enlightenment, which formerly had been *overreaching* itself and had been *extravagant*, began for the first time to develop *prosaically*. Under the government of the *Directory, bourgeois society*, freed by the Revolution itself from the trammels of feudalism and officially recognised in spite of the *Terror's* wish to sacrifice it to an ancient form of political life, broke out in powerful streams of life. A storm and stress of commercial enterprise, a passion for enrichment, the exuberance of the new bourgeois life, whose first self-enjoyment is pert, light-hearted, frivolous and intoxicating; a *real* enlightenment of the *land* of France, the feudal structure of which had been smashed by the hammer of the Revolution and which, by the first feverish efforts of the numerous new owners, had become the object of all-round cultivation; the first moves of industry that had now become free—these were some of the signs of life of the newly emerged bourgeois society. *Bourgeois society* [*bürgerliche* Gesellschaft] is *positively* represented by the *bourgeoisie*. The bourgeoisie, therefore, *begins* its rule. The *rights of man* cease to exist *merely in theory.*[2]

Thus, the Enlightenment had generated modern civil society, the *bürgerliche Gesellschaft*, with the consequent autonomy of the State and the formation of separate public and private spheres, all of which had caused a terminal crisis within the archaic type of organic and communal spirit that was still present in the *Ancien Régime*. This had given rise to a society made up of atomized human beings, who were egotistical, constantly engaged in conflict, dominated by a utilitarian kind of philosophy, separated from one another and alienated within the bosom of their own community. Denouncing these selfish men, who, in the course of the eighteenth century, felt that their actions were sanctioned by the empty rhetorical mask of the rights of man,[3] led to the creation of a typical nineteenth-century vein of ideology that found in individualism the authentic character of the Enlightenment. This indelible brand-mark was then eagerly picked up by both right-wing and left-wing polemicists, as well as by defenders of the Catholic tradition.[4]

Marx supported his Hegelian insights with a sophisticated analysis of the suprastructural dialectical moment represented by eighteenth-century materialistic theories.[5] In his *Deutsche Ideologie* (1845–1846), published posthumously only in 1932, he unmasked both the French and the English Enlightenments as expressing a bourgeois ideology with substantial class interests. On the one hand, that coarse and not as yet fully developed materialism concealed the positive function of traditional metaphysics in bringing about historical breaks with the past; on the other, it became obvious that it derived first and foremost from the bourgeoisie's need for a utilitarian theory of reality that would help it legitimize practices founded in the exploitation of man by man. From a historical point of view, Marx, like Hegel before him, considered the Enlightenment a decisive moment in the history of mankind's progress. However, dialectically, he also highlighted its limitations as an entirely political revolution that needed to become a social and economic one. The selfish bourgeois produced by the Enlightenment were destined to fall victim to their own specious liberty, as they exchanged the ultimate objective of human emancipation ("a *reduction* of the human world and relationships to *man himself*") for political emancipation ("the reduction of man, on the one hand, to a member of civil society, to an *egoistic, independent* individual, and, on the other hand, to a *citizen*, a juridical person").[6] In this respect, nineteenth-century reformist and democratic socialists were guilty of the same utopianism as their eighteenth-century predecessors, in that they reproduced, in the political arena, the impotence of Kant's having-to-be, and the abstract rationality of an intellect that is posited as absolute.

At the cusp of the nineteenth and twentieth centuries, this denunciation amounted to nothing short of a trial of the Enlightenment by the revolutionary left, complete with a summary condemnation and demonization of its limitations and partialities. At one end Engels prophesied that the final abode of Voltaire and his social-democratic followers would be the "dust-hole."[7] At the other end, Georges Sorel, in his famous *Les Illusions du progrès* (1908), piled on more abuse, which was gleefully received by the numerous right-wing reactionaries to be found throughout Europe. In fact the latter were at this precise moment unleashing their offensive against the legacy of the Enlightenment, a legacy that had been claimed as their own by a variety of liberal, socialist, and democratic currents.[8] One can assume that Marx himself would not have approved of such acrimonious critiques of the Enlightenment. After all, he remained a supporter of modernity and of the emancipation of man through man. His dialectical critique of the Enlightenment aimed instead at a form of "sublation" and a more profound rationalization of reality. Marx was fascinated by the boom of industry and commerce, and viewed capitalism itself as a fundamental, even heroic, stage in human progress towards communism. He would hardly have shared the reservations on the actual emancipation value of science and technology expressed by Lukács, Bloch, and Marcuse.

In the course of the nineteenth century, and then down to our own times, the view of the Enlightenment as the emancipatory project of modernity as outlined by Kant and, especially, by Hegel, has continued to fascinate generations of Western philosophers. One need only think of the numerous negative or positive verdicts on that model expressed by right-wing or left-wing commentators all over Europe, as well as of a great *Aufklärer* such as Jürgen Habermas, who has recently given us yet another update on the philosophy of the subject, developing the concept of "communicative reason." And yet one cannot overestimate the decisive role played by Friedrich Nietzsche in bringing about a radical transformation with regard to that issue and the way it was debated on the international scene at the end of the nineteenth century.

In the realm of philosophy, everything changed after the publication of Nietzsche's uncompromisingly revolutionary reflections on the real nature and purpose of the Enlightenment. His complex answer to the now century-old question *Was ist Aufklärung?* departed radically and iconoclastically from everything that had been said before about modernity, rationality, the individual, dialectic, values, emancipation, and the connection between the Enlightenment and the French Revolution.

Nietzsche was interested neither in the rationalistic theme of Hegel's dialectical sublation, which was beloved of Marx, nor in revisiting once again, in a more or less original form, the good old Western rationalistic metaphysic *à la* Kant. He instead confronted the very same subject-centered reason that had been Kant's starting point in his attempt to provide a preliminary definition of the problem, with something entirely "other" than reason itself. The theoretical scheme of Hegel's dialectics involved the sublation of the spirit's split and estranged forms through the pursuit of unifying philosophies in order to heal the wounds of an unhappy modernity. Nietzsche, on the other hand, effectively opened the way to the "postmodern" philosophical period by accusing modernity of producing the forgetfulness of being, of disregarding the real values and the authentic way of thinking of ancient man, of philologically inventing a false Ancient Greek *humanitas*, and of obfuscating through reason and rationality the true face of human nature and its dominant instinct, the will to power. Even today one feels a certain frisson in reading these reflections, in which Nietzsche unveils in the history of Western rationality an intrinsic vocation towards domination, and a tendency to deviate from the ancient paths it had abandoned, but which were still part of man's nature, such as myth and an aesthetic view of the meaning of life. It is as if one had climbed for the first time to the top of a very tall mountain and was finally surveying with clear and disillusioned eyes the abyss of history spread out below, so that it was possible now to discern the dark face of the Enlightenment that had up to now been concealed by all the various emancipatory ideologies.

In fact, the attack on modernity, and the consequent overall redefinition of the Enlightenment as a great philosophical issue, had begun as early as Nietzsche's first great work on the birth of tragedy (1872). Here the author had attempted to throw light on the genesis of art, seeing in its development the "eternal struggle between the theoretical and the tragic views of the world."[9] In the process, he identified the simultaneous presence in human beings of reason and myth, Apollo and Dionysus, the I and not-I. It was only through tragedy that myth attained its highest meaning: the tragic chorus represented the mass of the followers of Dionysus, the coming god in whose ecstatic exaltation of primordial instincts the subject element and the principle of individuation vanished into forgetfulness. In later eras that tragic spirit had been marginalized and its cult had been forced underground until "the gradual awakening of the Dionysiac spirit [. . .] in the world in which we live" (ch. 19, 94). This had been due to the rise of "logical Socratism" (ch. 13, 67), and of a "new, unheard-of esteem for knowledge and insight" (65). It was this clearly rationalistic and "enlightened" idea that was at the origin of modernity; namely, that only those who possess knowledge are virtuous and therefore capable of healing the perpetual wound of existence without having recourse to myth. Instead one could rely on "theoretical man"'s structural optimism.[10]

For many years Nietzsche scholars have studied what was assumed to be a positivistic and Enlightenment phase in his intellectual experience, and they have come up with contradictory ways of reading it.[11] This is a decisive question also for our present discussion. It is obvious that our Hegelian "Centaur" was more or less explicitly but thoroughly investigated by Nietzsche in several of his works, with surprising results, that he synthesized in his final proposition of an actual *neue Aufklärung* as a precursor to nihilism, and of a necessary transvaluation of all values in the modern world. In *Menschliches, allzumenschliches, ein Buch für freie Geister* (1878; *Human, All Too Human. A Book for Free Spirits*), dedicated to Voltaire on the centenary of his death, both the era of Humanism and Renaissance and the Enlightenment period were represented historically as consecutive phases of a single "cultural movement." Man's progress in this movement was opposed and eventually brought to a halt by two pairs of revolutionary-reactionary movements: the Protestant Reformation and the Counter-Reformation, and the French Revolution and Romanticism. Within that framework, which demystified several reference points of German historical consciousness in the wake of Hegel, the Reformation was disparaged as a serious obstacle in the development of European civilization, the "protestation" of a "German nature" incapable of educating itself at the great pagan school of the Italian Renaissance. Without Luther's medieval remonstrances, the Enlightenment would "perhaps have dawned somewhat sooner than it did and with a fairer luster than we can now imagine."[12]

Again from a historical point of view, in *Morgenröthe. Gedanken über die moralischen Vorurtheile* (1881; *Daybreak: Thoughts on the Prejudices of Morality*), Nietzsche demolished another of the Hegelian Centaur's strong points, i.e., the dialectical link between Enlightenment and Revolution. He maintained, in fact, that the autonomous progress of the former had been stunted precisely by the occurrence of the latter, with the subsequent rise in Europe, and especially in Germany, of a Romantic culture that was deeply opposed to the Enlightenment: "The whole great tendency of the Germans was against the Enlightenment and against the revolution in society which was crudely misunderstood as its consequence."[13] If it had not been stopped by the Jacobins' Reign of Terror, that civilizing movement, "left to itself, would have passed quietly along like a gleam in the clouds and for long been content to address itself only to the individual: so that it would have transformed the customs and institutions of nations only very slowly."[14] Nietzsche invited us therefore to "call back" "the spirit of the Enlightenment and of progressive evolution,"[15] and to fly again "the banner of the Enlightenment—the banner bearing the three names Petrarch, Erasmus, Voltaire."[16]

It is obvious that this *neue Aufklärung* had nothing to do with the traditional rationalistic and emancipatory project of modernity or of the historical Enlightenment that had been at the center of debates until Nietzsche's time. Its roots lay elsewhere, and they were entirely contained within an uncompromising acknowledgement of the centrality of man's will to power. They lay in that liberating and "progressive evolution" that found its symbolic representation in the figure of Voltaire, "one of the great liberators of the mind and spirit (*Geist*)," as he is called in the dedication that appears at the head of Part One in the original edition of *Human, All Too Human*. And indeed Voltaire had debunked Christian values with his fierce irony and opened the way for a pluralism of truths, which was followed by nihilism and that adult phase that constituted a necessary transitional stage before one could finally proceed towards an authentic and affirmative life founded on a complete transvaluation of classical Western values. Just as Christianity and the Church had betrayed the authentic message brought by the man Jesus, in the same way the historical Enlightenment was nothing other than a degenerate reiteration of the original "progressive evolution" that was linked to the will to power. The *neue Aufklärung* was born with the deliberate program of unmasking the damaging consolatory illusions of the subject's equality put forward by Kant and the hated Rousseau, the alleged natural rights put forward by the socialists, and in addition the vain hopes raised among the servile classes, the weak, and the "failures," by the followers of Christianity. As Nietzsche explained in his radically aristocratic critique of Western modernity as embodied historically by Christianity and by the Enlightenment and its rationalism, the modern world appears logical to us because we have dressed it in the language of logic. In fact, life does not in the least tend towards the pursuit of happiness but rather seeks power; it "prefers to *will nothingness*, than *not* will."[17] At the same time, the individual, Christian faith, and that reason beloved of the Enlightenment are nothing more than masks. They are the sheep's clothing in which the will to power shrouds itself. Faced with this delusory progress, one's only option was to live through the inescapable experience of the eternal return of the same with dignity and courage.

5

||||||||||||||||||||||||

HORKHEIMER AND ADORNO

The Totalitarian Face of the Dialectic of Enlightenment

WITHIN THE PARAMETERS described in the previous chapter, the philosophical issue of the Enlightenment was definitively transformed. This becomes obvious as soon as one reads Max Horkheimer and Theodor Adorno's *Dialektik der Aufklärung* (which they finished writing in the United States in 1944 and published three years later in Amsterdam). Here the old Hegelian Centaur was turned on its head. There were no noteworthy references to the Enlightenment as a historical period, or to the eighteenth century as its chronological and cultural context. The text revisited the classical dialectical paradigm and reformulated it, including all its dark sides, from the dawn of Western civilization onwards. It began with the adventures of Odysseus (the first *Aufklärer*), which exemplified the journey of the self through myth, and traveled on all the way to Hitler's totalitarianism and the American mass consumerism in their own day. This obviously precluded any attempt at historical criticism.

The main issue under investigation was entirely philosophical in nature. It directly addressed the nature and outcomes of the Enlightenment, and consequently the question of its culpability for the catastrophe that had hit the modern world with the horror of World War II. From its very first pages the book was a relentless indictment of what it saw as the historical failure of the Enlightenment's emancipation project, a project that had been in development over several centuries: "Enlightenment, understood in the widest sense as the advance of thought, has always aimed at liberating human beings from fear and installing them as masters. Yet the wholly enlightened earth is radiant with triumphant calamity."[1] Born with the intent of emancipating and liberating mankind from myth, that project had undergone a dialectical reversal that turned it, paradoxically, into a new form of myth, a totalitarian religion devoted single-mindedly to an instrumental rationalism whose final aim was the creation of a dehumanized society dominated by science and technology. The Enlightenment had hastened the crisis and the "collapse of bourgeois civilization" (xiv), thus catapulting the Western world into a "new kind of barbarism" (xiv) never recorded before in living memory. From this arose the urgent need to investigate the causes of the "enlightenment's relapse into mythology" (xvi), so as to expose at last its dangerous predisposition to self-destruction, a supposition based on the authors' thesis that a "tendency toward self-destruction [had] been inherent in rationality from the first, not only in the present phase when it [was] emerging nakedly" (xix).

It should be noted straightaway that Horkheimer and Adorno's text, rich as it is in literary elements, cannot be understood unless one takes into account the fact that, in writing about rationality and reason in connection with the Enlightenment, the authors are once again taking issue with the philosophy of the subject as described in Hegel (after all, that is the inescapable dialectical paradigm). To that effect, they appropriate both Marx's critique of ideologies and Nietzsche's unmasking of subjective reason as a smokescreen for the will to power. Adding a new ingredient in this explosive mixture, they also subscribed to the growing disenchantment with modern science, which by the early twentieth century was seen by large sectors of the European intelligentsia as having degenerated into the all-powerful dictatorship of so-called technoscience.[2] According to Horkheimer and Adorno, "[l]ike few others since Hegel, Nietzsche recognized the dialectic of enlightenment" (36). He had unveiled the close relationship of that phenomenon with domination and power. And now power had revealed itself as the evil face of technological society, where "the subjugation of everything natural to the sovereign subject culminates in the domination of what is blindly objective and natural" (xviii).

"Enlightenment [. . .] is the philosophy which equates truth with the scientific system" (66), with mathematical methods, and with the language of Galileo and Newton's theoretical thinking. However, over time these had been replaced by the pursuit of technological innovation and of organizational models that saw being only "in terms of manipulation and administration" (65). Developed with the intent that it be of service to man, technology was now well on its way towards dictating mankind's destiny. The tight dialectical process that reversed the relationship between man and technology was all already present in the initial core of the Enlightenment's very way of thinking, which was bent on "establishing a unified, scientific order and [. . .] deriving factual knowledge from principles, whether these principles are interpreted as arbitrarily posited axioms, innate ideas, or the highest abstractions" (63). The real spiritual father and true interpreter of this posture had been Francis Bacon, with his famous concept of knowledge as the absolute dominion of man over nature. The dialectic's ultimate results could be seen in the Enlightenment's proclaimed mission of vanquishing magic and myths by stressing man's finitude and the self-sufficiency of reason, a reason that was destined to be turned upside down in the instrumental reason propounded by the positivists ("modern mythologists" of scientific rationalism) and, more recently, by supporters of early twentieth-century pragmatism and American utilitarian philosophies.[3] Indeed, Horkheimer and Adorno's real objective was precisely the denunciation of this instrumental reason, which had been dehumanized, formalized into the theorems of logical neopositivism and programmatically detached from any kind of historical, metaphysical, or religious context; a reason whose sole intent was the pursuit of technological dominion over nature, and not the pursuit of truth. Abstract reason had proved incapable of constructing a solid rationalistic morality equipped with guidelines and principles that could rein in the subject's worst instincts and ensure peaceful coexistence on the basis of historically shared values. But the problem went further. For that reason had itself generated most of what was perverse in the modern world.

This was due to the fact that Kant's rejection of any and all authority principles had resulted first in the death of God, as proclaimed by Nietzsche, and then in the rise of the most unbounded individualism and utilitarianism, of consumerism and the commodification of every aspect of everyday life. The final, and inevitable, outcome could be seen in totalitarian regimes. Their intoxication with the will to power and lack of regard for human life are the natural offspring of instrumental reason's implicit totalitarianism. The Marquis de Sade and his *Philosophie dans le boudoir* perfectly exemplify the ultimate outcome of an Enlightenment project that had established man as absolute master of his own destiny and had, in so doing, allowed free rein to his propensity for domination and violence. The ideological nature of this dialectical reversal of the Enlightenment was also apparent in the American cultural industry, where artistic phenomena had been reduced to entertainment commodities and propaganda within the framework of a capitalistic system. This was the ultimate proof that the Enlightenment's original emancipation project was finally regressing into a dangerous form of mass mystification. Thus nothing seemed to escape the logics of domination deployed by the Enlightenment in modern technological society, in which "progress is reverting to regression" (xviii) and even economic well being leads to the spiritual bankruptcy of mankind.

Horkheimer and Adorno's *Dialektik der Aufklärung* was the work of two *Aufklärer*, who had been among the founders of the Frankfurt School and were now obviously disillusioned and disappointed by the crisis that the social sciences had suffered at the start of the century. They were also of course deeply affected by the tragic events of the 1930s and 40s. However, for many generations of activists and reactionaries alike, both left- and right-wing, as well as for the architects of the Vatican's cultural project (to be visited below), this text represented a veritable "black book" of modernity, one that provided them with an arsenal of ideas and suggestions that could be deployed without too much concern for historical accuracy. The few mentions of the original libertarian and emancipatory nature of the Enlightenment within the volume were hardly adequate to counterbalance its apocalyptic tone and unsubstantiated indictments, or the authors' unilateral pronouncements according to which "enlightenment is totalitarian as only a system can be" (18). Horkheimer and Adorno effectively threw away the baby with the bathwater. That is to say, they relaunched the paradigm of Hegelian dialectic within the framework of a radical and definitive condemnation of the modern world. They pronounced a crushing verdict, only partially relieved by their call for a *critical* rethinking of the philosophical issue of the Enlightenment, taking into account the negative effects produced by its historical action as well as its primary intent of pursuing truth rather than dominating nature. According to Horkheimer and Adorno, "the cause of enlightenment's relapse into mythology is to be sought not so much in the nationalist, pagan, or other modern mythologies concocted specifically to cause such a relapse as in the fear of truth which petrifies enlightenment itself" (xvi). Their book issues a peremptory warning, as it stresses "the necessity for enlightenment to reflect on itself if humanity is not to be totally betrayed" (xvii)

6

||||||||||||||||||||||||

FOUCAULT

The Return of the Centaur and the Death of Man

THE CRITIQUE OF MODERNITY as a nihilistic and openly antihumanist phenomenon that we delineated in the previous chapter enjoyed widespread currency
until quite recently. It gave rise to representations of this phenomenon that,
while undoubtedly interesting, are couched in such radically demonizing terms
that by comparison the anti-Enlightenment clichés of the late Romantic era
sound like mild reprimand.

Among the great European authors of the second half of the twentieth century, Michel Foucault was without a doubt the most original in reformulating
the very bases of the philosophical issue of the Enlightenment, within the radical strategy of unmasking and denunciation that we have been describing here.
Foucault's attack was directed at the very heart of the problem and moved from
a deliberate rereading of Hegel's Centaur (i.e., from the fusion of philosophy
and history), making no concessions, however, to his dialectic and phenomenology of spirit.[1] To that end, Foucault developed his own concept of history on
groundwork laid by Nietzsche, who was his true mentor. This concept aimed
at doing away with the subject, i.e., with Kant's "I think," and at refuting the
very idea of truth (the pursuit of which had still been a priority for Adorno and
Horkheimer), most especially the idea of the (presumed) scientific truth of the
traditional human sciences. This is at the root of Foucault's disconcerting advo-
cacy of the "death of man," that is to say the extinction of a rational platform of
knowledge along the lines developed by Kant and the Enlightenment at the end
of the eighteenth century, which still undergirded the modern *episteme*.[2] It was
to this task of conceptual deconstruction that Foucault devoted his formidable
intellectual energy. Thus, he called into question the idea of a necessary and

defining connection between knowledge and virtue, which had been the core identity of the Enlightenment. He also described the perverse and inextricable way in which power and knowledge were perpetually intertwined—"[t]he exercise of power perpetually creates knowledge and, conversely, knowledge constantly induces effects of power"[3]—and denounced the inexorable rise of disciplinary violence in the history of the Western world, and the way in which that violence was perpetually cloaked in a rhetoric of emancipation and appeals to truth that obscured the original will to power. This posed for both historians and philosophers a challenge that, whether we like it or not, is still unresolved to this day.

Foucault found himself in disagreement with the tradition of the *Annales* school, which was informed by a teleological and causal model and was considered still to be excessively influenced by a positivistic stance and by the single-mindedness of anthropological thought; but he also rejected the historicist brand of idealistic historiography that was ruled by the "I think," i.e., by a hermeneutical position that was programmatically opposed to the thesis that meaning is always derived from context, from something exterior, and that we do not produce thought but rather are the product of thought. Against these positions, Foucault developed his genealogical historiography, a new and original tool for the analysis of history. The boundaries and objectives of this new discipline were described thus by their author:

> One has to dispense with the constituent subject, to get rid of the subject itself, that's to say, to arrive at an analysis which can account for the constitution of the subject within a historical framework. And this is what I would call genealogy, that is, a form of history which can account for the constitution of knowledges, discourses, domains of objects etc., without having to make reference to a subject which is either transcendental in relation to the field of events or runs in its empty sameness throughout the course of history.[4]

Beginning with his first important work, *Folie et déraison: histoire de la folie à l'âge classique* (Paris, 1961),[5] Foucault applied his extraordinary heuristic and narrative creativity to a critique of the hidden negative consequences of rationality, in particular those produced by the much-touted humanitarianism of the Enlightenment, in the history of the Western world. Foucault denounced the dark and inhuman side of so-called scientific progress by taking as his subject the transformation of madness into a disease and the rise of modern psychiatry at the end of the eighteenth century, which led to the invention of lunatic asylums. These developments had brought to an end an entire historical phase in which madness had been considered as either evidence of sainthood or, as was the case during the Renaissance (for instance in Erasmus, Shakespeare, and

Cervantes), as a heightened form of ironic reason. Although meant as instruments for the treatment and reeducation of patients, the sharp differentiation between reason and nonreason and the wholesale internment of the insane (internment on a scale not seen in Europe since the time of the medieval leper hospitals) in fact signaled the abrupt end of the ancient dialogue between rationality and irrationality and heralded an era of segregation of the mentally ill. Ultimately, the birth of psychiatry had far more disturbing consequences than the mere confinement of bodies within purpose-built structures: the authoritarian monologue on madness delivered by the scientific reason of psychiatrists was answered now by the distressing and poignant silence imposed forever on mental patients. The result was a kind of monstrous mental segregation that matched the physical confinement. Reason's despotism was not content with locking up bodies: it claimed absolute control over the subject through the device of mental rehabilitation and reeducation.

Later works by Foucault are modeled on this same pattern, through which the author denounces the less commonly understood historical consequences of the power exercised by rationality and knowledge. These works include *Naissance de la clinique* (Paris, 1963)[6] and *Les Mots et les choses* (1966), an ambitious attempt at reconstructing the cultural codes, generative grammars, and "epistemes" that have emerged in Europe over the centuries as part of the processes of organizing knowledge. In the latter case too, Foucault's ultimate objective was to destroy delusory knowledge by calling into question the truth claims of the modern episteme, which was founded at the end of the eighteenth century on the "discovery of man" and the objectivity claimed by human sciences.

In 1975, Foucault published *Surveiller et punir. Naissance de la prison*, which he would call his "first book," perhaps not without cause, given its importance and the epistemological maturity he achieved with it.[7] For it was only with this work that he began to use the theme of the Enlightenment as a direct polemical instrument, on account of its role as historical background and point of reference for the modern technologies used to exercise power over the human body. The book focused on real, i.e., genealogical, history, specifically on the history of the enigmatic "gentle way" and of the ostensibly humanitarian character of the punishments advocated as part of the reformed penal code by Enlightenment figures such as Beccaria, Dupaty, and Pastoret. Here Foucault deliberately challenged established views by attempting to demonstrate a connection between the new human sciences, the emancipation ideals that supported the individual's assertion of his rights, and the rise of modern disciplinary society with its total institutions, such as prisons, mental asylums, factories, and military barracks. Foucault explores that society's growing need to rationalize, classify, measure, and train bodies, and to educate, treat, and punish them in light of new scientific notions, a need that had been felt with special urgency from the end of the eighteenth century on. He shows also how this need coincided with the discovery of the human body as object and target for the exercise of power, and with the natural development of domination technologies aimed at subjugating human bodies, so as to make them both docile and useful.

Foucault's analysis in *Surveiller et punir* points out that "[t]he 'Enlightenment,' which discovered the liberties, also invented the disciplines" and the coercion mechanisms of modern disciplinary society.[8] He attempts to outline the power effects of Beccaria's humanitarian philosophy from a historical point of view, and points to the birth of prisons as a prime example of the way in which the new power to punish ratified by the Enlightenment had metamorphosed within a few decades into the power to discipline and reeducate. Adorno and Horkheimer had already denounced the brutal symptoms of technological society's totalitarian project as offspring of the Enlightenment's utopian thought and philosophical deployment of instrumental reason. Foucault went further, claiming to furnish historical evidence of that process, a claim that sparked angry reactions among many specialists in the field,[9] and asserting also that he had documented the birth of the great total institutions that are still in operation today.

Foucault returned explicitly to the theme of the Enlightenment in a seminar that he gave at the Sorbonne in 1978 under the title "*Qu'est-ce que la critique? (Critique et Aufklärung)*" (What is Critique?—Critique and the Enlightenment), in a lucid and definitive reckoning that reopened the entire question, two centuries after Kant's famous formulation, in terms that were entirely original and that we would now perhaps call "postmodern." In 1983, just a few months before his death, Foucault continued the discussion in a lecture given at the Collège de France, this time explicitly entitled "*Qu'est-ce que les Lumières? Qu'est-ce la Révolution?*" (What is the Enlightenment? What is Revolution?). These were the crucial years of Foucault's last great historical and analytical effort, which was devoted to the history of sexuality and attempted to trace a genealogy at last of this modern subject, through the study of the technologies of the self. His research focused on the dawning self-awareness of the individual as the subject of a model of sexuality.

Thus, after writing on power *per se*, on the relationship between knowledge and techniques of domination, on mental institutions and on prisons, Foucault discovered the centrality of Christian man in the history of Western sexuality. The practice of confession *de facto* resulted in the birth also of the modern *scientia sexualis*, which was more interested in personalized control and in the surveillance of passion than in the pleasure techniques and *ars erotica* of the ancients. An essential aspect of that historical reconstruction was the recognition of the fundamental importance of the invention of truth as a Christian's precise duty. The denunciation of one's errors in the light of religious faith and the requirement to pursue the truth about oneself through the practice of confession had now replaced the pagans' art of living, thanks to an anxiety-inducing technique of the self aimed at achieving salvation on the basis of a form of introspective censorship. Foucault devoted much space to this revolutionary Christian politics of truth. He looked for traces of it in the ancient world, especially in ancient Greece. By "problematizing" more generally the thorny question of the genealogy of truth, he highlighted how one actually had to go back to Greece in order to trace the roots of both the analytics of truth as a rational activity aimed at establishing whether a proposition is true or false, and of *Parrhesia*, i.e., "truth-telling as an activity," as the active and concrete act of bearing witness. As Foucault points out, "With the question of the importance of telling the truth, and knowing who is able to tell the truth, and knowing why we should tell the truth, we have the roots of what we could call the 'critical' tradition in the West."[10]

All these themes concerning the *subject*, *power*, and *truth* were already present in the seminar Foucault had given at the Sorbonne. The aim was to separate a centuries-old history of critique from its generally accepted identification with Enlightenment rationalism,[11] and with related developments that had taken place in the course of the eighteenth century; namely, the rise of anthropology and man's installation on the throne of knowledge. Through those developments, critique had come to be identified with the subject's ability to distinguish between true and false, and with the role of critical reason in pursuing truth along the terms established by "Kant's great undertaking" in the development of modern rationalism. In putting forward his genealogy of critique, Foucault once again took as his starting point the decisive invention of truth by the Church, which "developed this idea—singular and [. . .] quite foreign to ancient culture—that each individual, whatever his age or status, from the beginning to the end of his life and in his every action, had to be governed and had to let himself be governed" in order to achieve salvation.[12]

St. Paul's directive that one believe in the truth revealed by Jesus Christ and in his teachings if one wishes to be saved, which was at the core of the Christian pastoral, had become in the course of the sixteenth and seventeenth centuries one of the necessary points of reference in a large process of "governmentalization" that still awaits proper study from a historical point of view. How to govern families, cities, States, armies, individuals, and consciences was the fundamental problem faced by ecclesiastical and secular authorities alike, as well as by that period's thinkers. Discipline and governmentalization had gone hand in hand. Historically, critique was born as "the art of not being governed quite so much,"[13] that is to say as an *ethos* of freedom, a specific attitude on the part of the subject that calls into question his relationships with truth and power. It had started as religious critique of the Biblical model of God-derived power, had moved on to political critique of the most archaic and violent modalities of the art of government by natural law, and finally launched a frontal attack on the effects of modern scientific truth as a locus of power.

Foucault had no qualms in asserting that, in the final analysis, "critique is the movement by which the subject gives himself the right to question truth on its exercise of power, and to question power on its discourses of truth. [. . .] critique will be the art of voluntary insubordination, that of reflected intractability."[14] This was, then, nothing to do with the model of rationality embodied by modernity, or with the primacy of knowledge as the antechamber of virtue. In Kant's answer to the question *Was ist Aufklärung?* this concept of critique coincided precisely with the first part of the reply, i.e., with the uncompromising definition of the *Aufklärung* as man's release from "tutelage" or minority through his rejection of any form of authority principle. On this, Foucault noted: "What Kant was describing as the *Aufklärung* is very much what I was trying before to describe as critique, this critical attitude which appears as a specific attitude in the Western world starting with what was historically [. . .] the great process of society's governmentalization."[15] Where Foucault diverged from Kant was in relation to the thesis that is constantly in the background in the German philosopher's 1784 text, and that identified the *Aufklärung* with a false idea of knowledge, and a precise model of rationality. Foucault openly disputed that thesis: "I am not attempting to show the opposition there may be between Kant's analysis of the *Aufklärung* and his critical project."[16] That opposition derived from a different concept of identity and of the function of critique as separate from any reference to Kant's reason.

And yet, it was precisely this explanation, based on separating the *Aufklärung* from "the critical undertaking" that was rationalism, that effectively opened the way to a kind of postmodern redefinition of the whole question. Foucault took the opportunity to draw up final conclusions from all his previous research, which had sometimes been quite alien to the thought of Parisian circles. He did so by distancing himself from the positions expressed by French historians of the Enlightenment, which he saw as epistemologically petrified, part and parcel of the traditional "block constituted by the Enlightenment and the Revolution,"[17] to the point of appearing now sterile, informed solely by ideology and aiming mostly at defending the values and legacy of the eighteenth century. As he would sarcastically say in his lecture at the Collège de France: "Let us leave to their pious meditations those who want to keep the heritage of the *Aufklärung* alive and intact. This piety, of course, is the most touching of all treasons."[18]

The correct approach had been followed only in Germany, beginning at the end of the eighteenth century, and consisted in focusing on the peculiar issue of the *Aufklärung* in its historical character as the great "problem of modern philosophy":[19] there "the *Aufklärung* was certainly understood, for better or worse [. . .] as an important episode, a sort of brilliant manifestation of the profound destination of Western reason" (52). Foucault further wrote, "[I]t is not because we privilege the 18th century [. . .] that we encounter the problem of the *Aufklärung*. I would say instead that it is because we fundamentally want to ask the question, *Was ist Aufklärung?* that we encounter the historical scheme of our modernity" (57).

A large number of German historians, as well as the European historians who followed their lead, had addressed the issue on the basis of precisely those premises. Foucault felt that he belonged to a tradition that went from Mendelssohn to Kant, Hegel, and Nietzsche, down to Husserl and the Frankfurt School in tackling the question of the *Aufklärung* from a historical and philosophical point of view. That philosophical tradition was particularly close to his own, especially from Nietzsche onwards. Breaking free from the spell of an apologetic history of the Enlightenment and of the Revolution seen as its fulfillment, it had long since focused on the power dynamics underlying rationalist emancipation discourse, and had denounced the presumptuousness of that reason and its pursuit of domination. The final challenge to the old image of the Enlightenment as a historical era and ideology informed by progress must now come from a new genealogy of the *Aufklärung* that, regardless of the specific historical contexts, could throw light in the first instance on the complex manifestations of the intersection between power, truth, and the subject. In order to do that, it was necessary to go back to the origins and revive the old German-derived paradigm of the Centaur. But to do so required clarifying the character of the new "historical-philosophical practice" (56) that must now move away as completely from Kant's reason as from Hegel's dialectic or Husserl's phenomenology.

In Foucault's view, the main characteristic of that "practice" was "to desubjectify the philosophical question by way of historical contents, to liberate historical contents by examining the effects of power whose truth affects them and from which they supposedly derive" (56–57). The objective, therefore, was to think the Centaur in postmodern terms by disenthroning man, getting rid both of the subject and of a rationalism that hid the pursuit of power behind the veil of scientific truth: that is to say, by certifying, once and for all, the death of the old Enlightenment. Only then would it be possible to uncover how the *Aufklärung* had been subsumed into the field of rationalistic critique and, above all, how completely the other possible reading of the Enlightenment had been lost; namely, the reading that identified it with critique, which was seen as the perpetual *ethos* of liberty and of the art of not being governed "too much." At the end of the day, both of these interpretations were already present in the answer that Kant had given to his own question. Foucault's main concern in his last works was how exactly to move away from that project, in which the modern world configured itself on a critical and rationalistic basis, so as to return instead to a Kant who was now seen from this perspective, and to the eighteenth-century origins of the Enlightenment question.

In the lecture read at the Collège de France in January 1983, Foucault's enquiry moved precisely in this direction. Two specific questions had been asked in 1784 and 1794, respectively: What was Enlightenment, and what was Revolution? For Foucault, these two questions constituted Kant's interrogation of his own present. What emerged from the question on the Enlightenment in particular was "the question of today, the question about the present, about what is our actuality: what is happening today? What is happening right now? And what is this right now we all are in which defines the moment at which I am writing?"[20] Before Kant, philosophy's discussion of history had drawn its coordinates from the ancient-modern opposition. With the reply given by the German philosopher a new and entirely original approach was born, seen as "the problematization of an actuality" and its exploration on the part of the philosopher, who belongs to and "has to position himself" in relation to it. Philosophy "as a discourse of and about modernity" (85), then, was not entirely identified with the rationalistic project of Kant's critiques. It was first and foremost a philosophy that offered plausible answers to the most burning questions: "What is my actuality? What is the meaning of this actuality? And what am I doing when I speak about this actuality? I believe that this is what this new examination of modernity is all about" (86). It was from this that Foucault's final thesis derived, according to which Kant was not only the revered father of the modern "analytics of truth," that is to say of a rationalism that originated in "the question of the conditions under which true knowledge is possible" (94); he was also the proponent of "what we could call an ontology of ourselves, an ontology of the present":

> It seems to me that the philosophical choice with which we are confronted at present is this: we can opt for a critical philosophy which will present itself as an analytic philosophy of truth in general, or we can opt for a form of critical thought which will be an ontology of ourselves, an ontology of the actuality. It is this form of philosophy that, from Hegel to the Frankfurt School, through Nietzsche and Max Weber, has founded the form of reflection within which I have attempted to work (95).

We have thus reached the current state of the art with regard to the philosophical question of the Enlightenment. On the one side we have those who continue to pursue Kant's Enlightenment tradition and his rationalistic project of modernity, those like Habermas, Rawls or Putnam, to mention only the most famous, who albeit with different nuances and interpretations, claim that "the problems generated by the Enlightenment are still our problems," from an epistemological point of view, as well as in relation to their historical and political foundation.[21] On the other side there is a vast and vociferous army of theoreticians of the postmodern, who for a while now have missed no opportunity to pronounce the death of the Enlightenment and the end of the modern world in the name and on behalf of relativism, nihilism, and the need for new beginnings and new philosophical dawns—the details of which are, of course, invariably yet to be revealed.[22]

However, this scenario is as yet missing a third, important protagonist: Catholic thought in the aftermath of the Second Vatican Council. More on this in our next chapter.

7

|||||||||||||||||||||||||||

POSTMODERN
ANTI-ENLIGHTENMENT POSITIONS

From the Cassirer-Heidegger Debate to
Benedict XVI's katholische Aufklärung

RICHARD RORTY OCCUPIES a position of special prestige and authority within the group of postmodern thinkers. His position is close to that of Michel Foucault, for he has argued for a need finally to separate the social and political project of the Enlightenment, which, however, in his view still constitutes a valid proposition, from its epistemological and philosophical project, which he declares a failure.[1] This position, which is particularly insidious and ambiguous, since its declared aim is to demolish the very basis of the Enlightenment's philosophical framework, was first articulated with great clarity at a meeting held in Davos, Switzerland, in the spring of 1929, where two important thinkers, Ernst Cassirer and Martin Heidegger, discussed the crucial theme *What is man?*—and thus, indirectly, the authentic meaning of Kant's philosophy.[2]

Above and beyond their academic skirmishes and the unbridgeable conceptual distance that divided them and would also affect their respective personal histories (Cassirer escaped from Germany to the United States, while Heidegger was a supporter of Nazism), what was really at stake was, even then, the very existence of the Enlightenment, and the legitimacy of its epistemological foundation. Cassirer attended that rendezvous as a prestigious exponent of early twentieth-century German Neo-Kantianism, a follower of the Marburg School, and of Hermann Cohen and Paul Natorp, who believed that current theories of knowledge were in urgent need of revision. In his research, Cassirer had endeavored to go beyond the old and controversial positivistic model of objective knowledge of the *thing in itself*, that was founded on the natural sciences, and to open up a united horizon of critique for the first time to the whole of human culture, embracing disciplines from psychology to linguistics, from ethnology to the history of ideas. Cassirer thus accepted the need to redefine the relationship between the *a priori* and experience, in view of an idealistic conception of Kantian transcendentalism that was both more complex and problematic. His position remained firmly within the universalistic tradition of Enlightenment humanism. At this very time, first in his pioneering studies on mythical thought, and then in his multivolume *Philosophie der symbolischen Formen*,[3] Cassirer was developing his original philosophy of culture, which focused once again specifically on man, who was seen as the privileged agent of an infinite production of cultural forms through symbolic language, forms that enabled him to understand himself within his world, and his world within himself. In the first paper he gave at the Davos meeting, on the subject of finitude and death, Cassirer immediately stressed the double nature, both material and spiritual, of man, and the crucial importance of the transcendental and extra-worldly dimension of human existence, without which no form of knowledge, and consequently no form of Enlightenment, would be possible: *"L'homme est certes fini, mais il est en même temps cet être fini que connaît sa finitude et qui, dans ce savoir qui lui-même n'est plus fini, s'élève au-dessus de la finitude."*[4]

Heidegger, on the other hand, came across as the great eliminator of the Enlightenment, which he saw as the final phase of that vilified trajectory of Western metaphysics that had finally brought about the enthronement of man—to use Foucault's famous metaphor in *Les Mots et les choses* (*The Order of Things*)—and had thus accelerated the rise of nihilism and the oppressive domination exercised by modern technological society. A pupil of Husserl, and believed by his contemporaries to harbor neo-Scholastic sympathies, Heidegger appeared to be the charismatic spokesman for a new concept of metaphysics, a concept that could only assert itself, as he wrote with an intentionally violent undertone, through the complete *"destruction de ce qui a été jusqu'ici les fondements de la métaphysique occidentale (l'Esprit, le Logos, la Raison)."*[5] It is likely that, in Heidegger's view, the key question of Enlightenment thought, *What is man?* which formed the basis of the Davos debate, was not in fact the decisive question to be posed if one is to achieve an understanding of the vicissitudes and destiny of mankind. For him, the fundamental question would have been instead that of ontology, that is to say of the meaning and essence of being: *What is being?* Why is there being instead of nothing? The lack of an answer to these questions and the consequent neglect of the issue of being, from Plato all the way to Nietzsche, were thus to blame for the wrong turning taken by Western metaphysics, which was leading it straight to nihilism. All the long series of "humanisms" in history, constantly characterized as they were by the assumption of man's universal and rational essence, merely confirmed the magnitude of this initial mistake.[6]

It was imperative to clarify this once and for all at the Davos meeting, before a philosophers' tribunal. Cassirer, who was an adherent of humanist thought, saw man as a transcendental being who was capable of attaining infinite knowledge and truth, and considered him to be both the main instrument and the ultimate end of a reflection Cassirer carried out in the tradition of the Enlightenment. Heidegger, on the other hand, assigned secondary importance to man compared to the vital question of the knowledge of being. For him, man was no more than a "shepherd of Being" and "the neighbor of Being";[7] he was the way and ontological instrument through which to interpret the meaning of being. To that end it was important to take into account the fact that the fundamental characteristic, the essence of the *humanitas* of *homo humanus* lay in the finitude of existence and in his inhabiting the truth of being—"the Being of man consists in 'being-in-the-world,'"[8] while truth was transformed from rational *adaequatio intellectus et rei* into the unveiling and manifestation of being: "deconcealing."[9] Man is thus defined as open to being (*Dasein*, "being there"), and therefore as part of a bigger picture. As such, he had inevitably fallen from the throne on which the Enlightenment had placed him. Contrary to what was claimed by the science and technology of the modern world, man was not in charge of being: in fact, it was man's "being-there" that was determined by being.

Both Cassirer and Heidegger had written important books on Kant, in 1918 and in 1929, respectively. The Davos seminar underlined further the irreconcilable differences between the two speakers, in particular their different interpretations of a text as fundamental as the *Critique of Pure Reason*. According to Heidegger, and contrary to common opinion, what was worth investigating within those pages was not Kant's critique of reason, i.e., his logic and methodology of the knowledge of positive sciences. Instead, Heidegger was interested in Kant as one of the first thinkers who had realized that one must go beyond pure logic to finally found an ontological metaphysics of man's being-there (*Dasein*). This would then entail investigating man's essence and the modality and meaning of his being-there in relation to being, rather than questioning how one could formulate a judgment on objects, or analyzing the limits and autonomy of reason in epistemological mechanisms. Kant had replied to the question *What is man?* by placing the problem of the finitude of human knowledge at the center of his critique of reason. That way of framing things was born out of the assumption that the finitude of man was a primary trait of his connection with being. From this came the provisional and derivative quality of human knowledge as well as its finitude, for it was subject to the temporality and mortality of being-there in relation to being. Intuition was therefore seen as a passive faculty, and intellect as merely re-productive rather than productive. Reason was finite and incapable of transcending experience in the pursuit of the realm of ends. Truth, far from being eternal, was finally revealed as the daughter of historical time. Heidegger's interpretation of Kant effectively tore the Enlightenment project to pieces. The dream of the emancipation of man through man, which saw man as being able to interact with his own destiny, had lost its sole and fundamental weapon, i.e., knowledge as developed by Western metaphysics. How could one go on believing in culture, or in man as the subject of a variety of formative activities and an ideal regulating force in their development? According to Heidegger, Kant had already realized all this, and he had retreated in fear and anguish from his own discovery. In the first edition of the *Critique of Pure Reason* Kant had indicated that the transcendental capacity of imagination was the fundamental faculty that unified sensibility and intellect within the mechanisms of ontological knowledge. However, in the second edition, he was frightened by this hypothesis, which questioned the very bases of a Western metaphysics that was founded on *Logos* and *ratio*, and he therefore abandoned this course, turning instead for his main theme to the centrality of the intellect and of logic rather than of imagination.[10]

Faced with this interpretation, which situated Kant within what we now call "the postmodern," Cassirer, who understood what was at stake, replied in strong terms. In a long review written in 1931, which in a way was the conclusion of the Davos disputation, Cassirer stressed again the overall import of Kant's philosophy, and the fundamental importance of the question of ethics and of moral law within that system of thought. It was within the world of morality that the categorical imperative was realized, which produced the miracle of man's creative knowledge and his exercise of the transcendental capacity of imagination towards the realm of ends: "the 'I' is at bottom only what it makes of itself."[11] Kant had always stressed how any analysis that was based solely on the "nature of man" would never be able to attain the transcendental idea of liberty and the creation of a universal ethics. Heidegger's crude and tragic monism aimed at bundling together phenomena and noumena, the sensible world and the intelligible world, since it considered it impossible to think of the human being outside time and finitude. Kant, on the other hand, was a dualist, and was trying to understand the relationship between *mundus intelligibilis* and *mundus sensibilis*. As Cassirer passionately pointed out, Kant's problem "is not the problem of 'Being' and 'Time,' but rather the problem of 'Being' and 'Ought,' of 'Experience' and 'Idea.'" Kant was not interested in the problem of the temporality of the subject, or in the theme of existential anguish in the face of nothingness, or in the interpretation of man's being-there in relation to the temporality of "being-to-death." What he was interested in was the "intelligible substrate of humanity" (18). For Cassirer, "Kant is and remains—in the most sublime and beautiful sense of this word—a thinker of the Enlightenment," as he "strives after light and clarity even when he contemplates the deepest and most hidden 'grounds' of Being" (24). Mankind owed to Kant a philosophy that pointed man on the one hand towards "experience," and on the other towards his participation in the "idea," and therefore in transcendence and infinity: that was his "metaphysics," his way of exorcising the "anxiety of nothingness."

What remains today of that famous debate? How will the confrontation between the modern and the postmodern end? And how will the philosophical question of the Enlightenment be transformed in the face of the obstinate attacks launched by those who want to do away with the subject and critical reason and proclaim the death of man—and this despite the fact that they are unable to point to any serious, feasible alternatives beyond those of nihilism or the return to more or less disguised forms of religious spiritualism?

These are difficult questions to answer. They are made all the more difficult by the reappearance of an unwanted third party, alongside postmodern and neo-Enlightenment thinkers. And this is a very powerful and fearsome party, about which very little is normally said: i.e., the Catholic Church. One of the most extraordinary effects of the war between the modern and the postmodern is without a doubt the philosophical and cultural resurrection of God. This has taken the form of an unexpected comeback of religions in the public arena of Western societies, which, having lost their way, now suddenly find themselves on the road to post-secularization.[12] One of the most obvious consequences of this comeback is the crisis that threatens the lay principle and Enlightenment concept of the separation between religion and politics, accompanied by the transformation, in many ways disconcerting and unexpected, of the philosophical issue of the Enlightenment into a new and complex theological issue. This is a problem that for too long has been underestimated by the heirs to the Enlightenment tradition, and which deserves instead our focused attention.

It is obvious that this radical change of scenery is not due solely to arguments adduced by postmodern philosophers, however insistent and persuasive those arguments may have been. Rather, behind the collapse of the great progressive ideologies and utopian philosophies of emancipation, which has been an incontrovertible aspect of the international scene since 1989, there are far-reaching economic, social, and political factors, compounded by errors and tragic delusions that history has laid to rest. And yet, it is certainly no coincidence that the radical theses, unsettling questions, and apocalyptic language of thinkers like Heidegger, Adorno, and Foucault have become an integral and crucial part of the arguments that Christian philosophers and theologians advance against the specter of the Enlightenment—which, incidentally, means that that specter, albeit now more diaphanous than ever, is still fearsome enough in their eyes.

The Catholic Church has updated its old anti-Enlightenment arsenal through intelligent and systematic reference to the dialectic of the Enlightenment itself, including the alleged responsibilities consequent to critical reason and the Kantian claim of man's moral autonomy. These positions have in fact been blamed for contributing to the genesis of totalitarianism, the commodification of goods, and the creation of our stressful technological society. Accusations have come from all quarters, ranging from John Paul II's encyclicals to the standard challenges posed by theologians, parish priests, and intellectuals alike, which have by now reached the status of cliché. It is worth noting that it is the paradigm of the Centaur, in its more recent and striking incarnations, that increasingly dominates major debates in the international public arena, while the historians' Enlightenment is consistently ignored. Within this framework, one may also cite how the philosopher Jürgen Habermas and the theologian Joseph Ratzinger recently concurred on the need for a dialogue between Faith and Reason, or between "lay rationality" and Christianity, in the light of a new postsecular society, in which religion occupies center stage in public life. The course of that dialogue has followed precisely the traditional Hegelian lines of censure aimed at the estrangement of modernity, a modernity that, moreover, is seeking its foundation and dialectical reconciliation with itself through religious Faith, just as the young Hegel had hoped.[13] In fact, this road remains the easiest in that it leaves open the possibility of future moments of convergence between reason and faith, and does so without dwelling too much on past history and dramatic events.

And yet the past is never completely gone and continues to affect our choices. For centuries the Catholic Church vilified, demonized, and used every means in its arsenal to impede an affirmation of the rights of man, of religious freedom, of toleration, and democracy. How can it now credibly present itself as a legitimate bastion, defending the Western world's precious political heritage without first taking serious stock of itself? It is not enough to invoke the "purification of memory" and to apologize for the misdeeds of the past, as John Paul II did, if one then continues to point the finger at the Enlightenment as the historical cause of the culture of death and all the other evils of the twentieth century.[14] It is not enough to proclaim to the four winds the universality of the rights of the human being, if the Church then negates those rights within itself, and refuses to confront the necessity to redefine the fundamental concepts of liberty and truth, also and especially on a theological level.[15]

As is well known—or rather, as should be well known but is not—it was only with the Second Vatican Council that the Church really began to respond to the modern political advances brought about by the Enlightenment. It took several varieties of totalitarianism, the tragic events of the twentieth century, and above all the Holocaust, which cast so heavy a shadow on the Catholics' attitude towards Jews, to shake the consciences of a hierarchy entrenched behind the certainties of the Council of Trent, to finally open up a dialogue between Catholicism and modernity.[16]

Already in 1930s France, a group of important thinkers linked to the Catholic avant-garde journal *Esprit*, including names such as Mounier, Daniélou, and Maritain, had in fact taken the first steps towards engagement with the modern post-Enlightenment world of the rights of man. However, their efforts went largely unheeded. These thinkers acknowledged at last the important positive contribution made by the Enlightenment, but they also advocated going beyond the "radical vice of anthropocentric humanism" pervading that movement.[17] They theorized the need to open the way to social rights, and to a "new Christendom" capable of taking in the positive aspects of modernity and Christianizing its very roots—or at least foregoing demonization of the modern based on preconceived notions. As Maritain wrote in his famous *Humanisme intégral* (1936), in which he outlined the foundations for a philosophy of the history of Christianity in the wake of historicist theories of "overcoming": "In the scheme of Christian humanism there is a place not for the *errors* of Luther and Voltaire, but *for* Voltaire and Luther, according as in spite of the errors they have contributed in the history of men to certain advances."[18]

After World War II, thanks to the efforts of progressive elements among the Church's European hierarchy and of the powerful Catholic Church of North-America under the direction of Cardinal Spellman, those ideas were reflected in the decree *Dignitatis humanae personae* of the Second Vatican Council, which strongly reflected the wishes of Pope Paul VI. In this groundbreaking document, the Catholic world defined for the first time the *ius ad libertatem religiosam* as an inalienable right of the human being, a right immune from both the "reason of State" and the "reason of the Church." On that occasion a "star witness," Karol Wojtyła, exclaimed: "It was a revolution!" He had immediately grasped that, beyond the significant theological and ecclesiastical departure that this constituted, the shift of emphasis from the rights of God to the rights of the human being could have important political implications in the fight against communism.[19] And indeed the Second Vatican Council seemed at one point to be headed towards an "anthropological turn,"[20] based on the works of some of the main exponents of the so-called *nouvelle théologie*, in which crucial attention was paid to a reconsideration of the historicity of Christianity and to the reevaluation of history and of human existence in time as a theological issue.[21] However, that position was soon abandoned in later interpretations of the outcome of Vatican II. A shortcut was adopted instead, which consisted in a form of hermeneutics that was entirely philosophical and theological, and which was, in the end, all that came out of that dialogue between Christian and Enlightenment humanisms that was heralded by the courageous questions asked in the encyclical *Gaudium et spes*: "What is man? What is this sense of sorrow, of evil, of death, which continues to exist despite so much progress?"[22] They thus abandoned the main road, which, though undoubtedly fraught with hardships and perils, would have led towards respect for historical truth, tolerance, and the reciprocal and respectful acknowledgement of each other by the two humanisms that have profoundly affected the history and identity of the Western world.

An important element that led to that approach being discarded was without doubt the dominant role played, in the last few decades, by the philosophical and theological culture of the German Catholic world within the intellectual horizons of the Vatican hierarchy. This was a strong and evocative culture, which found a crucial point of reference, especially for Pope Benedict XVI, in the work of Romano Guardini, who was born in Verona in 1885, but held the chair of Catholic theology at the University of Munich from 1923 until his death in 1968.

In his famous *Das Ende der Neuzeit* (1951), Guardini adduced solid philosophical arguments for proclaiming the end of "the modern world," that is to say of a modernity founded on values that went against the revealed religion of Christianity. Moreover, he detected in the postmodern era that was just underway unexpected and important grounds for God's reentry into the future history of mankind. In Guardini's evaluation, the experiment of modernity had been a terminal and resounding failure. With all its illusions and hopes, with all the bourgeoisie's "superstitious faith" in progress, in the autonomy of the individual, and in his capacity to enfranchise himself by his own means and without the need for God, what that experiment had finally led to were the horrors of totalitarianism, the Holocaust, and the terrifying prospect of science and technology out of control and able to produce only a "non-natural nature" and a "non-human man."[23]

Inebriated with power, an unconscious victim of his own uncontrolled and unlimited freedom, bowing under the weight of his own strength, modern man had led humanity to the brink of the abyss. "Without exaggeration one can say that a new era of history has been born. Now and forever man will live on the brink of an ever-growing danger which shall leave its mark upon his entire existence"—thus prophesied Guardini (110). Faced with the existential anguish wrought by the savage, primitive, and unbounded power of the modern world, in which "all the horrors of darkness are once more upon man [and he] stands

again before chaos" (111), humanity's only hope of saving itself lay in returning to a religious sentiment that needed to be built anew. In the new era that
was dawning full of uncertainty, the Church was called upon to assume the
supreme role of savior of humanity, to protect human beings and safeguard
their link with God through Revelation, which was seen as the foundation of
truth and of the historical meaning of being. The Church must bravely reenter
society, renew the sacred value of "the crucial events of life such as birth or
marriage or death" (117), and prevent the total secularization of the two forces
whose hybridization the Church fears and denounces more than anything, i.e.,
of biology and politics. Guardini was well aware of the difficulties and above all
of the ultimate eschatological meaning for God's people of the dawn of a new
historical era:

> Loneliness in faith will be terrible. [. . .] If we speak here of the nearness of the
> End, we do not mean nearness in the sense of time, but nearness as it pertains to
> the essence of the End, for in essence man's existence is now nearing an absolute
> decision. Each and every consequence of that decision bears within it the greatest
> potentiality and the most extreme danger (132–133).

In the aftermath of the Council, such thoughts pressed on the minds of Catholic intellectuals, bishops, cardinals and popes, as they faced the task of interpreting the "updates" put forward by Vatican II. John Paul II's general aversion
to today's Enlightenment-influenced modernity, for instance, bears deep traces
of this.[24] At a three-day seminar held at the behest of the pope at Castel Gan-
dolfo, near Rome, in August 1996, eminent scholars such as Paul Ricoeur, Reinhart Koselleck, Hans Maier, Stanley Rosen, and others deliberately launched an
entirely new era in the relationship between the Enlightenment and Christianity. The "today" of the seminar's title—"Enlightenment Today"—refers to the
post-1989 period, i.e., the new era characterized by the defeat of Communism
and the start of the third millennium.[25] In the proceedings we find the image
of the Enlightenment definitively ordained as the last stumbling block that remains before the pernicious and tragic experience of secularization can be top-
pled once and for all.

However, within those pages there are still many unresolved positions. One
senses a form of subdued and painful hesitation: on the one hand, there is acknowledgement of the by now historically undeniable merits of the Enlightenment, identifiable in the eighteenth-century rise of the ideas of liberty and
of the rights of man in the fields of philosophy, law, ethics, and politics; on the
other hand, there is the terrible accusation leveled by postmodern thinkers,
that, by denying God's role in history, the Enlightenment brought about the
rise of totalitarianism, the dominion of a dehumanized technology and science,

and a form of limitless individual freedom that was bound to degenerate into unfettered positivism. For instance, in Hans Maier's insightful paper, acknowledgement of the historical merits of the Enlightenment is accompanied by the claim that ever since the eighteenth century there had in fact been a "Catholic Enlightenment" and a "Christian 'Sapere aude!'," whereby the Catholic Church had worked alongside exponents of the Enlightenment at a common project aimed at educating mankind along the lines hoped for by Lessing (93). This being the case, a call went out to appropriate the most authentic legacy of Enlightenment-inspired humanism and to mobilize third-millennium religion in defense of its best values. In the words of one of the participants, Robert Spaemann, "in the aftermath of Nietzsche, we have now reached a point where only religion can save the Enlightenment [. . .] because religion understands the Enlightenment better than the latter understands itself" (232). Particularly noteworthy in this respect are John Paul II's concluding remarks, wherein he explores the religious origins of the metaphor of light and enlightenment. This validates in a definitive and authoritative way the strategy of appropriating the Enlightenment legacy, which itself follows the traditional pattern set by Augustine in his project of assimilating and surpassing the legacy of the classical world of Greek and Latin antiquity in the *City of God*.

In fact, many of these ideas were not new. They had been circulating for quite some time, ever since Vatican II. Among the thinkers who were most concerned with the complex relationship between Christianity and Enlightenment culture, both during and after the Council, was Joseph Ratzinger, the future Pope Benedict XVI. In his reflections, this became an important issue in terms both of theology and of the Church's political stance, so much so that the theme of the Christianization of the Enlightenment as a possible solution to the philosophical problem of the dialectic recurs obsessively in many of his writings. Ratzinger repeatedly points to the way in which the Church "in the dialectic of enlightenment does away with the conditions for enlightenment,"[26] prevents its degeneration into totalitarianism, and safeguards its original message of an emancipation generated by the *Logos*: "Christian theology, if it is functioning correctly, is to be seen as a force for enlightenment."[27] Ratzinger's hope that humanity can be rescued by a new holy alliance between faith and reason therefore rests on the common rationalistic foundation of the Enlightenment and of Christianity, as embodied in St. John's *Logos*. This can be seen clearly in texts such as the one drafted for a meeting with the academic staff of the University of Rome "La Sapienza" that was due to take place in January 2008 (but was subsequently called off). In this document, the constitution of a third-millennium humanism was to rest upon a number of agreed-upon principles, such as the fundamental vocation to the pursuit of truth and the rejection of myth in the name of reason that guided both Christian theologians and the thinkers based at European universities ever since their foundation, or such as certain pronouncements, at times somewhat questionable, on Islam's historical and genetic incapacity to embrace rational argumentation as the decisive horizon in theological discussion (as opposed to Christianity's greater openness in this respect).

And yet, one persistent obstacle to dialogue between the heirs of the Enlightenment and those of the Catholic tradition was Benedict XVI's constant oscillation between acknowledging the historical merits of the Enlightenment and condemning it as a dangerous "dead dog" in Western culture. In Ratzinger's stance we find, on the one hand, the admission that the Enlightenment has originated a modern lay culture founded on the beneficial institutional separation of Church and State: "In the broadest sense of the word, the term *laico* denotes spiritual membership in the Enlightenment."[28] On the other hand, there are constant references to the direct responsibility of the Enlightenment for the rise of totalitarianism. In the 2007 encyclical *Spe Salvi*, clearly following a pattern borrowed from Guardini's reflections, Ratzinger effectively proclaimed the end of the modern era and of the illusions of those who believed in the idea of "progress." He thus liquidated once and for all the Enlightenment's hope of emancipating man through man, and announced the definitive failure of Marx's communist prophecies. Even Kant was misappropriated as the first to raise serious concerns over the potentially catastrophic and apocalyptic consequences of human action in the latest periods of the history of mankind.[29]

The Catholic Church seems to have made a conscious decision to mix together history, theology, and philosophy along the lines of what we have called "the paradigm of the Centaur." One cannot help feeling that this will inevitably lead to a muddying of the waters and will make discussion of the issue in the public arena increasingly difficult. If the theological manipulation of the paradigm of the Centaur is carried beyond certain levels, it will elude or even mystify the rights of history, rendering discussion banal and straining belief. It is certainly not conducive to a helpful and clear discussion when Ratzinger asserts that there were three successive "ages of enlightenment" in history. In his account, the first of those ages occurred in ancient times, was adopted wholesale by Christianity and was instrumental in its victory over paganism. The second took place in the eighteenth century, had undoubted merits in its assertion of the rights of man and of human liberty, but was also responsible for chasing God away from the world. Finally comes Ratzinger's "second Enlightenment," which is currently in operation and which he characterizes as a dehumanized and Godless age, a product of that dialectic so well described by postmodern thinkers, and from which only the Church can save us.[30] This ambitious theological-philosophical vision can be considered a contemporary Catholic version of the Centaur. By these means, Ratzinger manages to take apart the whole universe of values developed by eighteenth-century Enlightenment culture. He bypasses the principle of the separation of religion and politics by applying Bellarmino's theory of *potestas indirecta* in the moral field.[31] He brings God back into the very center of public debate, and elevates the hierarchy and the sovereign pontiff to the role of guarantors of liberty and democracy in the Western world. He does all this in order to revitalize a Christianity that in practice continues to experience a profound vocational crisis, despite the huge crowds that gather in Rome.

Leaving aside the specific case of Benedict XVI's work, which stands out for its intellectual complexity and sophistication, the dangers of this conceptual device, and of that employed by postmodern philosophers, lie in the deliberate conflation of history, theology, and philosophy, at the expense of the rights of historical truth. And indeed the dominant element in contemporary variations on the theme of the Centaur is the theological principle. The Holocaust is used to explain, retrospectively, Rousseau's political ideas. Questionable products of mass culture are blamed on the rise of public opinion in the eighteenth century, and vice versa. Poor Voltaire would appear to have unwittingly opened the gates to Hitler and Stalin with his insistence on man's liberty and responsibility in the face of a distant and indifferent God. Rather than selectively studying the Enlightenment and the numerous metamorphoses that its legacy has undergone in the two intervening centuries, thinkers have resorted to an abstract and instrumental amalgamation of languages and disciplines. In opposition to this trend, the present volume focuses on the necessary distinctions between different contexts and eras, and above all between the philosophical and the historical aspects of the Enlightenment. It is hoped that this distinction will help us analyze these questions in a more productive way, as we reflect both on our historical knowledge and on whether or not the values developed by eighteenth-century culture have endured in time, above and beyond the shattered illusions and undeniably tragic aberrations and degenerations of the modern world. Only in this way will it perhaps be possible to escape the stranglehold of those who consider the legacy of the Enlightenment and its values as nothing more than an anachronistic relict, and therefore invite us (with a malicious smile) to choose between skepticism and moral authoritarianism, between God and nothingness.

PART II

||||||||||||||||||||||||

THE HISTORIANS' ENLIGHTENMENT

The Cultural Revolution of the Ancien Régime

8

||||||||||||||||||||||||||

FOR A DEFENSE OF HISTORICAL KNOWLEDGE

Beyond the Centaur

THE CORRECT QUESTION to ask a historian is not "What *is* the Enlightenment?" but rather "What *was* it?" We should ask what is it that we know about its significance in the history of Europe during the *Ancien Régime*. Conversely, the historian questioned should resist the disastrous temptation—for someone in this business—to think of the Enlightenment as a kind of *philosophia perennis*. That perspective risks making it impossible to distinguish with true intellectual honesty and philological rigor between the specific historical identity of the eighteenth-century phenomenon and its legacy in the following centuries, down to our own times.[1]

In fact, however, this kind of attitude is very common today, amid the prevailing confusion of languages and ideas, and the constant spin of political communication, which jumbles together in the most indiscriminate manner historical and philosophical questions, and radically different periods and events, simply in order to fuel public debate. Today we seem to forget that the questions and answers of historians are different from those asked by Kant on the subject of the Enlightenment, as he reflected, as a philosopher, on his own times. Nor are they the same as those posed by Hegel, who was concerned with creating an absolute foundation for the modern world, or by Marx, in his determination to find in history an ideological and philosophical continuum on which to found his political project for the emancipation of mankind.

It cannot be denied that in the past it was this very interweaving of history and philosophy—the phenomenon of the "Centaur" described in the first part of this book—that most contributed to the advancement of our knowledge, thanks to the powerful images it presented. Today, however, this way of thinking about history raises some concern, especially if it is not accompanied by a clear awareness of a phenomenon's original premises and final objectives. That kind of blinkered vision leads more and more often to manipulations and misunderstandings, as in the case of the bold historico-theological reconstructions put in place by Benedict XVI on Adorno and Horkheimer's dialectic of Enlightenment. At other times it takes the form of a philosophical travesty of the history of the Enlightenment, which poses a significant risk, not least in an epistemological sense, to future historical research. This makes it imperative that we go beyond the current state of things to attempt clarifications and distinctions, insofar as possible, and that we uphold, humbly but firmly, the autonomy and prerogatives of historical knowledge in this field.

It should be noted straightaway that in the past the need to go beyond this dual way of thinking did not present itself with the same urgency as it does now. The double nature of the Hegelian Centaur was often interpreted with great wisdom and admirable results by many eminent historians, and without causing any problems. One need only mention how, in the study of the ancient world, some scholars have deemed it useful and legitimate to see the rationalism of the Greek sophists as an early enlightenment phase in Western thought. Eminent scholars like Momigliano and Droysen made use of this idea with critical intelligence and awareness, as they compared Voltaire's anti-religious mentality with a similar stance in Xenophanes, or as they detected significant common traits between Hellenism and the eighteenth-century Enlightenment, to the point where the latter served as a model for the establishment of the former as a category.[2] Finally, it is impossible to deny that much of the best twentieth-century historical research on the Enlightenment was conducted under the spell of the Centaur, and with very positive results.[3] A few examples will suffice.

Carl Lotus Becker's celebrated study, *The Heavenly City of the Eighteenth-Century Philosophers* (1932), a foundational work for American historical scholarship on these issues, deliberately mixed together history and philosophy. Becker subscribed to Dilthey's thesis of a basic continuity between the medieval *Weltanschauung* and that of the Enlightenment, seeing in the former an attempt to secularize Augustine's City of God on the basis of a rationalistic outlook that was found to be substantially the same in Thomas Aquinas as in Voltaire. Among the works that carry out a philosophical critique of the Enlightenment along Hegelian lines, in the wake of Adorno and Horkheimer's radicalization of Hegel's theses, we find two important historical studies, both published in 1959: Lester G. Crocker's *An Age of Crisis*, and Reinhart Koselleck's ingenious though debatable *Kritik und Krise*, which until recently was still enjoying great international popularity.[4] As a French literary historian, Crocker's focus was on demonstrating the historical role played by the Enlightenment in bringing about the moral crisis of the modern world, within a perspective that saw the birth of nihilism and totalitarianism as the inevitable consequence of the *philosophes'* attempt to emancipate man through man, while renouncing the idea of God as a fundamental philosophical premise.

Koselleck, on the other hand, was an expert in social and political history. His aim was to trace the beginnings of the modern world, and of the devastating political and social conflicts that afflict us to this day, back to the rise of critique as the exercise of reason and to its application in every field by European adherents of the Enlightenment, freemasons and literary figures alike. Arising in the period between two civil wars (the wars of religion that had ended in the seventeenth century and the French Revolution), the Enlightenment is depicted by the great German historian as dialectically intertwined with the rise of the absolute State. That crucial metamorphosis of the modern State was originally meant to ensure peace and security through repressive and disciplinary mechanisms. In the event, however, it aided the Enlightenment's reaction against that State by attempting to separate morals and politics, and by reducing man to a subject and appropriating all private space devoted to the exercise of critique. This resulted in the dialectical rise in the Western world of a crucial historical phenomenon, which was identified by Marx as the autonomization of bourgeois civil society from the State, and which consisted in the widespread use of critique together with the practice of Masonic secrecy and set up oppositions between morals and politics, and between the rights of the individual and the interests of the absolute State. The critique had thus revealed itself to be an insidious weapon. It was originally intended to reassert the rights of morality over politics and to unveil the *arcana juris* that hid from view the drive towards domination on the part of the Church and individual sovereigns. However, according to Koselleck, through its own perverse internal logic, which was informed by the overriding need to achieve transparency and rationality by means of judgment and doubt, the practice of critique, "via counter-criticism, arrived at super-criticism, before finally declining into hypocrisy" of a moralistic kind.[5] This negated the autonomy of the "political," as theorized in the 1930s by Koselleck's university tutor Carl Schmitt, and set in motion the current unstoppable crisis of the Western world, which is now incapable of escaping the state of permanent revolution and ideological civil war that was unleashed by the utopian theories of the Enlightenment at the end of the eighteenth century, and by the French Revolution.

It is interesting to see how this pattern, based on the philosophy of spirit and on the study of the Enlightenment as a moment in the history of Western rationality, has continued to influence scholars whose research ostensibly

has no link whatsoever with our Hegelian Centaur. These scholars seem determined to defend the Enlightenment against the accusations issued by the age
of Restoration and by the Romantics in the wake of Hegel's authoritative pronouncements. This applies, for instance, to a study by historian of ideas Peter
Gay, *The Enlightenment: An Interpretation*, which was published in two volumes subtitled *The Rise of Modern Paganism* (1966) and *The Science of Freedom*
(1969). Born in Berlin, Gay had fled from Nazi Germany to the United States.
In his introduction, he immediately reveals his debt to dialectical thought, as he
identifies the moment of thesis with the "appeal to antiquity" contained in the
works of the European Enlightenment, and the moment of antithesis with their
"tension with Christianity." The synthesis, on the other hand, consisted in their
determined "pursuit of modernity."[6] Another and more important example is
Ernst Cassirer's now classical 1932 study, *Die Philosophie der Aufklärung.*[7]

Cassirer's theses were widely accepted in the past and continue to exercise
a significant influence on international Enlightenment scholarship. However,
this is due to a disconcerting and persistent misunderstanding that accompanied the success of those theses from the very beginning. Cassirer's dense study
is as admired on the level of its civic engagement as its research is considered
dubious and, nowadays, obsolete.[8] He was concerned not with the nature and
characteristics of the historical Enlightenment in general, but only with the
new way in which it understood philosophy. His aim was, first and foremost,
that of providing a modern version of the Centaur in Kantian terms, in open
opposition to the negative pronouncements of Hegel and his followers on the
European Enlightenment's abstract "philosophy of reflection." Cassirer states
this quite clearly in his introduction. After linking his present book explicitly
with some of his previous works on the history of philosophy, including his
Individuum und Kosmos in der Philosophie der Renaissance,[9] Cassirer indicates
how "the movement to be described is not self-contained, but looks before and
after beyond its own confines. It forms but a part and a special phase of that
whole intellectual development through which modern philosophic thought
gained its characteristic self-confidence and self-consciousness." Both this
study's frame of reference and its approach to the history of philosophy, then,
explicitly looked back to the traditional model of the Hegelian Centaur: "Such
a presentation of philosophical doctrines and systems endeavors as it were to
give a 'phenomenology of the philosophic spirit'; it is an attempt to show how
this spirit, struggling with purely objective problems, achieves clarity and depth
in its understanding of its own nature and destiny, and of its own fundamental
character and mission."[10]

For Cassirer there was no doubt that the Enlightenment had created an entirely new form of philosophical thought, which was founded on the methods

of the natural sciences and on the systematic use of scientific reason in every field. That made it meaningless to pursue original philosophical content, great new works of metaphysics and visions of the world according to traditional criteria. Cassirer replied to any accusations of superficiality, eclecticism, and a lack of speculative originality levied against eighteenth-century philosophers by stressing above all the value of their redefinition of the very identity and tasks of philosophy itself. For philosophy had now become a powerful tool for the analysis and transformation of reality via the articulation of knowledge, effecting a momentous shift from seventeenth-century *esprit de système* to a vibrant new *esprit systématique*.

The core of Cassirer's reconstruction, and the fundamental thesis that would profoundly influence subsequent debates, resided in his firm declaration of faith in Kant and Newton's scientific rationalism, in which he saw the decisive and unsurpassed manifestation of modern rationalism. This is why Cassirer completely turned on its head Hegel's negative pronouncement on modern science, which Hegel saw as the ultimate basis for a "philosophy of reflection," that is to say for the narcissism of the subject that looked at itself in the mirror, as embodied in the assumption that man and the methods of natural sciences ought to be the sole points of reference and truth criteria:

> The philosophy of the eighteenth century takes up this particular case, the methodological pattern of Newton's physics, though it immediately begins to generalize. It is not content to look upon analysis as the great intellectual tool of mathematico-physical knowledge; eighteenth century thought sees analysis rather as the necessary and indispensable instrument of all thinking in general. This view triumphs in the middle of the century. However much individual thinkers and schools differ in their results, they agree in this epistemological premise.[11]

Whether or not one is prepared to share these theses—which are in any case too schematic and reductive with respect to the real intellectual life of the European Enlightenment (more on this below)—Cassirer's work eventually dominated the scene of international historiography and was at the center of harsh polemics. In Italy, Furio Diaz and Franco Venturi did not hesitate to distance themselves from it. They pointed out how in Cassirer's analysis there was no reference to the general context, or to questions such as those relating to political economy, to reforms, or to government, which were all crucial factors in any correct definition of so complex a historical phenomenon. In his Cambridge *Trevelyan Lectures* of 1969, Venturi denounced the way in which "[f]rom Kant to Cassirer and beyond, our understanding of the European Enlightenment has been dominated by the philosophical interpretation of the German *Aufklärung.*" The only difference was that, among the numerous more or less conscious followers of that paradigm, Cassirer at least "was sincere and entitled his book *Die Philosophie der Aufklärung*."[12] Nevertheless, it is worth analyzing the contents of Venturi's absolutely correct denunciation, in order to understand also the limitations preventing historians, both then and now, from really coming to terms with the foundations of the Centaur paradigm. The specific source of that denunciation was a problematical and empirical concept of historicism that could be traced back as far as Ranke, Droysen, and Meinecke, as opposed to so-called "absolute historicism." The latter was a form of logical and providentialist historicism, of a kind that originated with Hegel and seemed to survive in isolated cases as far as Benedetto Croce's late works, such as his *History as Thought and Action*.[13] It also at times resurfaced in the writings of those who, like American historian Carl Lotus Becker, tended always to "fuse history and philosophy in the Enlightenment,"[14] thus arbitrarily creating a "retrospective history" (4), tracing "history backwards in order to explain an idea or an event" (3), and (as in the case of Delio Cantimori and of Eugenio Garin) postulating the very existence of a kind of long Enlightenment, "from Petrarch to Rousseau" (5). Such scholars tend to forget that although philosophers "are tempted to push upstream until they arrive at the source," historians "must tell us how the river made its way, among what obstacles and difficulties"; that is to say, they must respect the logic of the historical context and judge phenomena *iuxta propria principia*.

Venturi denounced in similar terms also the scholars engaged in the new social history of the Enlightenment, such as Daniel Roche, whom he accused of writing about history from an ideologized standpoint—"in the light of the writings and opinions of Marx, Engels and their school" (10)—on the links between the Enlightenment and bourgeois rationalism. These were serious accusations, and in fact rather ungenerous. It was not by chance that Venturi's final target are the adherents of a French style of social history, with their "pretension of creating a total history, a vision of society as a global structure able to reveal its inner logic, the laws governing its own existence, if it is submitted to a suitable interpretative instrument, whether it be the class struggle, quantification or structuralism" (16). Ironically, these accusations reveal all the limitations and insuperable weaknesses of Venturi's polemics against philosophers. Indeed, he never questions the main thesis of Cassirer's book, that of the complete identification between the philosophy of the Enlightenment and the modern scientific rationalism of Galileo, Kepler, and Newton. Nor does he address in any significant way the *vexata quaestio* of the differences between historical knowledge, its foundations, and the modalities of philosophical knowledge in epistemological terms, even though that would have been the only really effective way to undermine the received wisdom and go finally beyond the paradigm of the Centaur.

Much has changed in the intervening half-century, but the clash between philosophers and historians is still with us. It has now taken a new form, however, and refers largely to different theoretical horizons and research questions. Whether we like it or not, the "postmodern" virus has left its mark, attacking previously solid organisms, creating widespread uncertainty and raising questions that should not be underestimated.

As we saw in part 1, the great challenge for historians of the Enlightenment today comes above all from the work of Michel Foucault. More specifically, it comes from Foucault's attempt to revive the paradigm of the Centaur as "historico-philosophical practice" in the wake of the great German historiography of the *Aufklärung*. He focused on new and insidious themes that represent typical postmodern concerns, such as the subject, power, and above all truth, which is now unveiled in its quality as will to power, a rhetorical exercise that aims at domination, but remains devoid of all real knowledge. After Foucault, and more specifically after his frontal attack on the traditional way in which scholars following in the wake of Nietzsche and Heidegger view the Enlightenment, the issue that needs to be resolved if we are to go beyond the Centaur and emancipate historians from the philosophers' claim to primacy in this field, is definitely that of upholding the epistemological status of historical knowledge. Obviously, this must be done without any great claims to a glorious past, but with the awareness that history is not in any way inferior to any other form of knowledge, and therefore has the potential to achieve original and autonomous results towards solving the historical problem of the Enlightenment.

As is well known, in the course of the sixteenth and seventeenth centuries historical knowledge and its cognitive foundations in European culture faced a huge challenge. The rapid spread of a new historical Pyrrhonism, more generally the so-called "crise pyrrhonienne," had infiltrated many aspects of human knowledge.[15] This attitude of total skepticism, which called into doubt the possibility of attaining any real form of knowledge, originated with the translation into Latin of the works of Sextus Empiricus in 1569, and spread across the Republic of Letters with the success of Montaigne's *Essais*. It gathered momentum with the religious controversies between Catholics and Protestants, who were desperately in search of a truth criterion by which to distinguish between the tradition of the Church, the pope, and the Councils, on the one hand, and the sole authority of the Scriptures on the other. After affecting theologians, scientists, and jurists, eventually it called into question the authority of historians as well. This crisis revived ancient and disturbing questions, first asked by skeptic philosophers at Plato's Academy during the third century BC: Could man reasonably aspire to the possession of truth? And if so, on what basis was this knowledge justified? Mabillon, Bayle, Huet, Le Clerc, Muratori were some of the protagonists of the debate on the validity and truth of the testimonies of the past, and more generally on the epistemological autonomy of history as a discipline.[16] The heated debates on *fides historica* and the decisive role played by new auxiliary sciences, such as philology, diplomatics, and numismatics, that were supposed to validate historical evidence (or, as the saying went, *historicis argumentis fidem faciunt*), culminated in foundational texts such as J. M. Chladenius's 1752 *Allgemeine Geschichtswissenschaft*, in which it was the evidence of common sense grounding testimonies that defined the precise boundaries within which it was possible to ascertain the truth of past events from an epistemological and philosophical point of view.

Historians triumphed over the attack from seventeenth- and eighteenth-century skepticism thanks mainly to the work of antiquarians who for the first time provided the solid bases needed for the new critical-philological method that has come down to us through the later syntheses and analyses of such great scholars as Gibbon, Ranke, and Droysen. As Arnaldo Momigliano wrote, "Antiquarians rescued historians from skepticism, even though they were not writing history books. Their preference for original documents, their acumen in detecting forgeries, their expertise in collecting and classifying sources and, above all, their boundless love of culture are the antiquarians' important contributions to the historians' 'ethics.'"[17]

In the last few decades the postmodern has posed another challenge to the work of the historian, one no less disturbing and insidious than that of seventeenth-century Pyrrhonism. This time, the issue was raised by supporters of the theory of the "linguistic turn," or "rhetorical turn," and by deconstructionists and relativists of all stamps.[18] It is, fundamentally, a postmodern skeptical stance that recognizes only narrative or rhetorical dimensions in historiography and rejects any claim to truth-finding on its part, and it is currently flourishing. Moreover, dangerously, it is acquiring more and more credence worldwide, and for reasons that it is vital not to underestimate. In the first instance, there is a widespread desire to forget the horrors of our recent past, such as the Holocaust and the different varieties of totalitarianism, and with it an attendant temptation to relativize historical truth to the point where it is rendered meaningless and banal, all in the attempt to anesthetize painful memories. This has given rise to negationist and relativist currents, with the latter attitude reaching so extreme a nihilism that its proponents deny the existence of any kind of factual truth and perpetuate the law of the strongest, being once again inspired to see the will to power as the sole and ultimate truth and the explanation for the very essence of man. Nietzsche can perhaps be seen as the spiritual father of this—to historians rather worrying—new episode in the history of skepticism. As Carlo Ginzburg has shown, it was specifically a reflection

by Nietzsche on truth and falsehood that in the 1970s inspired several exponents of the "linguistic turn." The philosopher's poignant remark deserves to
be quoted in full:

> What then is truth? A movable host of metaphors, metonymies, anthropomor-
> phisms: in short, a sum of human relations which have been poetically and rhe-
> torically intensified, transferred, and embellished, and which, after long usage,
> seem to a people to be fixed, canonical, and binding. Truths are illusions which
> we have forgotten are illusions, they are metaphors that have become worn out
> and have been drained of sensuous force.[19]

Ginzburg has given a very effective reply to modern Pyrrhonists, in which
he pointed out how the pursuit of truth already played an important role in the
Aristotelian view of rhetoric, and then in the writings of Quintilian, Valla, and
Maurini, and how the status of proof constituted the rational core of the original concept of rhetoric, which had subsequently been set aside in favor of the
current reductive view of rhetoric as merely the art of argumentation.

There have also been other, no less important replies to the new postmodern
skepticism's stand against the idea of history as the pursuit and testimony of
truth. Indeed, it is not enough simply to point out that a historian, while he or
she can be considered a kind of rhetorician, is also expected to *prove* his or her
argument. Furthermore, we must also realize that skepticism and relativism
are not an absolute evil *per se*, and that they have always been at the origin of
every serious reflection on truth over the course of the centuries. All in all, we
should always keep in mind that there are different kinds of relativism, and
different types of skepticism.[20] The moderate skepticism of thinkers like Gas-
sendi, Descartes, and Hume is at the origin of modern philosophical thought.
In the same way, there is a form of empirical and problematical historicism
that is characterized by programmatic relativism, eschews any kind of nihilistic extremism, and has long existed alongside the modern concept of truth as
daughter of time and within reach of human objectives and capabilities. This is
the position adopted by all of the sciences. As Lessing used to say (though he
remains as largely unheeded today as he was in his times), absolute and eternal
truth pertains only to God.

A clear example of this stance is found in discussions of historical methods
by Koselleck and Momigliano. Both authors acknowledge the inevitable coexistence, in the work of historians, of objective source criticism and their own
subjective points of view, which themselves operate in history.[21] There has always been some unease over the idea of historicism as, in Momigliano's words,
"the acknowledgement that each one of us sees past events from a certain point
of view, or at least that our perspective is influenced by our individual and

changeable collocation within history." He also points out that, while "this is an uncomfortable view, because it implies the danger of relativism," it does not in any way invalidate the cognitive status of historiography. In fact, all forms of knowledge are subject to the same condition, for the very reason that they are human constructs. What matters are the rules of the game within the discipline itself, i.e., the verifiability of all data and conclusions. "Like that of all common mortals, historians' work is verifiable in so far as it is falsifiable: i.e., they can get it wrong and they can be shown to be wrong." It follows that "since all we can do is study change from a changeable point of view, we might as well do it properly," which means always searching for historical truth through a rigorous critical study of sources, elaborating new issues and models of analysis, and then verifying them with incontrovertible proof, always keeping in mind that "the inevitable corollary of historicism is the history of historiography, that is to say the awareness that historical issues have themselves a history."[22]

Other eminent philosophers, such as Paul Ricoeur, Hilary Putnam, and others, have also made important contributions, especially from an epistemological point of view, to the exploration of the conditions for a new critical realism of historical knowledge and of its legitimacy from the starting point of the rules of self-government that apply within the scientific community.[23] The outcome of this new search for objectivity, conducted against the new Pyrrhonists and in the context of rampant nihilism and strong skepticism towards the very idea of historical truth, seems to me to be well summarized in the peremptory and entirely welcome assertion by Roger Chartier, according to which "it is necessary to state with all our strength that history is ruled by the intention and principle of truth, that the past that it takes as its object is a reality that is external to its discourse, and that its knowledge is verifiable."[24]

THE *EPISTEMOLOGIA IMAGINABILIS* IN EIGHTEENTH-CENTURY SCIENCE AND PHILOSOPHY

THERE IS UNDOUBTEDLY one omission in our discussion of the Enlightenment so far, particularly as regards our aim of allowing historians to go beyond the very premises of what we have called the paradigm of the Centaur (according to Cassirer's final version, in which the Enlightenment mainly coincides with the paradigm of Newtonian physics). More attention ought to be devoted to the final outcome of an ancient debate that for nearly two centuries has dominated discussions of historical knowledge within the ancient quarrel between the moral and natural sciences.

Indeed, we should reflect in greater depth on the fact that today our way of thinking of and defining science has radically changed compared even to the recent past. The change in science's image and the revelation of the philosophers of science's so-called *epistemologia imaginabilis* have been due especially to the research carried out in recent years by historians of science.[1] This happened, however, only at the end of a difficult, centuries-old process, which can be only briefly summarized here.

Many things have changed since the day when the extraordinary results obtained by Kepler, Galileo, Descartes, and Newton effected a critical rethinking of all traditional forms of knowledge in the light of the scientific revolution. From Hobbes to Leibniz, to Hume and Diderot, many eminent scholars have engaged in the epistemological debate over extending the methods of the natural sciences to the study of human experience. For instance, in the course of the eighteenth century much hope was placed on the application of probability calculus to the social sciences. In his 1777 *Essai d'arithmétique morale*, Buffon theorized the existence in nature of "vérités de différents genres, des certitudes de différents ordres, des probabilités de différents degrés,"[2] thus opening the way to Condorcet's social mathematics, despite Diderot's reservations about d'Alembert's mathematical imperialism.

The idea of the unity of knowledge across all disciplines on the basis of scientific methodology reached its apex with Kant. However, we should not forget that at the start of the eighteenth century Giovan Battista Vico's critique of Descartes, Locke, and Newton had laid the foundations for a different epistemological view of the various forms of knowledge, one based instead on the distinction between sciences of the spirit and sciences of nature.[3] It is well known how, throughout the nineteenth century, historical knowledge was pitted against the prestige of scientific methodology. Countless scholars from every corner of Europe were questioning whether history should be considered a "science," or whether it was more a form of "art," closely related to rhetoric and literature.

In Italy, in 1893, Benedetto Croce wrote an essay with the emblematic title "La storia ridotta sotto il concetto generale dell'arte," or "History Brought under the General Concept of Art." The purpose of this brief study was to revisit this topic in light of the positivistic crisis at the end of the century, and to reply to an article written by Pasquale Villari in 1891, which had appeared also in German and French translation, in which the historian abruptly asked "Is History a Science?" The question seemed to have been convincingly settled once and for all by Droysen's brilliant epistemological solution, set out in the three editions of his *Historik* (the last of which was published in 1882). However, this was before the so-called *Methodenstreit* broke out in Germany, with the intervention of Simmel, Dilthey, Rickert, and Weber, and revived the old dualism of the different forms of knowledge under new terms.[4]

In his famous handbook Droysen had clearly reasserted the primacy of *Verstehen*, that is to say of historical science as a form of knowledge that aims to achieve "*understanding* by means of *investigation*."[5] This was a kind of historical science that was mindful of the specificity of the moral world and of the liberty and will of man as the primary subject in history, and it stood in polemical contrast to attempts by positivists like Buckle to extend to history the methods and objectives of the natural sciences.[6] The hermeneutical interpretative method and the traditional separation between sciences of the spirit and sciences of nature seemed to have won out also in the organization of university courses.

In fact, if one traces all the complex vicissitudes and echoes of the *Methodenstreit* across Europe, it will be easy to see how completely entangled all of the different positions and interpretations became as a result of the crisis of positivism and the start of the momentous revision of the epistemological foundations of the image of science. The traditional definition of science itself was called into doubt. This happened especially in France, following the work of

Mach, Avenarius, Duhem, Boutroux, with Bergson's and Le Roy's harsh polemics against Poincaré at the end of the century. Once a static and normative matter of objective mathematical laws that were set once and for all and could be explained and predicted according to the rigorous deterministic model of Galileo and Newton's rational mechanics, science came to be seen as a historically determined assemblage of hypotheses and theoretical explanations of a conventional and probabilistic nature. It needed to be verified empirically and then, if necessary, to be constantly "consumed" and replaced in the course of a process based on truths that were only ever partial and relative.

This undermined the nineteenth-century positivistic myth of science as absolute truth, dealing with laws that were universal, static, and eternal and that claimed to describe reality as the thing itself, objective and independent of the observer. That myth began now to crumble and was replaced by a "humanized" image of a science defined first and foremost by its method and practice, and by the creative role played by the researcher who formulates hypotheses and verifies each new theory in turn.[7]

Among the great historians, Marc Bloch was certainly the one who best understood the intellectual revolution that was at its most intense during the first few decades of the twentieth century, and the role that such a radically new conception of science could play in redefining and reviving the legitimacy also of historical knowledge. The real substance and originality of Bloch's famous short work, *Apologie pour l'histoire ou métier d'historien*, which he wrote during the tragic years of World War II, lies in its passionate defense of the concrete bases of historical knowledge in the light of the heated epistemological debate on the nature of science that had taken place in the 1930s.[8] In that context, Bloch's text stands not only as a kind of closing chapter in the historians' long-standing engagement with the natural sciences but also, and especially, as a fascinating manifesto in support of the unity of function of all sciences, and of their fundamental methodological and epistemological connection. The locus of this unity was the central position occupied by man, in accordance with the tenets of the Enlightenment and against the German dogma of the dualism of *Geisteswissenschaften* and *Naturwissenschaften*. More than half a century later, Bloch's pages still come across as full of insights and of civic passion. While reading them, we should always keep in mind the so-called "crisis of reason" that profoundly affected intellectual life in Paris in the first few decades of the twentieth century. Nor should we forget the great debates organized by the *Centre de synthèse*, whose executive from 1925 included figures such as Rutherford, Einstein, and Volterra, alongside representatives of the humanities. And we should remember also the week-long conferences and seminars organized between 1929 and 1939 by Lucien Febvre, Paul Langevin, Abel Rey, and Henri

Berr, on topics such as *Evolution, Civilisation, Relativité, Théorie des quanta, Science et loi,* and *Statistique.*[9]

Bloch certainly made good use of those very high-level meetings, encounters in which several Nobel-prize winners took part, and which had as their aim redefining the very idea of rationality and knowledge in every field of human knowledge. Their utility to Bloch went further, for he hoped to find here a way to go finally beyond what he saw as the historians' centuries-old tendency to feel "rather small beside their colleagues in the laboratory," i.e., before the protagonists in the field of experimental science. Bloch sets this out very clearly at the beginning of his essay, where he describes his work program. In relation to the hegemonic role played by the old positivistic model of nineteenth-century science, Bloch remarks:

> Our mental climate has changed. The kinetic theory of gases, Einstein's mechanics, and the quantum theory have profoundly altered that concept of science which, only yesterday, was unanimously accepted. They have not weakened it; they have only made it more flexible. For certainty, they have often substituted the infinitely probable; for the strictly measurable, the notion of the eternal relativity of measurement [. . .] Hence, we are much better prepared to admit that a scholarly discipline may pretend to the dignity of a science without insisting upon Euclidian demonstrations or immutable laws of repetition. We find it far easier to regard certainty and universality as questions of degree. We no longer feel obliged to impose upon every subject of knowledge a uniform intellectual pattern, borrowed from natural science, since, even there, that pattern has ceased to be entirely applicable. We do not yet know what the sciences of man will be someday. We do know that in order to exist—and, it goes without saying, to exist in accordance with the fundamental laws of reason—they need neither disclaim nor feel ashamed of their own distinctive character.[10]

Consequently, the whole of the *Apologie pour l'histoire* is built around a point-by-point parallelism between the science of history and the new concept of natural sciences. Bloch's stated objective was to stress the common epistemological and methodological matrix of all forms of knowledge, despite their individual languages and objects of investigation, a unity founded on their common ability to construct hypotheses and theories in order "to arrive at new certainties (or very strong probabilities), which are thenceforth duly proved."[11]

As Bloch pointed out, referring to Augustin Cournot, "[H]istorical criticism is like most other sciences of reality, except that it undoubtedly deals with a more subtle gradation of degrees."[12] Like other sciences, it too aimed at the pursuit of objective truths, formulated hypotheses and conjectures in relation to specific problems, oriented its observations on the basis of theories to be proved, and studied the traces and signs of any phenomenon that was too elusive to be examined directly:

> It matters little whether the original object is by its very nature inaccessible to the senses, like an atom whose trajectory is rendered visible in a Crookes tube, or whether through the effect of time it has only become so in the present, like the fern, rotting for thousands of years, whose imprint is left upon a lump of coal, or like those long-abandoned ceremonials which are painted and explained upon the walls of Egyptian temples. In either case, the process of reconstruction is the same, and every science offers a variety of examples of it.[13]

The "historian's craft" and methods for the pursuit of truth, and the specific language that was employed in that process, must therefore be subjected to critical rethinking in the light of new advances in the fields of atomic physics and quantum mechanics, of the discovery of the indeterminacy principle, of the rejection of the concept of cause, and especially of the importance acquired by new probability-based prediction mechanisms, which rendered the traditional concept of scientific law and legality entirely obsolete. Many instances of this can be found within Marc Bloch's slim volume, which was left unfinished and was published only posthumously in 1949, after the death of the author under Nazi torture. The most important thing for us now, however, is not so much to document his original defense of history's epistemological status, but rather to register Bloch's early awareness of the epistemological revolution that was taking place in those years of great discoveries and astounding interpretative innovations.[14] That revolution was, in fact, redefining the very notion of science, taking as its starting point those very discoveries and the "crisis of classical reason" that they had directly fostered via Kant and Newton.

In 1934 Gaston Bachelard published in Paris *Le Nouvel esprit scientifique*. By means of psychological and philosophical analyses, Bachelard's work underlined the importance to scientific activity of the scientist's imagination. He also showed how the "scientific spirit" took a discontinuous form from the philosophical point of view, as it was constantly having to overcome the epistemological obstacles and obstructions created by the latest research. Frequent references to Heisenberg, de Broglie, Bohr, the *Schola quantorum*, and Einstein bolstered Bachelard's thesis. His original philosophical view of the scientific enterprise was, thus, founded on his belief that with the theory of relativity the scientific spirit had become the judge of its own spiritual past.[15]

Also in 1934, but this time in Vienna, Karl R. Popper published his famous *Logik der Forschung*, which clearly addressed the crucial issue of those years, that of *demarcation*: What are the boundaries of science? Popper described empirical science as a "system of theories," i.e., networks of hypotheses and universal statements with which to capture the "world," so as to rationalize it and rule over it. The logics of knowledge and of scientific discovery, seen as a "theory of theories," found its philosophical demarcation criteria in the falsifiability of those theories from every possible point of view: mathematical, logical, technical. That is to say, the criteria consisted in their self-correcting character, whereby the more a theory was falsifiable the higher its "scientificity" rate, because it meant that that theory explained more and so brought our thought closer to reality.

Popper thus entered into a fervent polemic with the conventionalist views of science, which at the time had a strong foothold in France and Italy, and especially with the sophisticated verificationist views of the Vienna Circle, whose members favored a form of logical empiricism whereby science manifested itself as a system of mutually consistent assertions and linguistic statements that were absolutely and irrevocably true.[16] In contrast with that position, Popper claimed that his criterion of falsifiability had solved the classical problem of induction formulated by Hume. In 1970, he was again pointing out how, in order to move from facts to theories, our reason has to go through confutation and "falsification." In fact, for decades following the first edition of his famous work, Popper persevered in his implacable polemic against logical neopositivism and the reduction of empirical science to enunciations and linguistic systems to be verified at the logical level. In Popper's view, we should stop worrying about words and meanings and think instead about criticizable theories and reasoning, and about their validity.[17]

The other polemical target in Popper's book, and also in most of his subsequent works, was obviously the "Copenhagen Geist," that is to say the attack launched by the supporters of quantum mechanics against scientific determinism and the principle of an objective reality and of scientific legality, the position strenuously defended by Einstein.[18] The metaphysical view of reality as fundamentally unknowable, which is implicit in Bohr's complementarity principle, caused Popper to fear the onset of an irrationalistic drift within the very concept of empirical science. And yet, if we look closely, we realize that, despite the wealth of subjects with which it engages, Popper's work seems strangely silent about important aspects of the wide debate that was taking place in those years in Europe. For instance, Popper never refers to the change in the images of science, in terms of the amount of importance now given to the historical context in which scientific discoveries took place and to science's unavoidable relationship with the logical and philosophical context of justification. And yet this was a crucial issue that was beginning to fascinate historians of science, sociologists, philosophers, and scientists alike, all of whom were determined to go beyond the conclusions reached within the remit of logical empiricism.

The fact that times were now ripe for a change in this direction was confirmed by the publication in 1935 of *Entstehung und Entwicklung einer wissenschaftlichen Tatsache*, the masterwork of a Polish doctor-philosopher of Jewish origins, Ludwik Fleck. The title itself was intended as a challenge: How could a "scientific fact" be subject to "genesis" and "development"? A fact was a fact, and nothing more. And yet, by painstakingly tracing the modern concept of syphilis from the Renaissance to our day, Fleck revealed the changes that our way of seeing and interpreting this phenomenon had undergone in the course of the centuries through the elaboration of new theories. He showed also how each of these theories was variously influenced by astrology, political and religious beliefs, or by the needs and technological instruments of the time.

By examining the succession of different theories, from the earliest hypotheses that saw syphilis as a form of just "punishment," to the discovery of the Wassermann reaction, Fleck was able to outline a whole new way of thinking about science, based on the importance of the historical context of each discovery, and not simply of its justification, as Popper and the members of the Vienna Circle had maintained, relying on logical models of analysis. In the creation of scientific knowledge, data could never be set apart from theories, and the latter were profoundly influenced by the "thought style" of the time and by the ruling "belief system." Any scientific discovery was, in this sense, first and foremost the result of a change in a society's "thought collective."

Fleck's inquiry into a theory's historical development thus revealed that, in the final analysis, science was the result of an intellectual community at work, that is to say a public, not a private, fact. For the same reasons, rationality criteria were also a product of their time and of the scientists' cultural horizon. In Fleck's analysis, "[c]ognition is the most socially-conditioned activity of man."[19] "No medieval chemist could understand a modern law of chemistry in the same way that we do today and vice versa" (54). He pointed for example to the gap between the eighteenth century's view of phosphorus and the modern idea of that element (128–133).

Thus the facts uncovered by Fleck, together with his historical analysis, completely invalidated the epistemological stance of those who favored an abstract logical and philosophical model of science. Fleck himself was very clear about this:

> Biology taught me that a field undergoing development should be investigated always from the viewpoint of its past development. Who today would study anatomy without embryology? In exactly the same way epistemology without historical and comparative investigations is no more than an empty play on words or an epistemology of the imagination [*epistemologia imaginabilis*]. (20–21)

Fleck's views were grounded in the work of such authors as Max Weber, Karl Mannheim, Lucien Lévy-Bruhl, Georg Simmel, and Wilhelm Wundt, and they followed from the theses of *Gestaltpsychologie*, according to which, from a logical and psychological point of view, observations made in isolation from their cultural premises did not make any sense. And yet, even though they admirably summarized an epistemological revolution that had been underway for quite some time, those pioneering ideas did not spread quickly. In fact, they remained the preserve of only a small number of specialists, and did not take a definitive hold in debates and general opinions until after World War II, and especially in the 1960s.[20] It was only in 1962 with Thomas S. Kuhn's short work, *The Structure of Scientific Revolutions*, that this epistemological revolution was finally complete, changing for good the traditional image of science inherited from nineteenth-century positivism.[21]

Kuhn placed at the center of his investigation the issue of scientific development and of the change wrought in our ideas of science by the historical model of analysis, as opposed to the traditional logical and philosophical model. He identified outright the realm of discovery with that of justification. The introduction to Kuhn's work was significantly subtitled, "A Role for History." And indeed Kuhn's epistemological observations centered on the history of science and on the conflict among the different theories that had held sway over the course of time, and this emphasis remained a constant theme also in his subsequent works.[22] In contrast to the image of scientific progress entertained by philosophers, science, as described by Kuhn, progressed historically through a series of revolutions, breakthroughs, and discontinuous events that represented real cultural transformations in our view of the world, changes that arose alongside new images of science. As he said, with an indirect reference to Wittgenstein's *Philosophical Investigations* and to the *Gestaltpsychologie* movement, "[T]the marks on paper that were first seen as a bird are now seen as an antelope, or vice versa."[23]

Science was not a logical phenomenon of a cumulative and continuous kind. It was, rather, a product of historical and social factors that was discontinuous and controversial in nature. Its theories and images were diverse and mutually "incommensurable." They were constant human approximations to a relative (certainly not an absolute) idea of truth: "[T]truth and falsity are uniquely and unequivocally determined by the confrontation of statement with fact" (80). As for development, this consisted in an alternation of phases of so-called "normal" science, which was dominated by winning theories that turned into pervasive and influential cognitive paradigms, interspersed with periods of crisis and revolution caused by problems within or without the scientific community, or by unexpected events, such as the discovery of oxygen, which set in motion Lavoisier's chemical revolution.

For instance, one could not derive Newton's science of dynamics from Einstein's relativistic dynamics, nor would it be possible to find any logical connections in the move from geocentrism to heliocentrism, from phlogiston to oxygen, or from corpuscles to waves. Any talk of scientific progress in the traditional sense postulated a process of evolution towards a final purpose. But does nature have a purpose? In Kuhn's words, "Any conception of nature compatible with the growth of science by proof is compatible with the evolutionary view of science developed here" (173).

From these considerations arose a lively intellectual debate on the foundations of knowledge, which is still open today, and which sees historians of science and philosophers of science on opposite sides. Having cast his lot with the former, Kuhn was unjustly accused of relativism, and of opening the door to a variety of irrationalistic drifts, forms of mysticism and epistemological anarchy, by postulating that paradigm changes and the very definition of science were determined first and foremost by historical reasons.[24] In fact Kuhn's book finally acknowledged that any absolute criteria for the validation of scientific theories had long disappeared, and that it did not make sense to continue to search for a mythical language that was entirely neutral and universal, a language that was purely descriptive and free from all interpretation.

In the general opinion of scholars, science is now seen everywhere as an assembly of conflicting theories and images of reality that certainly cannot be summed up as a logical totality of true propositions. Since Kuhn, it is no longer necessary to fight against the old distinction between *Geisteswissenschaften* and *Naturwissenschaften* in order to uphold the venerable thesis that originated with Descartes and was subsequently reformulated and updated by figures of the caliber of Marc Bloch, according to which there is a living unity across all sciences. This is a unity that transcends the differences in the specific languages of the different sciences and is based on a common research method founded on hypotheses and proof. The traditional nineteenth-century question, whether history is a science or not, has finally become meaningless.

Just as Bloch had predicted, the defense of historical knowledge in direct comparison with other disciplines has become much easier since the first few decades of the twentieth century. There is no longer an absolute truth that is the preserve of the natural sciences. All knowledge has been absorbed into the realm of human activity. First we saw a humanized theology, then came the humanization of science. In the light of these developments, historians of the Enlightenment ought to pay closer attention to the work and the results achieved by historians of science in the past few years. These scholars have brought down all barriers between the study of scientific theories and other cultural phenomena, and they have contributed significantly to the redefinition of the very concept of science, which is now based on the concept of truth as something that comes within the compass of human objectives and capabilities.[25] But more than that, they have also prepared the groundwork for the definitive demise of the Centaur in the name and on behalf of the primacy of context and the historical method.

Today we no longer share Ernst Cassirer's reductionist views on the identification of Enlightenment philosophy with the "paradigm of Newtonian physics" that formed the basis of Kantian rationalism. Historical research on the European fortune of Newton's mechanistic universe has demonstrated the importance of social, political, and religious factors in helping that paradigm become established, and have highlighted the existence of other, quite different images of science.[26] The study of the historical phenomenon of the scientific revolution in the West and its development over the course of the centuries has unveiled both points of contact with, and significant points of divergence from the development and objectives of the Enlightenment movement.

Over the course of the eighteenth century, modern science underwent several crucial transformations, as it became an institution and acquired definitive legitimacy as a new form of knowledge. Significant changes also occurred in the mechanisms of formation and professionalization of its protagonists which were based on a corporate logic in the style of the *Ancien Régime*, a style that, paradoxically, contributed to its success despite the fact that that logic represented an antiquated view of society and its institutions. The old *natural philosophers* turned into modern *scientists*, along the lines of the Royal Society's privatist model. At the same time, Parisian *dilettantes* became prestigious and privileged exponents of the *corps savant*, on the model of the Académie des Sciences. It was these kinds of transformations that gave rise to the first truly international scientific community.[27] Further developments contributed to what has been called "the triumph of sciences" in Europe. These included the rise of an extensive academic circuit, mostly financed by individual governments, a system of gazettes and scientific journals that kept public opinion abreast of new developments, and the establishment of a common language and shared practices, as well as the creation of a historical identity of the world of science through academic memoirs and the commemoration of famous scientists. Science became a global phenomenon *à la mode*, thanks to events such as the success of the Montgolfier brothers' hot-air balloons, the chemical revolution brought about by Lavoisier and Priestley, Volta's electricity, the new rational mechanics of Lagrange, and Spallanzani's discoveries.[28]

However, it was a mixed triumph, marked by conflict and furious clashes. It called into question the very identity of the modern scientist and brought up for the first time the crucial epistemological issue of demarcation: What is science? Who sets the criteria of truth? Who are scientists and how do you become one? How can we stop the powerful system of academies, with its *Ancien-Régime* style of corporate privileges, from transforming knowledge into a mechanism in the service of power and exclusion? These were the questions that were asked, for instance, by Brissot de Warville in his 1782 pamphlet, significantly entitled *De la vérité*. And he certainly was not alone. These issues sparked heated debate in the pages of gazettes and journals throughout Europe, echoing the old clashes between d'Alembert and Diderot, and between Voltaire and Rousseau. They were at the root of the frenzied struggle that broke out in the 1780s between Mesmer's followers, Marat and Brissot, on the one hand, and, on the other, Condorcet and Vicq d'Azyr, who adhered instead to the Galilean and Newtonian paradigm represented by the triad *numero, pondere et mensura*.

This was a clash between two different ideas of the scientific profession—one based on vitalistic and organic views of nature in the wake of Francis Bacon, the other on the Newtonian paradigm and its physico-mathematical mechanicism. Far from signaling the end of the Enlightenment, as some writers have suggested, these two opposing views made clear the error of those who even today tend to identify the Enlightenment with a single scientific paradigm, and above all with a single criterion of rationality and demarcation.[29]

The fact that the world of the Enlightenment has dramatically split in two over these issues, to the point of postulating entirely different images of science, should make us pause. It is not by traveling once again down the foggy and imaginary path of the phenomenology of spirit that we will arrive at a clear understanding of what the Enlightenment truly was. This is amply demonstrated, on the one hand, by the centrality of man in relation to all his instruments of knowledge, including from an epistemological point of view, as is clearly illustrated by the tree of knowledge placed at the beginning of the *Encyclopédie*, with its basis in a new Enlightenment humanism. On the other hand, it is also evidenced by the necessity to exercise one's reason freely in a critical and public way in every field, starting with the numerous challenges posed by the historical context.

Maybe the Centaur is now obsolete, even from a philosophical point of view. What is certain is that in the eyes of historians of science, who are set on realism and devoted to philological criticism, the Enlightenment does not entirely fit the pattern of a modernity modeled on the science of Newton's *Principia*, as was maintained first by Hegel and then by others, all of whom were bent on linking the Enlightenment indissolubly and polemically with a specific image of modern science and with the subsequent positivistic period, regardless of the danger of anachronism.[30] In fact, as we shall try to demonstrate below, the Enlightenment comes across instead as a complex laboratory for a modernity that had to come to terms with the nooks and crannies of the historical context.

It was a thorough-going process of cultural reorientation, similar to Kuhn's scientific revolution, that affected our perception of the world and of man, with multiple, mutually-exclusive options. Here the dramatic and fascinating project of emancipating man through man on a cultural and political level came up against the challenges posed, in the first instance, by the historical context of Europe under the *Ancien Régime*.

But before examining this question in further detail we must make another detour. We need to look at the huge influence exercised by the historiographical tradition in which generations of Enlightenment scholars were raised and continued to work. With regard to that tradition, we must examine both what kind of political and ideological weight it brought to bear on historical discourse, and how methods of research were transformed in the course of the last century.

10

|||||||||||||||||||||||||||

THE ENLIGHTENMENT–FRENCH
REVOLUTION PARADIGM

Between Political Myth and Epistemological Impasse

IN ORDER TO RETHINK the Enlightenment and create the epistemological premises for new directions of research, it is not enough to try and go critically beyond the Centaur based on a more up-to-date defense of historical knowledge
that stresses the importance of the historian's craft and methodology. On the
contrary, one must concentrate on the rules to be followed if one is to respect
the logic of context, and on the numerous interactions with the various mechanisms that determine the meaning of events.[1] It is also necessary to reflect on
the fact that, while a historian's ideas derive entirely from history, a cultural
phenomenon "can never be understood apart from its moment in time,"[2] and
that no point of view is ever neutral. Hence the necessity to avoid both the
fundamental danger of anachronism (*omnia tempus habent*), when one is offering a critical interpretation of the relationship between past and present, and
the undisputed dominance of tradition. One must instead constantly scrutinize
the validity of current research hypotheses, and especially call into question the
extraordinary longevity of a historiographical paradigm that has dominated a
large part of the international debate, and continues to do so to this day. I mean
the paradigm that rests on the link between the Enlightenment and the French
Revolution, whereby the former is studied first and foremost as the origin and
genesis of the latter, thus denying the historical world of the Enlightenment its
own autonomous and specific identity.

The first thing that must be said is that very little has been done so far to
question the obviously teleological nature of this research hypothesis that seeks
to understand the past from the point of view of future developments—even

though that teleological nature has always been evident to all. The strength of the paradigm has not been diminished in any way, even though first Droysen and then many others consistently denounced in their handbooks the myth or "demon" of origins, as Bloch called it;[3] that is to say, the dangers that are inherent in a disregard for the logic of context. It was almost as if the French Revolution was not subject to the same rules that apply to other fundamental historiographical issues.

In fact, there were far more complicated causes than a simple and neutral, albeit persuasive, research hypothesis behind the persistence of this paradigm, which soon became an immovable historiographical tradition and then a foundational element in the historical consciousness of the Western world, following a process that has yet to be studied in all its details. At stake were extremely sensitive questions, relevant to the memory and national identity of republican France, the political myth of the demise of the *Ancien Régime*, or the political, social and ideological roots of virtually all the most important projects of emancipation produced by modern Europe as a republican and democratic entity.

Indeed, there is no doubt that, as a momentous event that radically changed the whole history of Europe, the French Revolution immediately became a kind of powerful magnet capable of radically redefining a before and after, and of transforming historical figures and events. In this context, the view of the Enlightenment as a specific and independent historical phenomenon, in its original cosmopolitan and European dimension, and nothing to do with the Revolution, did not stand a chance.

It all began with the so-called *panthéonisation* of Voltaire and Rousseau, in July 1791 and October 1794, respectively. In terms of propaganda and of political and ideological struggle both within and outside France, those grand popular ceremonies forever established the *philosophes* as fathers of the French Revolution in the eyes of the whole world. Despite differing opinions of everything else, reactionaries and revolutionaries alike agreed in linking the *philosophes* to the genesis of the Revolution.[4] In the following years, at every anniversary and through a variety of ceremonies and unveilings of monuments, they were made the object of obsessive declarations of perpetual hatred or sincere gratitude (depending on the point of view) in front of huge crowds.[5]

With the Third Republic, the Enlightenment-Revolution paradigm became a sort of grand ideology of identity, supported by a militant Dreyfusard historiography of State, and an essential component of the new civic religion of the secular republican homeland.[6] In fact, ever since the end of the eighteenth century, the progressive diffusion and consolidation of the political and ideological use of the paradigm, with its attendant pre-judgments and acritical defenses, was supported by the a series of prestigious and important historiographical

studies. In the course of the nineteenth century every important French figure wrote on this, within and outside the academic world. The *Lumières*, seen
as the breeding ground of the Revolution, became the object of justly famous
analyses by Madame de Staël, Constant, Chateaubriand, Comte, Désiré Nizard,
and Sainte-Beuve, down to Villemain's research and the debate between Ferdinand Brunetière and Gustave Lanson.[7] One went from paranoid investigations
of the conspiratorial and Masonic origins of the Revolution, which Barruel attributed to a direct intervention on the part of the hated *philosophes*, to Taine's
sophisticated analysis of the ideological origins of an abstract and unhistorical
esprit classique, which had been embodied by Descartes, Voltaire and Rousseau
before descending into its tragic but inevitable epilogue with Robespierre and
the Reign of Terror. There followed Mornet's analysis of intellectual origins,
and finally, on the occasion of the bicentenary of the Revolution in 1989, Roger
Chartier's study of its cultural origins.[8] One cannot but be amazed at the staying
power of this paradigm, which was subject to metamorphoses but certainly
never exhausted in its substance. This has led Roger Chartier to speculate,
rather tongue-in-cheek, that the historiographical discourse on the Enlightenment might actually have been nothing more than an invention on the part of
the Revolution itself as it sought to create a noble origin for itself. On a more
serious note, however, Chartier also acknowledged the existence of a problem:

> Whether we like it or not, then, we have to work within the terrain staked out
> by Mornet (and before him by the revolutionaries themselves) and consider
> that no approach to a historical problem is possible outside the historiograph-
> ical discourse that constructed it. The question posed by [Mornet's] *Les Orig-
> ines intellectuelles de la Révolution française*—the question of the relationship
> of ideas formulated and propagated by the Enlightenment to the occurrence of
> the Revolution—will serve us as a set of problems that we both accept and place
> aside, that we receive as a legacy and continue to subject to doubt.[9]

In fact, before definitely abandoning that road, we should perhaps evaluate more closely the pros and cons of that paradigm, and highlight both its
appreciable—and established—historiographical results and its now obvious
limitations. For instance, the paradigm has been usefully applied by eminent
scholars such as Robert Darnton to the study of the mechanism that leads to
the formation of a revolutionary mentality, or to gain a better understanding
of such a crucially important event as the rise of modern forms of "intellectual
power" in the Western world, starting from the role played by self-conscious
minorities in historical processes.[10]

This hypothesis was first formulated in 1790, in Edmund Burke's famous
Reflections on the Revolution in France, which within a few years became a

bestseller throughout Europe. This was an angry but intelligent denunciation of the *philosophes*, assigning them direct responsibility for the overthrow of the old political and religious order through their conscious manipulation of a nascent public opinion. Burke saw this historical phenomenon as being limited to the French capital, and in particular to the specific social dimension of the philosophical party created by figures such as Voltaire and Diderot. Those French "political men of Letters" had become a dangerously arrogant community, thanks above all to the unfortunate cultural policies of control put in place by France's absolute monarchy, which transformed the sixteenth-century "Republic of Letters" with its essentially private nature into a belligerent *Ancien Régime* corporation that was independent and enjoyed public recognition via the system of academies and the workings of the State privileges and pensions originally instituted by Richelieu.[11]

Since then, the analysis of the ideas and actions of the party of *philosophes*, headed by Voltaire and Rousseau, was a constant in all historiographical research on this matter. According to this theory, an intellectual movement made up of men of letters and philosophers at first arose alongside political society, and then took over, creating horrendous revolutionary fallout with its abstract quality and its entirely literary mentality. Variously formulated, this view is found in Guizot, in Tocqueville, in Taine, and in many other writers. As conflicts grew more serious, this criminalization of intellectual power increasingly undermined historical truth. For instance, seen through the distorting lens of the political myth of the great Revolution and of the unleashing of contrasting ideological passions, the Enlightenment went from being a great European phenomenon of a markedly cosmopolitan and reforming character to being a specifically French national event.

This careless though understandable generalization turned the undoubted primacy of the Parisian scene in eighteenth-century European culture into the natural basis for an overall Frankification of the Enlightenment. Finally, the tragic collateral effects of the instrumental use of the Enlightenment by the armies of the *Grande Nation*, determined to use their weapons in order to "export" the republic, democracy, and the values promulgated by Rousseau and Voltaire, further overshadowed the importance of eighteenth-century Enlightenment circles in places such as Naples, Milan, Madrid, Berlin, Saint Petersburg, Vienna, London, and Edinburgh.

After Napoleon and his violent imperial wars of conquest, in every corner of Europe (from Jovelanos's Spain to Beccaria's Italy, Lessing's Germany, and Radishchev's Russia), all followers of the glorious Enlightenment tradition were considered nothing more than slaves to the French invaders, who were antipatriotic and, at best, extraneous to the nascent cultural and political nationalism.

Among the most significant consequences of the Revolution, and of the various forms that the paradigm took on in the course of time, we should also mention the beginning of a parallel process of "nationalization" of the Enlightenment at the historiographical level. This was done mostly with "good" intentions, with the aim of safeguarding at all costs certain established conquests, and eventually "going beyond," in a positive way, those values of liberty and tolerance produced in the eighteenth century, with a view to new syntheses that would draw inspiration from liberal, and therefore more moderate and balanced, attitudes. As a result, various schools of European historians of the Age of Restoration began to explore and underscore the national character of individual historical incarnations of the Enlightenment.

In fact, Hegel himself had opened the way to this process. With his *Vorlesungen über die Philosophie der Geschichte*, the German philosopher had been the first to establish a clear-cut historical distinction between the original traits of the *Lumières*, with their anti-Christian and vehemently radical stance, and the religious, moderate character of the *Aufklärung*. In Germany this interpretative strategy asserted itself especially after Bismarck, when the need to construct a new national historical consciousness was felt with particular urgency. This strategy is thus present in the work of Troeltsch and of Dilthey, and, in particular, in Friedrich Meinecke's *Weltbürgertum und Nationalstaat*, in which the *Aufklärung* was presented as the noble and, though partial, dialectically indispensable premise, of the birth of *Historismus*, that great glory of post-Reformation Germanic *Kultur*.[12] In Italy a similar attempt to distinguish between the dangerous abstractions of the French *philosophes* and the concrete and moderate reformist action of the Italian Enlightenment is found in the early twentieth-century writings of Giovanni Gentile and Benedetto Croce.[13]

However, the most important and startling aspect of this nationalization of the Enlightenment is its persistent influence on the sophisticated but deceitful metamorphoses that concept underwent in the writings of Anglo-Saxon and German historians. Two works that stand out in this respect are the *Lexikon der Aufklärung*, published in Munich in 1995, and the volume *The Enlightenment in National Context* (Cambridge, 1981). The theses expressed in those books, which privilege first and foremost studies of national manifestations of the Enlightenment, as opposed to its cosmopolitan dimension, have been rekindled by such authorities in the field as J. Pocock and P. Higonnet.[14] Of course, there was no shortage of polemical replies. However, one has the distinct impression that the dangerous old nationalistic historiography that caused so many problems in the past is not at all out of the picture yet. Far from it. In its current travestied and adulterated manifestations, which are indirect and in any case negative outcomes of the Enlightenment-Revolution paradigm, the debate on this matter is bound to remain alive and, if anything, to grow in the next few years, given the tensions and unease it has brought to national communities searching for strong identity mechanisms at the historical level.

In fact, the first doubts about the truthfulness and usefulness of the Enlightenment-Revolution paradigm had already begun to emerge at the start of the nineteenth century, and in France of all nations. However, they were no more than that. For instance, in her work *De la littérature considérée dans ses rapports avec les institutions sociales*, Madame de Staël did not hesitate to describe the Revolution as a mortal danger for the Enlightenment itself and for a proper understanding of it: that is to say, as a most regrettable interruption in that great independent emancipation project that had always been entrusted to writers and thinkers.

There have always been numerous European historians of moderate and liberal persuasion who have viewed the Revolution as a setback in the Enlightenment's progress towards reform. However, this aspect has always been in the background, without leading to new research. This has been the case, for instance, with those theses that aim at separating the events of 1789 from those of 1793, in an obvious attempt to somehow rescind all links between Voltaire's world and the culture of the Terror and reassert the independence of the former from the latter. In Italy, on the matter of the autonomy of the Enlightenment as category, Benedetto Croce did not hesitate to write: "The triumph and the catastrophe of the [E]nlightenment was the French Revolution; and this was at the same time the triumph and the catastrophe of its historiography."[15] In Germany, it was Nietzsche who first and most importantly denounced the artificial and ideological character of this paradigm, and its role as a serious epistemological block at a historical level, a position authoritatively reprised by Ernst Troeltsch. In an important work of 1897, *Die Aufklärung*, the great German historian asserted the full autonomy of the historical world of the Enlightenment and its centrality as the very essence of the modern Western world. These research hypotheses were also supported by Dilthey's reflections on the concept of epoch (*Epochenbegriff*) and on the need for historians to focus on "representations of the world" (*Weltanschauungen*) that did their work of interpreting the past while grounded in specific historical contexts.

In France, the strongest criticism of the Enlightenment-Revolution paradigm came from Michel Foucault, who drew support from Nietzsche's reflections and from an articulation of the need to eliminate a political myth that had by now become an obstacle to research.[16] However, this polemic achieved only limited results. Although many important contributions have been made in the twentieth century by both European and American historians (C. L. Becker, P. Hazard, F. Venturi, P. Gay, J. Starobinski, R. Mauzi, A. Dupront, to mention just a few), who have sought to investigate the peculiarities of the historical world of the Enlightenment, the paradigm's field of attraction remains strong to this day. Far too strong, in fact. It is true that a great historiography on the French Revolution has developed alongside the exponential growth of Enlightenment studies. And it is also true that this historiography has uncovered other and no less important intellectual "origins" of the Enlightenment, for instance in the field of religion, or that it has finally focused on the specificity of the Revolution as a historical phenomenon.[17] However, the political myth and the epistemological stumbling block created by the *panthéonisation* of the *philosophes* as fathers of the Revolution still linger in the background: they remain part of our common historiographical grounding and continue to influence our very way of thinking of the history of the Western world.[18]

In fact, the way ahead for our future research on the Enlightenment lies elsewhere. We must move away from the abstract constructions of philosophies of history, as well as from the temptations of a neonationalistic historical stance and from the distortions of revolutionary historiography. Instead, we should be ever-mindful of the delicate balance that exists, in the realm of cognitive processes, between points of view and proofs, and between the historian as a subject that observes and reflects on the past and an objective and measured perception of our operational domain. And we should finally acknowledge that the principal object of history is not the "spirit" but rather man in time, in his social and individual dimensions—including, and indeed especially, when we are dealing with vast historical categories.

Instead, we have marginalized the primacy of context. We have forgotten that human beings resemble their own times more than they resemble their fathers—as Bloch used to say, quoting an Arab proverb.[19] This has left the field open to widespread anachronism, and to new and more sophisticated Centaurs, creating a situation that discredits the whole idea of the study of the past. Our new working hypotheses, therefore, must be built on an awareness of the autonomy of the historical world of the Enlightenment and on the investigation of its specific qualities as both critique and product of the *Ancien Régime* in its eighteenth-century phase. We need to finally acknowledge the Enlightenment as an original cultural system that represented a major breakthrough in the comparative history of modern Europe.

We need to reconstruct the guiding principles of that historical world and uncover its value system, language, representations, practices, institutions, forms of sociability, and communication mechanisms. We must question its protagonists, keeping in mind the influence exercised by the context and the persistence of traditions, but also the creativity and originality of the new élites, paying attention to the emancipation projects that they represented, to their cosmopolitan and universal vocation, and to their reformist drive as well as to their utopian views. Only a vast undertaking of this kind will be able finally to bring again to light the indelible signs of a great transformation, that is to say of the true cultural revolution that is at the basis of modern Western identity. The study of that world in terms of cultural history might allow us to revisit the dawn of a new concept of man and of a new way to experience reality.[20] We may then gain an understanding of both the conscious and the unconscious aspects of a fundamental venture in the history of European civilization: a project that, because of its multifaceted legacy both in the long and in the short term, is comparable only to Christianity's break with the ancient pagan world.

11

||||||||||||||||||||||||

THE TWENTIETH CENTURY AND THE
ENLIGHTENMENT AS HISTORICAL PROBLEM

From Political History to Social and Cultural History

THE OPENING OF Paul Hazard's 1935 study of the crisis of European consciousness between the seventeenth and the eighteenth century is justly famous, and
deserves to be quoted at length:

> Never was there a greater contrast, never a more sudden transition than this!
> An hierarchical system ensured by authority; life firmly based on dogmatic
> principle—such were the things held dear by the people of the seventeenth cen-
> tury; but these—controls, authority, dogmas and the like—were the very things
> that their immediate successors of the eighteenth held in cordial detestation. The
> former were upholders of Christianity; the latter were its foes. The former be-
> lieved in the laws of God; the latter in the laws of Nature; the former lived con-
> tentedly enough in a world composed of unequal social grades; of the latter the
> one absorbing dream was Equality.
>
> Of course the younger generation are always critical of their elders. They al-
> ways imagine that the world has only been awaiting their arrival and intervention
> to become a better and a happier place. But it needs a great deal more than that, a
> great deal more than such a mild troubling of the waters, to account for a change
> so abrupt and so decisive as that we are now considering. One day, the French
> people, almost to a man, were thinking like Bossuet. The day after, they were
> thinking like Voltaire. No ordinary swing of the pendulum, that. It was a revolu-
> tion. [. . .] For a civilization founded on Duty—duty towards God, duty towards
> the sovereign, the new school of philosophers were fain to substitute a civilization
> founded on the idea of rights—rights of the individual, freedom of speech and
> opinion, the prerogatives of man as man and citizen.[1]

One could not wish for a better description of the dawn of a new civilization—in this case, of the beginning of what we have defined as the Enlightenment's cultural revolution. And yet today we are still faced with the fundamental historical problem of how to gain an understanding of the specific traits that were original to that great cultural transformation, which took place in less than a century. How and why did that transformation occur? Who were its protagonists, and what were its crucial events? What was its chronology? Its geography? What shapes did a change so rapid and decisive take on throughout the process, starting with its *Ancien Régime* context? Finally, how can we evaluate the corpus of projects and ideas put together by the self-conscious and belligerent minorities that brought about that change, a corpus that went hand in hand with the autonomous unfolding of new cultural practices? And what of the unfolding of the institutional, social, and economic logic of that radical historical transformation? To sum up, how did this new hegemony arise—as Antonio Gramsci would have said—over the intellectual, political, and social life of eighteenth-century élites, so as to produce a cultural revolution so profound that would change the life of every European?

Any historians who might undertake to trace the web of possible unifying factors within this steady rise of a new civilization must acknowledge the fact that they are dwarfs standing on the shoulders of giants. Consequently they must start anew, working from the results already achieved by twentieth-century historians, especially from Franco Venturi's pioneering research, which best sums up this extraordinary and terrible historiographical period—a period that coincided with an era of totalitarianisms. These historians must therefore effect the move from political to social history before they can tackle the fundamental issue of the new cultural history of the Enlightenment, which has now become the indispensable tool for the success of any future research.

The great Venturi consistently interpreted the Enlightenment as the "history of a movement, which has its own origins and roots, its development, its internecine struggles, its moments of crisis, of rebirth, of dissolution." It was a movement of a political nature, one created by self-conscious intellectual minorities: "The work of men who know that they have elements in common, who seek and create new forms of organization, of coming together and of action. Men who think and act on the basis of those new forms and who, as they go along, become aware of their own activity in the world around them and create the consciousness of the place they occupy, in society and in history."[2] Venturi believed that, in order to understand this momentous change, it was necessary to pay the utmost attention to the ideas put forward by these men, and to the circulation of these ideas and how it was that they were able to take on political form in every corner of Europe.

Venturi knew perfectly well that on the surface there was nothing new in his proposal to go back to a view of the Enlightenment as a movement and as a fundamental chapter in the new history of intellectuals, a discipline that had taken a fresh shape at the beginning of the twentieth century, after the *affaire Dreyfus* and the first occurrences of the term "intellectuals."[3] He openly admitted as much in his 1969 *Trevelyan Lectures*, where, in open polemic with other interpretations, he wondered quite frankly whether it would not be better to "*return* to the interpretation of the encyclopaedists as *philosophers* and as people who lived for their ideas, and who found a way of changing the reality which surrounded them."[4] The fact that this view represented the prevailing—or textbook—interpretation in twentieth-century historiography is also demonstrated by the opinion of the eminent Robert Darnton, who recently discussed how, from the historical point of view, the Enlightenment ultimately remained "a movement, a cause, a campaign to change minds and reform institutions."[5] In fact, even a cursory comparison between the great nineteenth-century historiography on the *philosophes* and Venturi's monumental oeuvre immediately reveals their profound differences, especially in relation to their view of the *philosophes'* actions and way of thinking.

When writing about ideas, politics, intellectuals, or a movement, Venturi means something completely different from his predecessors. If we must attempt a synthesis of his thought, which is quite complex and still largely to be deciphered,[6] we could say that in his eyes the destiny of men is never determined by history: on the contrary, the former are responsible for shaping the latter. Venturi was a revolutionary intellectual who had gone underground and taken up arms against the Fascists, a man who would do anything to uphold the right to freedom against tyranny. First and foremost, he was a product of the great period of European and Italian idealism of the first half of the twentieth century. This was a vitalistic and multifaceted idealism, one that had passionately debated the link between thought and action, will and freedom, and had analyzed the terrible hold exercised by political myths over the masses, as well as the issue of the secular religion and political faith that inspired those intellectuals who were devoted to the revolutionary cause. After all, was not religion itself a form of philosophy, or rather a powerful world picture, an ethical and moral experience perceived as a belief and as such capable of instigating political action and thus creating history? This attitude characterized thinkers as diverse as Croce, Gentile, and Marx in his revolutionary and antipositivistic aspect, which was particularly appreciated by Lenin and Sorel (who in his theses on Feuerbach had announced that the philosopher's task was no longer to interpret the world, but to change it). It also informed Rosselli, Gobetti, Salvemini, and these are only a few of the authors that inspired Venturi's reflection on the vacuum created with the end of the positivistic worldview and the crisis of reason in the years between the two world wars. From that crisis a new and disturbing idea of man had been born, a man who was virtually omnipotent in his boundless autonomy or, in Garin's incisive formulation, "a point of absolute freedom, total risk and infinite possibility."[7]

Anyone who had the fortune and privilege to know Franco Venturi is well aware of how much he cared about issues of liberty and of the political creativity and will of the individual, as opposed to reductionist deterministic or economistic stances, to the primacy of social conditioning, and to any kind of leaning towards the sociology of knowledge. These issues and values were for Venturi much more than objects of faith to be observed with religious sentiment and passion. They formed the basis for a program to which he would devote an entire lifetime of study as well as action. In this regard, the preface to his *Jeunesse de Diderot*, published in Paris in 1939, already contained his original interpretation of the French and European Enlightenment, which derived from precisely this kind of idealistic stance: i.e., his view of the essentially "political" character of the Enlightenment as a historical event—even though, as Venturi immediately pointed out, "[I]t is necessary to give the term 'political' a wider meaning than it normally has at present."

In Venturi's view, politics was not something to do primarily with royal courts, reason of State, intrigues, and diplomacy. Nor was it a matter of institutions and wars. It consisted in new ideas with the ability to change our reality and our entire view of the world and of the human condition. What he was proposing was, obviously, an idealistic reading of politics as a creative act of will and as revolutionary energy capable of joining together thought and action. To "return" to the study of the Enlightenment in the twentieth century therefore meant to study the rise of a new political force that was full of meaning and of human life. This was why Diderot's ideas should be considered more from the point of view of their effectiveness and of their immediate intent than in terms of their philosophical origins, which was instead the course of research taken by earlier historians and philosophers in France and Germany.[8]

In his work, Venturi never lost sight of the power of ideas as a creative and driving force in historical processes. He also put to good use the suggestions he derived from the theory of élites, which had been formulated in Italy by Pareto and by Mosca and had become an invaluable model of social analysis, one that could be applied to the history of intellectuals within Benedetto Croce's "ethico-political history."[9]

In 1952, on the occasion of the publication of his famous volumes on Russian populism, Venturi again vehemently upheld the right to study the great movements behind the formation of modern revolutionary élites in a new and different way, i.e., as specific and original historical phenomena. This involved leaving aside all constraints imposed by economic or social history, or by the history of philosophy, or by the study of ideology. Instead, one would concentrate on the human and psychological element and come to recognize the truly original aspect of the Russian populist movement, that manifested itself especially in the creativity of ideas and in the individual figures' obstinate and self-conscious determination to put them into practice. Who more than the men of the *Narodnaja volja* had attempted to marry together thought and action, going as far as the tragic extreme of terrorism in order to assert their belief in freedom and in their mission as democratic revolutionaries?[10] Obviously, the history of the eighteenth-century Enlightenment had taken a different and less dramatic course. However, it showed the same militant spirit and the same obstinate will to change the world through ideas. A common thread, that of a modern political passion, linked Herzen to the young Diderot, who had exclaimed: "Imposez-moi silence sur la religion et le gouvernement et je n'aurai plus rien à dire."[11]

Venturi was quite clear about this: the task of historians of his generation was to understand how the figure of the intellectual, who for centuries had remained confined within the restricted circles of the Roman Curia, the courts, and the universities, had finally attained full and self-conscious autonomy of political action, and had begun to guide nascent public opinion to the point where, with the Enlightenment, it became a powerful political force and a subject capable of changing the course of Western history. Venturi's project for a political history of the Enlightenment, which he constantly updated and developed further, thus started from the premise that the study of the "movement of the Enlightenment" must always remain "a problem," and not something that can "be taken for granted or used as an historical presupposition."[12] Therefore, it was necessary to study the biographies of its protagonists, highlight its key ideas, trace their circulation in every corner of Europe, and understand the political and historical role that those ideas had played in shaping the conscious action of Enlightenment thinkers in Europe.[13]

In the course of half a century, Venturi's research gave rise to several fundamental works and led to historiographical discoveries that remain essential points of reference for the study of these issues. One example is the important set of lectures given in Cambridge on the Enlightenment's transformation of the republican ideas of the ancient world, thanks to the work of Montesquieu and Rousseau, and on the far-reaching consequences of the European debate on the right to punish that was set in motion by Beccaria. Other seminal works by Venturi include *Le origini dell'Enciclopedia* (1946), and his 1954 study of the intellectual vicissitudes of Alberto Radicati di Passerano. Venturi's research finally culminated in his multivolume work on the eighteenth-century reformist spirit in Italy, *Settecento riformatore*, in which he studied "only and exclusively revolts, reforms, conquests and borders, markets and streets, coins and laws, political and economic ideas, land registers and contracts to tender."[14] By these means, Venturi highlights the ways in which men of letters in the Enlightenment period had demonstrated their political concerns through the reforms with which they had sought to govern and to transform reality. Through the political application of a form of rational critique that encompassed every field of knowledge, such men had come increasingly to represent the new ruling class of the Western world. They constituted an alternative to the traditional élites based on nobility of blood or allegiance to the sovereign, but at the same time also acted as witnesses and interpreters of the crisis and fall of the *Ancien Régime*.

And yet, these incredibly insightful and fascinating books are nonetheless products of their time. They bear the marks of its political passions and of the harsh ideological debate between liberals and communists.[15] On the one hand, Venturi's work did indeed elucidate the historical role played by the Enlightenment and underlined the originality and singularity of the values and key ideas of its intellectual project. However, he failed to answer the crucial question concerning the ultimate reasons for the extraordinary success of the Enlightenment in the course of the eighteenth century. Why did the Republic of Letters and its greater and lesser protagonists suddenly become so important and so terribly effective that they gave origin to a kind of cultural revolution that transformed Western identity? And why did it only happen in the eighteenth century?

The fervent political determination of a handful of heroic protagonists and the creativity and originality of their ideas is not sufficient to explain such a profound and lasting transformation of the culture and society of the élites and of our world's very identity. We know today that this complex historical phenomenon, with its numerous implications, grew rapidly to reach significant dimensions thanks also to institutions like Freemasonry and to forms of sociability, such as the academies and salons, which now took on shapes quite different from those of the past. Another important factor was the rise of a new and original communication mechanism built around the creation of the modern "public," and of a public opinion seen as an arena for the exercise of critical reason in the world. It was a space that was free and open to all, and it expanded yet further with the growth of the periodical press, with new reading practices, and with the improvement and strengthening of publishing circuits. As we shall see below, the triumph of Enlightenment culture in the last quarter of the century directly involved vast sectors of eighteenth-century society, which laid the foundations for modern "civic society" and transformed virtually every field of knowledge, from philosophy to religion, and on to literature, music, painting, theatre, and architecture. In this respect, we now may smile at the lack of interest openly shown by Franco Venturi towards novelists, theater practitioners, adventurers, and writers such as Goldoni, Alfieri, or Casanova, whom he regarded as irrelevant to a real understanding of the profoundly political nature of the Enlightenment.

The rise in the 1960s of a social history of ideas applied to the study of the Enlightenment, with its rigidly positivistic and quantitative model of explanation, seemed designed to irritate someone who, like Venturi, had always focused on the self-consciousness and creative freedom of the individual, rather than on the influence of the mental structures of any particular period.[16] Such a method of research seemed to him a dangerous return to the past: a step backwards even with respect to the more problematic positions of Bloch and Febvre on these issues. And all in all he was probably right.

The attitude criticized by Venturi was clearly not a course of action that would win out in the end. It placed the emphasis on the study of social structures and on the unconscious and serial dimension of mentality, especially in quantitative terms. But at that precise moment the history of science and Kuhn's modern epistemology were scrutinizing the processes that led to innovation and paradigm change, and their results assigned a wide scope of action to individual creativity and to the influence of context and of cultural practices as opposed to that of styles of thought and of the so-called normative and rational phase of "normal science." And indeed, in the next decades, the traditional ranking in the relationship between social and cultural effects was basically overturned. This was due to the rise of new epistemological premises and to the acknowledgement of the limits of both intellectual and social history, which had in fact been subjected to constant critical review.[17] No one today would analyze the circulation of the ideas of the *philosophes* using the same methodology as Daniel Mornet, who had studied discourses and representations as separate from cultural practices. No more would anyone think of ideas as an objective and neutral corpus, something autonomous and transparent in itself, whose circulation became quantitatively evident, especially in the progressive widening of the social milieus in which those ideas were accepted. Equally obsolete now is the model applied by Augustin Cochin, who derived specific ideological forms from the logic of sociability practices and concluded that the Jacobins' ideology of Terror was the outcome of the practice of direct democracy in the Enlightenment's "thought societies," such as lodges, academies, and salons.[18] And the same applies to Venturi's opposite approach, which postulated a kind of direct continuity between thought and action, between intellectual life and the social dimension, as if practices could be deduced from the discourse that justifies them and on which they are founded. In fact, the discourse of emancipation does not always translate into liberal practices that benefit the individual. This was highlighted by Foucault in *Surveiller et punir*, which opened the way to reflections on a topic fundamental to any attempt at dealing with cultural transformations; namely, the issue of the creative appropriation of texts and of the production-consumption of new ideas by individuals and institutions.[19]

The new cultural history that developed from the 1980s onwards has not yet found a clear and precise model of investigation that is unanimously acknowledged. However, it has made good use of the critical reviews that have underlined especially the epistemological limitations and errors of past theories. It has thus embarked on a complex series of experiments and research projects that are still in progress and whose results are yet to be decided, with the aim of reconstructing the world of the Enlightenment as cultural system and object. To this effect, it is exploring several paths, all of which are legitimate as well as innovative, that start from different theories and ways of thinking about the phenomena of acculturation as a historical process.[20] Thus, the new cultural history analyzes the strategies of social communication and of symbolic attribution of forms of meaning to reality,[21] or the relational dynamic between practices and representations, between the mechanism of social distinctions and the influence of cultural fields, between discourse and context, or between linguistic innovation and the transformation of institutions. It also reminds us that cultural and historical facts are in any case "a system and a process, institutions and individual acts, expressive reserve and significant order."[22] As far as possible, practices and representations should be considered together from the historical point of view, as elements that are indissolubly linked in their definitory interaction. Among the numerous possible research strategies that have been deployed so far, this seems to us the one that is most likely to lead to an understanding of the unity of practice and discourse. This goal can be achieved by examining the values, the ideas, the social environment and the global context of the world of the Enlightenment, which can then be seen historically as the founding event of modern Western identity.[23]

12

||||||||||||||||||||||||||

WHAT WAS THE ENLIGHTENMENT?

The Humanism of the Moderns in Ancien Régime *Europe*

THE PHENOMENON OF the Enlightenment in the context of *Ancien Régime* Europe represents a complex acculturation process, and its historical reconstruction is not a straightforward operation either. But we need to start somewhere. An analysis of the dynamics of representations and practices as a means of understanding specific cultural transformations always requires us to choose from among a number of different priorities.[1] Normally, our choice is determined by our specific competencies and dispositions, as well as by our acquired knowledge, and by the contemporary historiographical debate. But in this case it is intellectual history, along with the numerous important attempts at achieving a unified image of the Enlightenment that have been carried out under its aegis, that undoubtedly constitutes the best starting point. Obviously, intellectual history needs to be rethought in new terms. We can no longer see it simply as the specific and traditional history of the corpus of key ideas found in the main texts of the most famous authors—ideas like the critique of religious fanaticism, the enormous emphasis on religious and civic tolerance, the new faith placed by scientists and philosophers in observation and experimentation, the critical and unfettered analysis of the customs and institutions of men and societies all over the world, the reformulation of social and political ties on the basis of the idea of the natural liberty of man, the definition of a universal form of natural morality, to name just a few. Intellectual history must now also look further, toward any kind of intellectual horizon that leads to concrete action and any system and original style of thought capable of influencing action and reflection. It must include a Kuhnian paradigm made up of shared problems and solutions, based on a common understanding and mode of interpretation within a precise historical context.[2] This is what we shall attempt to do in the course of this chapter, as we outline a hypothesis that we will attempt to verify later in specific works.

We must begin by highlighting the effects of the traditional reading of Kant's philosophy, which views it as an attempt to delineate a specific form of Enlightenment reason within a history of Western rationality that bore the stamp of the scientific revolution. In this regard, we must also mention the similar effects of the focus that has been placed on this reason's specific operational modalities and on its much-proclaimed public and critical use in every field. Both of these elements have for a long time resulted in the marginalization of what was in fact a fundamental issue: namely, reason's principal object, which has always been man, his progressively awakening consciousness of his fundamental autonomy and finitude, as well as of his liberty and, at the same time, his responsibility towards himself and towards others. On the other hand, if we must seek a common factor, a unifying principle that is actively present in the intellectual field of the Enlightenment, then we will definitely find it in eighteenth-century humanism. All the protagonists of that world demonstrated an obsessive and stubborn determination to question, above all things else, human nature and the human condition. They were intent on investigating man's limitations and potentialities, taking man himself as their starting point, even to the extent that they offered ammunition to those who, in subsequent centuries, talked a little too abstractly of the Enlightenment's myth of a Godless humanity, a humanity that was polemically opposed to Christian humanism. What needs to be studied as the truly defining trait of the Enlightenment style of thought is, therefore, not only critical reason in its various historical metamorphoses, but first and foremost man's brave and unbiased reflection on man: in short, we must shift the emphasis from "critical reason" to man as the defining factor.

In fact, the eighteenth century produced no end of volumes and pamphlets whose very titles show their interest in that peculiar creature, the human being, and its existence at both the individual and the social level. What is man? What can I know? What must I do? What am I allowed to hope? These precise questions, that ultimately go back to Kant, were much more common in European cultural environments in those decades than is normally realized. We know that there have been several "humanisms" in the course of history. Nevertheless, maybe Foucault is right to stress that it was only in the eighteenth century that the entire Western *episteme* was turned upside down, with man being placed "on the king's throne" and all forms of knowledge converging on him. In earlier times, "there was no epistemological consciousness of man as such":[3] he simply "did not exist—any more than the potency of life, the fecundity of labor, or the historical density of language" (308). "Renaissance 'humanism' and Classical 'rationalism' were indeed able to allot human beings a privileged position in the order of the world, but they were not able to conceive of man" (318) himself "as a primary reality with his own density, as the difficult object and sovereign subject of all possible knowledge" (310), because they were unable to think the finite starting from the finite itself.

From the historical point of view, many have insisted on the continuity between fifteenth- and sixteenth-century humanists and their Enlightenment successors. And indeed, there are plenty of elements in the work of eighteenth-century writers to support this view. For instance, in *Le Siècle de Louis XIV*, Voltaire had drawn a confident portrait of a succession of golden ages for mankind, starting with the Greece of Pericles and Plato, through the Rome of Caesar and Cicero, proceeding to a celebration of the Renaissance of Valla and Erasmus, whom he considered the true spiritual fathers of the modern Republic of Letters, and on down to the time of Bayle and of Louis the Great. In his *Esquisse d'un tableau historique des progrès de l'esprit humain*, Condorcet had not hesitated to reiterate these theses. However, this was clearly an intriguing rhetorical scheme that aimed above all at establishing noble antecedents and at outlining a philosophy of the history of mankind's progress that reflected well on their own achievements.

On the other hand, we now see more clearly the historical discontinuity between the humanisms of earlier centuries and Enlightenment humanism. It is not enough to stress the common centrality of the new critical and philological method for the pursuit of truth in all of these iterations, or their common interest in the ancient pagan world, to conceal the profound differences attributable to changes in context. Obviously, there were points of contact between figures like Valla and Erasmus on the one hand and Voltaire, Gibbon, and Lessing on the other. These included "the pursuit of a truth that was critically ascertained through the unbiased study of texts and of reality,"[4] as well as an awareness of the limitations that applied to the very possibility of this research. These commonalities led these thinkers to a similar view of man, one that involved the renewed centrality of reason, knowledge, and a critical spirit. However, in the earlier period we do not as yet find some of the crucial elements and links that characterize the specific brand of Enlightenment humanism. First among these is the definitive rise of the scientific revolution, with all of the transformations that ensued. Then, there was the birth of a new historical consciousness and of a kind of knowledge that was capable of finally redefining the relationship between the ancients and the moderns, between sacred history and lay history, and thus of radically undermining the traditionally undisputed primacy of theology. In fact, scholars should reflect on the implications, at the historical and ideological level even more than at an epistemological and philosophical one, of the triumph of the scientific and experimental method. They should also pay increased attention to the reorganization of research in supranational terms through the continental circuit of the new scientific academies, particularly research into the redefinition of the essence and nature of the human being, and of man's cognitive limitations and potentialities. Such research has, for instance, led to a comprehensive redefinition and revival of the cosmopolitan bias of ancient Stoicism.[5]

In the course of the seventeenth century and in the early eighteenth century, many things had already started to change as a result of the rejection of the supernatural and of the Hermetic knowledge of Renaissance magi in favor of a kind of knowledge that was universally comprehensible and verifiable. This is borne out by Bacon's statement, in his 1620 *Novum Organum*, that his new "way of discovering sciences goes far to level men's wit and leaves but little to individual excellence, because it performs everything by the surest rules and demonstrations" (CXXII).[6] Bacon's remark highlights the abyss between the modern scientific "enterprise," with its institutional system of academies, the replication and verifiability requirement for experiments and for the results of research in every field, on the one hand, and on the other, the ineffable mystical wisdom of the Renaissance magi. This "democratic" and public way of pursuing truth was comprehensible to all because it could be communicated to and be verified by everyone. With the press further contributing to its diffusion, it also helped directly modify the way in which the succession of events was generally seen, and thus to put an end to the centuries-old *querelle* of the ancients and the moderns, which was adjudicated now in favor of the latter.

It was not only the acknowledgement of the cumulative quality of scientific knowledge and of the cultural heritage available to man that led to the triumph of the moderns and to the projection of man's history and autonomy into the future. An important contribution to this cause came also from the related realization that the ancients had been faced with different problems related to their own times, and that the moderns could now rely for their solutions on new and much more powerful knowledge than was available in the past. Too many things are in fact overlooked when mechanically mapping on the same level, without qualification, the Enlightenment's sympathetic view of the ancients and that entertained by fifteenth-century humanists. The latters' focus was above all on the groundbreaking rediscovery of the pagan world after more than a thousand years of enforced oblivion, and on producing learned and philologically exact critical editions of those fascinating and hitherto-forgotten texts. The main concern of the former, on the other hand, lay in the use and cultural consumption of those documents, in a historical context that now appeared as thoroughly new and entirely projected towards the conception and realization of the future.

We should not forget that the stereotype of the constant confrontation between the ancients and the moderns derives in fact from the literature of the Enlightenment. Constant's famous remarks, in the course of the nineteenth century, on the liberty of the ancients and the liberty of the moderns were often anticipated in the previous century. And indeed the eighteenth-century style of thought constantly deployed the mechanism of opposing and contrasting the past with the present with the aim of constructing the future, and evolved a skillful way of reworking the values and ideas originally developed by Ancient Greece and by Republican and Imperial Rome.[7] In fact, a large part of Enlightenment thought relies on the philosophical arguments put in place by the Stoics and the Epicureans. Voltaire's repeated invitation, "Remember thy dignity as a man,"[8] comes directly from Cicero's *De officiis*, which was a foundational text for the many Enlightenment authors who pursued a universal morality based on the concept of *humanitas*—a concept that had been developed in the pagan world, especially by such authors as Epictetus, Seneca, Sallust, Lucretius, Marcus Aurelius, and Julian.

In this regard, even more than Horace's *sapere aude*, the real motto of the Enlightenment is no doubt to be found in Terence's words, "homo sum, humani a me nihil alienum puto," which were made popular by the famous "Philosophe" entry in the *Encyclopédie*.

The great Renaissance humanists—Erasmus for instance—philologically restored ancient texts and then used them mostly in an effort to reform medieval Christianity and restore it to its true evangelical origins, thus reversing St. Augustine's victorious pathway. However, the Enlightenment's recourse to the ancient world was by now selective and had different objectives from those that guided Renaissance scholars. Enlightenment thinkers were not overly concerned with Augustine's clever operation of assimilating the whole of classical thought, from Plato to Cicero, within the Christian providential scheme. Their sympathies lay with the critical spirit of ancient Greece and Rome rather more obviously than with the Judaic and Christian traditions, whose revelations and beliefs were founded on divine inspiration. The pagan world, in fact, met their needs far better than the world of Christianity. With its tolerant polytheism, its philosophical quest for truth and universal values at both the ethical and the political level, a quest that was carried out through man and for man, paganism was for them a much more precious heritage, one that could be revisited and culturally transformed within the new Enlightenment humanism—that humanism which proudly defined itself as "of the moderns."

This dualism and opposition between the primacy of the theology of Judeo-Christian culture on the one hand, and the primacy of the philosophy and critical spirit of Greco-Roman culture on the other occur prominently in all eighteenth-century debates, especially when the argument is advanced that the philosopher is better suited than the theologian or priest to the task of providing spiritual guidance. This is borne out by Enlightenment takes on the myth of Socrates, seen in all European circles as the hero of the eternal struggle between religious superstition and the philosophical pursuit of truth. Which means that there is much to be said for Peter Gay's thesis according to which, from the point of view of intellectual history, "the Enlightenment was a volatile mixture of classicism, impiety, and science; the *philosophes*, in a phrase, were modern pagans."[9]

In fact, eighteenth-century humanism showed from the beginning entirely original traits compared to any previous movement, and those traits had a strength and vigor never seen before, particularly because they were the result of extraordinary events such as the terrible wars of religion that afflicted Europe in the course of the sixteenth and seventeenth centuries. We should never forget the horror and the vast and dramatic consequences of those events, which left a lasting mark on the historical memory and the very identity of the Western world.[10] From the massacres during the struggles between Huguenots and Catholics in France to the 1598 Edict of Nantes, and then on to the Thirty Year War, that began in 1618 in the middle of Europe, the entire continent was torn to pieces and left in a state of profound crisis. The thousand-year-old *Respublica christiana*, once a great "oecoumene" (united church), became a series of scattered and divided Churches, sects, and confessions that had nothing to do with one another. Nothing was ever again the way it had been before those horrors. In the German regions of the Holy Roman Empire that had been most affected by the horrendous sequence of wars + epidemics + famine, the population decreased by more than two thirds. Unending lootings, murders, vendettas, and devastations of town and country caused demographic damage that would not be repaired for half a century. The war was of a new type, radically violent because it was characterized by unquenchable hatred and scorn towards the enemy, and because it was fought in the name and on behalf of religious truth, and thus eschewed political mediation. The only solutions it admitted were recantation and the "religious cleansing" of territories through the principle of *cuius regio eius religio*. This inevitably led to a rethinking of the relationship between politics and religion and of the primacy of theology in human affairs, a course of reflection that would shake the old world to its very foundations. The dire predicament in which Europe found itself in those years through its self-destructive obstinacy created the conditions for the main invention that we owe to the Enlightenment: that of the rights of man.

One of the spiritual fathers of the Enlightenment was Pierre Bayle, who had been forced to flee to the Netherlands after the Edict of Nantes was revoked. Without the terrible wars of religion, Bayle might never have found the courage to formulate the radically new thesis that he put forward in his 1682 *Pensées diverses, écrites à un docteur de Sorbonne, à l'occasion de la Comète qui parut au mois de décembre 1680.* Bayle's idea of a so-called republic of atheists and of the virtuous atheist postulated the existence on earth of peoples who could lay the foundations of an entirely human moral and political order, without having to resort to religion. Although it was seen by many as paradoxical, monstrous, and preposterous, this thesis reappears in every major work of the eighteenth century. It thrived in the Enlightenment climate of thought, marking a drastic and permanent break with the prevailing Christian humanism that defined man's profound nature and identity solely on the basis of a providential scheme in which the "son of God" heeds his Father's message mediated through Christ. It was a view of man as *homo viator* and pilgrim in the world, or *saeculum*, as famously described by St. Augustine: a being spiritually extraneous to the world and devoid of any real autonomy, since the "world" itself, seen in Platonic terms and according to the alluring theory of the immortality of the soul put forward in the *Phaedo*, was nothing more than a transitory passage towards the Other World.

It is probably true that the religious question remains one of the crucial issues in the philosophy of the Enlightenment and in its reflection on the human condition. However, we must break free once and for all of all those anachronisms and historiographical clichés that largely privilege the study of the materialistic component and of the atheistic propaganda of small groups of turn-of-the-century intellectuals or of the Parisian anti-Christian circles of the second half of the eighteenth century. In fact, these positions forget the far more significant impulses directed towards religious reform, as represented, for instance, by Voltaire, Rousseau, Lessing, Filangieri, and, above all, by the main figures of the European Masonic movement, which ultimately was the very heart of a large-scale rethinking of Western religious sensibility.

An obvious contribution to the so-called de-Christianization of the Western world and the crisis of the *Infâme* came from the great editorial project undertaken in the 1760s by the *coterie holbachique*, which reissued all the classic materialist texts by the Continental libertines and by English freethinkers like Toland and Collins.[11] By circulating books like the *Brunus redivivus*, the *Militaire philosophe*, or the *Traité des trois imposteurs*, the so-called Radical Enlightenment—the importance of which will be discussed below—undermined the foundations of every great revealed religion, exposing the alliance between altar and throne and unmasking once for all the support given by religion to the *arcana imperii*. However, the very nature of that new wave of radical and materialistic propaganda coming from Paris, and the comparison between that current and previous movements that were more directly linked to the positions of the libertines and of Spinoza, should make us consider more carefully the complexity and chronology of the religious history of the Enlightenment, which is a question that still needs to be properly studied.

An entirely new and original phase opened with the posthumous publication of Nicolas Boulanger's influential writings.[12] Boulanger altered the very meaning of the question originally raised by Bayle of the possibility of a republic of atheists, because his scientific analysis of man's religious feelings suggested that they had been in evidence since the beginning, manifested in a series of myths linked to the common idea of the Great Flood. Questions that were previously unheard of, foreign to the old libertine tradition, suddenly seemed licit and of great contemporary relevance. For instance, could the need to follow a religion, which had been documented by the new history of religion and the nascent sciences of man, be used for political ends, in order to emancipate the masses? Could mythical and rational thought coexist? Could philosophy and religious enthusiasm cooperate in advancing the project of human civilization, thus assigning new meanings and objectives to religious belief, and values different from those of traditional Christian humanism? These questions gave rise in the 1770s and 80s to important reflections on modern civic and political religions. Indeed, many authors followed the example set by Rousseau's *Contrat social* in dealing with this issue, and their thinking led to the genesis of an "eternal religion of the Enlightenment" (so called by Gaetano Filangieri in his *Science of Legislation*), conceived as a powerful new *religio laica* in the service of a more equitable and just society.[13]

In fact, the Enlightenment was also, and perhaps first and foremost, an extraordinary religious revolution. It radically changed the Western way of seeing the relationship between man and God, for it overturned the hierarchy of primary interests, exploring man's autonomy and liberty and consequently his responsibility instead of taking the traditional providential view of human existence. From the historical point of view, this was due not so much to the Enlightenment's atheistic and materialistic propaganda—which was a fairly circumscribed phenomenon, despite its importance—as to its redefinition of the image, function and meaning of God and religion. Its critique had a direct influence on German rationalistic Protestantism (as evidenced by the rise of the so-called Christian *Aufklärung*), on Italian Regalism and Jansenism, and on the various Latitudinarian currents in England. Lastly, it attacked the very theological and historical foundations of every revealed religion in the name of a natural religion that applied to every people in every corner of the earth.

As Franco Venturi put it, in the first half of the eighteenth century the current that goes under the generic name of Deism divested "the old God of all his legendary, mythical, personal and human attributes, turning him into a great logical or logistical principle." However at the same time "another, generally lesser-known but equally interesting current attempted to turn the Biblical God into a 'tangible' being, that lived the life of passions and of sense among men." The two currents converged into a sort of double death of the old God, who, on the one hand ascended higher and higher into the sky and became simply a witness of men's actions, while on the other he descended into nature and became entirely enmeshed in it. The latter idea of the sacred drew upon Spinoza and, in the first instance, upon quietism. It was a major influence on the eighteenth-century Enlightenment, from Fénelon to Ramsay, to Shaftesbury, Radicati di Passerano, Rousseau, Genovesi, and many others.[14]

Voltaire's life and intellectual progress provide a useful example of how the critique of traditional revealed religions was ultimately at the core of the Enlightenment's humanism of the moderns.

Voltaire subscribed neither to the atheistic propaganda of the *coterie holbachique* nor to Rousseau's political theology, which inclined to quietism. Instead, he promoted a view of religion that became vastly popular among those who followed the Enlightenment style of thought. It saw religion as a necessity and a useful tool in the life of man. It banished all Churches and hierarchies, all phantoms and intolerance, and was hostile towards the plague of theological controversies. It was rational, universal, and contrived to bring mankind together rather than cause divisions. Voltaire did not have much time for Bayle's theories on atheistic nations, but maintained instead throughout his life that if God did not exist he would have to be invented: "It is then absolutely necessary for princes and people that the idea of a Supreme Being—creating, governing, rewarding, and punishing—be profoundly engraved on their minds."[15] Of course, if compelled to decide which posed the greater social danger, an atheist or a fanatic, he would have had no hesitation in denouncing the horrendous crimes of the latter. As he gleefully pointed out at every opportunity, religious history was full of bloodshed caused by fundamentalists and by superstitious people. Only a madman could prefer fanatics to atheists. The latter are harmless thinkers "who reason ill and, unable to comprehend the creation, the origin of evil, and other difficulties, have recourse to the hypothesis of the eternity of things and of necessity."[16] Voltaire did, however, subscribe to Bayle's thesis that there was no need for a religious foundation based on the revelations of Moses, Christ, or Mohammed in order to establish a new universal morality. In fact, the latter was more likely to produce men of a meek and tolerant temper if it was built on empirical and rational bases. He wrote at the end of his 1734 treatise on metaphysics, "Those who must have recourse to religion in order to behave righteously are much to be pitied."

Moral principles common to the whole of mankind were instead to be found in nature, which was "everywhere the same," and therefore in a new universal concept of a natural religion that was valid for all times and for all the peoples of the earth. Like many others in the early eighteenth century, Voltaire was fascinated by Isaac Newton's amazing mechanistic universe, whose law of gravity, interpreted *ad maiorem Dei gloriam*, legitimated the image of a rational God, devoid of mystery, in the context of an immobile nature subject to mechanical laws.

Voltaire found himself in profound agreement with the Deism and natural theology of the Boyle Lectures, which were vehemently opposed to any materialistic reading of Newton's *Principia*, such as the one attempted by the Freethinkers, followers of John Toland. However, despite all of these ostensibly moderate positions, which he shared with several important sectors of liberal Protestantism and Catholicism,[17] Voltaire's withering criticism of revealed religions, and especially of Christianity, was nonetheless vocal and devastating, whilst remaining always functional to his project of religious reform, as summarized in the *Profession de fois des théistes*.

This reform found an extremely effective tool in historical research, whose philosophical bases had been critically revised by Enlightenment thinkers themselves. An example is the way in which Voltaire used concrete philological evidence to expose the false premises of Christian theology, demonstrating that "the Catholic, apostolic, and Roman religion is, in all its ceremonies and in all its dogma, the reverse of the religion of Jesus."[18] In fact, Jesus Christ had been both a great and admirable man and an amazing prophet of peace and love. He would never have countenanced the cruel laws promulgated by the medieval Church against heretics, nor (as Voltaire argues in chapter XIV of his *Treatise on Toleration*) would he have built the Inquisition prisons or appointed their executioners. In his Dictionary, the *philosophe* gives a vivid and sarcastic description of the first chaotic councils of the Church, where fanatical theologians tore one another to pieces and gradually deformed the original message of the Gospels to yield a collection of contradictory dogmas and alleged religious tenets. It was through this process that God was transformed into three different persons of one substance, and the figure of the pope became a "vice-god," taking on spiritual, and above all temporal, powers of a kind unheard of in primitive Christianity: "Jesus has not given the pope either the march of Ancona or the duchy of Spoleto; and, notwithstanding, the pope possesses them by divine right."[19]

We often forget that Voltaire was one of the first in the Western world, together with John Locke, to publicly invoke the Gospels' exhortation, "Render unto Caesar the things that are Caesar's, and to God the things that are God's" (Mark 12:17), to uphold the principle of the separation of politics and religion and of Church and State, and to exclude priests from any form of civic authority.[20] Voltaire's historiographical dismantling of the theological certainties of the main revealed religions spared nothing and no one. Judaism and Islam too suffered at his hands. This highly caustic and openly ironic critique belonged by rights to a more general movement of antireligious ideas circulating in the texts of a clandestine literature that had grown in volume and strength during the decades of the so-called crisis of European conscientiousness. However, Voltaire's position also appeared truly original, especially in reviving reflection on the ancient and fundamental theme of the presence of evil in history, a reflection that was now carried out in new and evocative terms within the framework of the Enlightenment.

Voltaire undertook an analysis of the inevitability of evil for human beings living in an increasingly disenchanted world, and carried it to its extreme consequences. He went far beyond the traditional division between sacred and lay history adduced by Renaissance humanism, and put together an imposing work of critical and philological reflection on the veracity of the Bible, on sacred chronology, and on the secularization and subdivision of the history of nature and the history of nations into periods that began with, among others, Isaac Lapeyrère, Spinoza, Richard Simon, and Augustin Calmet. Voltaire's 1759 novel, *Candide*, went through seventeen print runs to reach a total of twenty-five thousand copies in the first year alone of its anonymous publication. In the novel, the scandalous existence of evil finally lost its absolute character and was brought back down to the realm of the relative and the human. It became a natural fact within a "philosophy of history" that took issue both with Leibniz's assurance that *tout est bien* and with the religious myth of the earthly paradise and the Fall, as well as with St. Augustine's invention of the theory of original sin as the ultimate explanation for the existence of evil. This critical juncture for Enlightenment humanism has rightly been called the shift from a *théodicée* to an *anthropodicée* where, "disconnected from Providence, the human adventure must discover its own purpose and its own resilience."[21] In Voltaire's view, as in that of many European Enlightenment circles, man was finally and realistically acknowledged as part of nature. He was seen in a concrete and empirical light, beyond metaphysics, in the autonomous greatness and dignity of a being determined to pursue happiness outside of any providential scheme. This image was, however, accompanied by an awareness of the painful limitations that were imposed on man by nature itself, and by the simultaneous presence of good and evil within it. It did not obscure from view either the concurrence of the positive potential man derived from his use of reason or the impassable limitations due to his finitude and to the unavoidable elements of tragedy and evil present in the human condition. Man was thus obviously a creature with boundaries, but also one capable of emancipation. He had suddenly realized that he was free to pursue either his own happiness or his "surplus" of society-produced evil. In short, he knew his responsibility for his own destiny on earth, and was ready, finally, to live through the tragedy of life with freedom and responsibility.

It must be said that on these themes twentieth-century historiography was less successful than it was in its rediscovery of the Enlightenment in general. Overall, it simply inherited and augmented a caricature of Enlightenment humanism that had grown out of the ideological and philosophical distortions of the previous century. It was an image built on eudemonism and on an abstract and deterministic idea of progress. In fact, there was little that was historically reliable in this representation of the Enlightenment style of thought. It was simply a replaying of rough and ready clichés about reason, progress, liberty, and optimism, without any further investigation into how those ideas were actually conceived and put into practice.

Recent studies have uncovered a world very different from the one constructed by the research of early-twentieth-century neoidealist scholars, who depicted the *philosophes* as in thrall to utopian visions and to a view of the omnipotence of man and his determination to shape the world according to his wishes.[22] The question of man's limitations was keenly debated throughout the eighteenth century. The revival of tragedy as a literary genre took an unexpected turn. Even the most utopian will to reform was always held in check by an awareness of the limitations of man's thought and actions.[23] There are countless pages in which Voltaire determinedly reiterates this idea of the finitude of man's thought and spirit, as he refers to his beloved Montaigne and to the modern rediscovery of ancient skepticism: "It is impossible for us limited beings to know whether our intelligence is substance or faculty: we cannot thoroughly know either the extended being, or the thinking beings, or the mechanism of thought."[24] Above all, it is impossible for us to know the ultimate causes of our destiny. As for progress itself, in the eighteenth century it was hardly even seen as the engine of history, or as mankind's destiny, as if mandated by some deterministic law of the universe. It was rather seen exclusively as possibility, as a great opportunity offered by nature to man. Condorcet and Kant, with their belief in the inevitable improvement of mankind, are rather an exception. The great thinkers of the Neapolitan Enlightenment saw things differently, in the wake of Giovan Battista Vico.[25] And they were not alone. Once again, it is Voltaire who voices a common feeling among Enlightenment thinkers when he reflects: "To ages of civilization succeed ages of barbarism; that barbarism is again expelled, and again reappears: it is the regular alternation of day and night."[26] It was, then, up to free man to take on part of the responsibility for his own destiny, relying on the hypothesis of the natural perfectibility of being.

There is very little eudemonism in these words of a man who did not hesitate to see men as ridiculous beings, extravagant, bloodthirsty, abominable, the mud of this world, even—weak creatures lost in immensity and imperceptible to the rest of the universe, leading a painful and transitory existence.[27] And yet, the ultimate meaning of Enlightenment humanism perhaps lies in this very image of humanity, an image that is as unexpected as it is realistic and sorrowful. For it is in this form that humanism reveals its determination to thoroughly investigate the consequences of man's realization of his finitude and of his inevitable and contradictory oscillation between the promise of happiness and the fatality of evil.

Voltaire's famous *Letters Concerning the English Nation* (1734), which became the first great bestseller of Enlightenment culture in Europe, offer a striking example.[28] In these letters, Voltaire dares to write "in defence of [his] fellow creatures" (introduction, 198), taking on Blaise Pascal with the same courage with which in late antiquity the British monk Pelagius had dared to oppose Augustine and his dramatically pessimistic vision that saw man as weak, damned from birth, naturally unhappy, and entirely dependent on the grace of God. The questions being asked in Voltaire's letters were clear and uncompromising: What is a human being? To what extent is his existence dependent on God? What is the true picture of the human condition? Against Pascal, who saw men only as "wicked" or "wretched" (198), and who found the solution to the enigma of man and the fatality of evil in the theory of original sin, Voltaire advanced the idea of the naturalness of evil and of the autonomy, liberty, and responsibility of the individual in his pursuit of happiness:

> Man is not an aenigma, as you figure him to yourself to be, merely to have the pleasure of unriddling it. Man seems to have his due place in the scale of beings. [. . .] Man is like every thing we see round us, a composition in which good and evil, pleasures and pains are found. [. . .] If man was perfect, he would be God; and those contrarieties, which you call contradictions, are so many necessary ingredients to the composition of man, who is just what he ought to be. (III, 203)

It is obvious that if we look only at the misery, wars, natural catastrophes, and violence that are omnipresent in the history of peoples, it can only confirm the thesis of the natural unhappiness of our condition as weak and mortal beings, and therefore of our necessary dependence on divine grace. But in fact, moments of happiness, though rare, do occur. As Voltaire points out, men "are as happy as it is consistent with their nature to be":

> Why should endeavours be us'd to make us reflect on our Being with horror? Our existence is not so wretched as some persons would make us believe it to be. To

consider the universe as a dungeon, and all mankind as so many criminals carrying to execution, is the idea of a madman (VI, 209).

> The natural condition of man is not to be either chain'd or murther'd; but all men, like animals and plants, are sent into the world to grow, and live a certain period; to beget their like, and die. [. . .] Instead therefore of wondring at, and complaining of the infelicity and shortness of life; we ought, on the contrary, to wonder that our happiness should be so great, and of so long duration, and congratulate our selves on that account. (XXVIII, 230)

Voltaire could not accept a religion that invited us to do nothing other than love and worship God, and to subordinate earthly life and the pursuit of happiness to incomprehensible dogmas, purported revelations, and rigid eschatological schemes invented by prophets in good faith but now being reinterpreted as instruments of power and domination. Pascal's famous "wager"—Why not live as though God did exist? "If you win, you win all; if you lose, you lose nothing" (V, 206)—seemed to Voltaire a blasphemous and disrespectful pronouncement: we should recognize the existence of God not in order to save our souls, or to ensure the survival of the papacy or the priests, but to emancipate and help make man a little happier on this earth: "It is incumbent on man to love, and that with the utmost tenderness, the creatures: it is incumbent on him to love his country, his wife, and his children; and this love is so inherent that the Almighty forces a man, spite of himself, to love them. To argue upon contrary principles wou'd be a barbarous way of reasoning." (X, 214).

There was an abyss between Voltaire's new religion—natural, universal, rationalistic and church-free—and Pascal's Augustinian religion. Voltaire's view of a far-away God justified and legitimated Newton's mechanistic universe by continuing to satisfy our natural religious sentiment when faced with the mystery of the sacred. On the other hand, this view of God also opened the way to the emancipation of man through man, by leading to the rise of an original culture capable of radically transforming values and ideas which dated back to the ancient world, such as equality, toleration, liberty, happiness, as well as by creating new practices, languages, representations, and modes of communication. This overturned the respective positions of God and man in the hierarchy and made the latter responsible for pursuing his own happiness on earth, a change that quickly became one of the most effective and characteristic intellectual tenets of modern Enlightenment humanism. Man's ultimate objective was without a doubt to live freely and with dignity and responsibility the drama of life, as far as the limitations imposed by his finitude allowed, and to make the most of the few moments of happiness that were granted to him on this earth. Once he had reached this conclusion, the main issue became finding the way, means, and tools necessary for that purpose. Like many other thinkers, Voltaire had no doubt that the first thing to do was to redefine the different forms of knowledge and exchange theology for philosophy, the primacy of tradition for a critical spirit and the desire for knowledge, and grace with reason, as was urged in the entry for "Philosophe" in the *Encyclopédie*. Finally, it was necessary to study human beings from the standpoint of nature, so that the sciences of man could at last see the light:

> 'Tis false to say, that it is possible for a man to be diverted from thinking on the condition of human nature; for to what object soever he applies his thoughts, he applies them to something which is necessarily united to human nature; and once again, for a man to reflect, or think on himself, abstractedly from natural things, is to think on nothing (XXXVII, 238).

The epistemological and philosophical project of the *Encyclopédie*, that magnificent intellectual war machine, arose as a direct expression of this new style of thought. Diderot and d'Alembert consciously outlined a tree of knowledge according to a view shared by many. Their tree was not in the least concerned with tracing God's intervention in the world, as previous encyclopedic works had always done. On the contrary, it studied man at work and in the process of building his own happiness. Knowledge was achieved not thanks to Revelation or to the Church but through the senses and reasoning.

Man and his faculties were at the origin of all knowledge. Reason imposed order on the proceedings and combined together empirical data furnished by the twin faculties of memory and imagination. The schematic tree represented this quite clearly. Philosophy formed the main trunk, being now the cognitive tool *par excellence*. Theology, on the other hand, was mercilessly deposed and relegated to a minor and peripheral branch: next to black magic, no less.[29] The end result was a genuine epistemological revolution, in that it amounted to the public consecration of a new view of the world and of human knowledge.

In the fifth volume of the *Encyclopédie*, published in 1755, Diderot gave an honest account of the difficulties the authors had encountered in finding a plausible synthesis between different images of science, such as his own, which was founded on a vitalistic and transformative view of nature, and that of d'Alembert, who was a follower of Newton and a supporter of mechanism, and whose idea of science was based on mathematical phenomenalism. Any hope of arriving at a definitive and sure method in the systematization of knowledge soon ran up against harsh reality. What we now call modernity was turning out to be mostly a work in progress, a fascinating laboratory with no absolute certainties. Every possible classification hid some obvious arbitrariness. As Diderot conceded, the universe could be represented from "an infinity of points of view."

How could one then deny the obvious incompatibility between the historical and the philosophical order of intellectual processes, when even a "positivist" like d'Alembert was openly admitting it? The admission that every encyclopedic classification was *filia temporis* soon became a cliché among Enlightenment thinkers, who strove to study the history of the obvious links between the rise and development of the sciences, and the social and political order of civilizations.[30] Hence the introduction of a new and decisive element absent from earlier interpretations of the scientific revolution: i.e., the assumption of the absolute centrality of man as the criterion for the construction and definition of knowledge, and the main criterion determining the usefulness of a science for the purposes of man's emancipation. "Man is the sole point from which to begin, and to which all must be brought back," as Diderot passionately urged in the entry "Encyclopédie" itself:

> [I]f man or the thinking, observing being is banished from the surface of the earth, this moving and sublime spectacle of nature is nothing but a sad and silent scene. The universe is dumb; silence and night overtake it. Everything changes into a vast solitude where unobserved phenomena occur in a manner dark and mute. It is the presence of man that gives interest to the existence of beings; and what could we better have in view in the history of those beings, than to yield to this consideration? Why not introduce man into our opus, as he is placed in the universe? Why not make of him a common center? Is there some point in infinite space from which we could more advantageously originate the immense lines which we propose to extend to all other points? What stirring and agreeable reaction of those beings towards man, and of man toward them, would not result?
>
> This is what has led us to seek in the principal faculties of man, the general division to which we have subordinated our labors.[31]

One could not have hoped for a better description, from the epistemological point of view, of the triumph of the individual and of the rise, through the Enlightenment, of the humanism of the moderns, with its new interpretation of the scientific revolution. According to this view, the different sciences were all defined and evaluated in terms of their usefulness to man, rather than vice versa as in the positivist period, when a rapid process of professionalization changed everything. In this regard, it is too often forgotten that it was only in the course of the eighteenth century that certain new and meaningful expressions such as "the sciences of man," "civilization," and "public opinion" first appeared and then quickly came into widespread use.

As for the first of these expressions, which has yet to be studied in detail, we note that it was David Hume, in his 1739 *Treatise of Human Nature*, who argued for the need to extend the experimental method to a future "science of man."

Subsequently, Mandeville, Montesquieu, Rousseau, and many others, including Genovesi and Beccaria, called for an in-depth scientific analysis of the human being as an individual and a subject that could be studied in his social dimension for the purpose of redefining our concept of morality and politics. This was not simply a linguistic phenomenon. Compared to the previous century, which focused on the natural sciences, assigning primacy to the language of physics and mathematics, and to mechanism, the eighteenth century and the Enlightenment extended the domain of the scientific revolution to unexplored worlds. New disciplines came into being, such as political economy, and the foundations were laid for modern, rational sociology and anthropology. History and law were radically transformed, their theoretical bases redrawn from the viewpoint of the subject.[32] The groundbreaking invention of "the rights of man" as central to the political vocabulary of the moderns is itself part of the historical developments that made up this brand new cultural system.

No less meaningful was the simultaneous appearance of the term "civilization" (*civilisation*, *Zivilisation*, *civiltà*) in Enlightenment circles in France, Britain, Germany and Italy at the end of the 1750s. This neologism, as used by Boulanger, Diderot, Condorcet, Genovesi, Robertson, Herder, summarized the very essence of the new style of thought of the Enlightenment. It encapsulated its claim to universality and its view of the philosophy of history. The latter was seen at one and the same time as an evolutionary process ordered by stages that ran from the natural society of savages, through the violent society of barbarians, before reaching modern civil society, and also as a project for the future cultural transformation of man and society away from their *Ancien Régime* models.[33] The entry for "Philosophe" in the *Encyclopédie* already insisted that the only "divinity" that the philosopher recognized on earth was "civil society," thus defining the ultimate political objective of an entire generation of intellectuals.[34]

If we look at the uses of the word "civilization" in the famous works of Raynal and Filangieri, which were trying to influence European public opinion, we can see the ideal and moral value that the term progressively took on, and observe how synthetically and effectively it represented the Enlightenment emancipation project, which aimed at creating a civil society of the moderns: i.e., a society without slaves, that was cosmopolitan, egalitarian, and founded on justice, the rule of law, and the rights of man. In 1761, we see Diderot also moving in this direction, with the same energy he had previously devoted to the *Encyclopédie*'s task of transforming the very concept of human knowledge. In putting forward a sort of political manifesto of the Parisian salons, which, with their radical and atheistic stance, were now publicly asking for the substitution of religion with philosophy, Diderot provided a clear explanation of the extremely ambitious program for a radical cultural reform of the European identity that was implicit in the Enlightenment idea of civilization: "On a dit l'*Europe sauvage*, l'*Europe payenne*, on a dit l'*Europe chrétienne*, peut être dirait-on encore pis, mais il faut qu'on dise enfin l'*Europe raisonnable*."[35]

We are now in a position to understand that the unifying element, and the ultimate defining trait of the Enlightenment style of thought lies in this common intellectual project, which pervaded the new humanism of the moderns. The groundbreaking implications of this project in religious, moral and epistemological terms came to light in the individual contributions offered in different forms and at different times by the various Enlightenment groups in Paris, Berlin, Edinburgh, Naples, Milan, and Amsterdam. However, even this realization constitutes only a beginning. Historians should at this point investigate the protagonists, the reasons, and the modalities behind the unprecedented rise of a strong intellectual power and of a new élite in the history of the Western world, which has been seen as a sort of "consecration" of the writer, to the extent that this figure stood now as a counterweight opposed to the evocative *sacre* of the kings of France in Reims cathedral.[36] What could have given such courage, self-awareness and power to the *hommes des lettres* in Paris and more generally in Europe in the second half of the century?

If we turn once again to the *Encyclopédie*, a few considerations immediately present themselves. This ambitious editorial project, begun in 1751 by a small gathering of writers and artists (as indicated in the frontispiece), underwent a dramatic crisis in 1759, when it came under attack and was temporarily halted by the combined action of the Parliament in Paris, the King's Council, the Jansenists, and the Jesuits, and placed on the Index of forbidden books by Clement XII. However, in the subsequent decades it was so resoundingly successful in terms of both public affirmation and earnings as to give rise to what has been described as the "business of Enlightenment."[37] The movement had now become big business in economic terms, thanks to the burgeoning publishing industry. Indeed the first folio editions of the *Encyclopédie* were immediately imitated by similar publishing enterprises on the part of Swiss and Italian printers, and, from the late 1770s on, numerous editions of the *Encyclopédie* in quarto and octavo format sold over twenty-four thousand copies all over Europe. This raises the issue of the printing industry's pivotal role in revolutionizing traditional communication systems, which in turn amplified the social consequences and political importance of the new style of thought.

In fact, something similar had happened two centuries earlier in the case of the Reformation. It is doubtful whether its rapid diffusion and the bloody conflicts that arose as a result would have taken place had it not been possible to print hundreds of thousands of copies of the Bible, newly translated from Latin into the various national languages, as well as copies of illustrated pamphlets denouncing the Church of Rome. As has been rightly noted, it was only the invention of the printing press, and the speedy development of mass media that it made possible, that enabled Luther to successfully mobilize his multitudes and to avoid ending up like Peter Waldo or John Wycliffe. Instead, he managed to split Christianity in two and put the Church on the defensive, so that it responded with the Council of Trent, whose effects are still felt today, despite Vatican II.[38]

In the eighteenth century, the expansion of the printing industry had a similarly powerful impact. The industry reached incredibly high levels in terms of production and influence over authors, the reading public, and ways of reading. This led to the rise of new genres, such as the novel, and to the proliferation of newspapers and gazettes. In Germany, for instance, book catalogues for the Frankfurt Book Fair record a steady increase in the number of available titles: 1,384 for 1765; 1,892 for 1775; 2,713 for 1785; 3,257 for 1795.[39] England went from 21,000 titles in the first decade of the century to 65,000 in the 1790s, and similar levels of growth are recorded in France and in Italy.[40]

Everywhere in Europe, religious books lost ground to literary and scientific texts. From the 1770s onwards, so-called *livres philosophiques* became especially popular.[41] Those years also saw remarkable developments in the history of literature, due not only to the general increase in production, but also to the diffusion of small-format books (including 12mo, 16mo, and 18mo). The so-called pocketbook was easier to handle and affordable by a wider public. Thus the act of reading itself became more independent, daring, and irreverent, pandering to that typically eighteenth-century reading "fury," whereby books were "consumed" as soon as they became commercially available. Reading, which traditionally consisted in the intensive and repeated study of great folio volumes, gave way to a new extensive form of reading, characterized by rapid shifts from one volume to another. The old collective and public mode of reading, carried out in front of the family, at first accompanied and then gradually gave way to a silent, private reading style, which underscored the existence of the individual, whose needs within a new civic society differed from those of previous generations.

The spread of the Enlightenment was greatly aided by these transformations in the communications system. In fact, without the press it would never have come into being. We should however try to avoid presenting the Enlightenment as simply a chapter in the history of the book, of reading, and of means of communication in the modern era, albeit a very important one. As we shall see below, from the 1770s onwards, the Enlightenment became very fashionable in literary circles, salons, lodges, and courts throughout Europe. Thus, one might think that it would not make much sense to ask whether that historical phenomenon had itself played a major part in the rise of the press as mass media, or whether it had simply profited from it for the diffusion of its own style of thought. It sounds a little like asking which came first, the chicken or the egg. There is no doubt that the *Encyclopédie*, the numerous *livres philosophiques*, and the Enlightenment novel were instrumental in the growth of the publishing industry in the eighteenth century. Works like Marmontel's *Bélisaire* or Rousseau's *Julie*, however, were much more than bestsellers whose importance was limited to the field of the social and economic history of the book. It is important to consider as well the narrative intent of these texts. In addition to their status as works of considerable literary merit, they had the further objective of spreading both the ideas and the values of the Enlightenment and encouraging cultural practices based on the public and critical use of reason in every field. They wanted to make people think as they read, so that they too might become *philosophes*.[42]

Thus, leaving aside the great economic success of these books, they represented an absolute cultural novelty. They directly affected the role, identity, and tasks of the writer. A literary figure was now part of a revolutionary current of ideas and cultural practices, but also, paradoxically, part of a specific *Ancien Régime* corporation that was fighting against other bodies and communities in order to assert its own social prestige and political power. As we know, in the course of the eighteenth century, social mobility increased throughout Europe with the decline of the old élites and the rise of new ones. Among the latter were men of letters, who were sometimes openly treated as though they constituted a new aristocracy.[43] The history of the Enlightenment is inextricably intertwined with the rise of this powerful élite.

Maybe more attention should be devoted to these issues of social and institutional history, which are linked to the metamorphosis of what has been proudly called the "Republic of Letters" ever since the humanists first used that term in the early fifteenth century. This expression, which was to have a considerable run, was first used in Italy, under the Latin form *respublica literaria*, in the correspondence between Francesco Barbaro and Poggio Bracciolini.[44] It referred in general to both individual scholars and their disciplines and to the new international community of scholars and men of letters, a rapidly expanding group whose members would soon be "authors" of printed books and the undisputed protagonists of the new communications system.

Certainly in the course of the sixteenth century the works of figures like Erasmus had created the myth and ideal of an international intellectual community that would heal the wounds of religious conflict and create a universal and irenic *respublica literaria christiana* of free and equal citizens. However, in the seventeenth century this utopian view had started to come to terms with reality. Questions were being asked about the specific nature of the new scholar produced by the rise of the press. Also under scrutiny were the implications of the widening of the social group to which that figure belonged, along with the changes that were taking place in the institutions dealing with the new forms of knowledge. These included the academies, and a plethora of new journals devoted exclusively to collaboration and communication among scholars, which bore such revealing titles as *Nouvelles de la République des Lettres*, *Relationes Reipublicae literariae*, *Republyk der Geleerden*, and *Giornale de' Letterati*.

Given the extent of this phenomenon, parallels were inevitably drawn between these associations of writers and older, traditional institutions and social entities, so that the former came to be variously dubbed a "nation of men of letters" or the "invisible Church" of men of letters. Some began to speak of the new institutions as an unprecedented kind of sovereign State, entirely different from the confessional absolutism founded on the *cuius regio eius religio* principle, or on rigid *Ancien Régime* hierarchies. Pierre Bayle explained this in the entry for "Catius" in his 1720 *Dictionnaire Historique et Critique* as follows: "That Republic is a very free State. No other authority is there acknowledged but that of reason and truth; under their Auspices men may make war innocently against any person whatsoever. [...] Every one is there both sovereign and accountable to every one."[45]

However, it was especially in the eighteenth century and through the Enlightenment thinkers' efforts at self-definition that a new phenomenon arose that could be described, in terms borrowed from Marx, as modern class-consciousness. This consisted in a full awareness of the identity and of the public function of this new social group (and consequently of its political function as well). In discussing the constitution of the Republic of Letters in 1751, Charles Pinot Duclos was one of the first to acknowledge that it had split into at least three main categories. The first of these was the old-style learned humanist, with his undaunted encyclopedic ambitions: as late as 1694, the definition of "Lettres" in the *Dictionnaire de l'Académie Française* referred to "every kind of knowledge and learning," with no distinction drawn between the humanities and the sciences. The second was the scientist, a figure who had started to emerge in response to the rapid process of professionalization and the entry of the natural sciences into the powerful network of European academies, with their emphasis on the universalizing language of mathematics, of physics, and of the experimental method. Finally came the famous writers and the "wits," among whom Duclos included the philosophers of the Enlightenment.[46]

This latter group constituted a determined and increasingly self-conscious avant-garde, determined to assert cultural domination. It is this group that is largely the focus of Voltaire's entry on "Gens de Lettres" in the *Encyclopédie*. By a "man of letters" Voltaire meant a scholar-figure who was knowledgeable in every field, including the natural sciences. The author underlines the differences and asserts the superiority of this figure when compared with both the "wits" and the old humanist scholars of previous centuries. Whereas the former were only capable of witty conversations at court or in the salons, and the latter, ensconced behind piles of dusty folios, devoted themselves solely to philological criticism, modern men of letters had a specific social function and identity. This derived above all from the courageous, no-holds-barred critique they applied in every field, a critique that was informed by a new philosophical spirit that inspired them to take center stage in political and intellectual life. As Voltaire wrote:

> Previously, in the sixteenth century, and well before the seventeenth, literary scholars spent a lot of their time on grammatical criticism of Greek and Latin authors; and it is to their labors that we owe the dictionaries, the accurate editions, the commentaries on the masterpieces of antiquity. Today this criticism is less necessary, and the philosophical spirit has succeeded it. It is this philosophical spirit that seems to constitute the character of men of letters; and when it is combined with good taste, it forms an accomplished literary scholar.[47]

This philosophical spirit was nothing other than the acknowledgment of the autonomy and centrality of man. It was embodied in the free and public use of human reason; in the establishment of the reign of critique; in the acknowledgement of man's rule over every aspect of reality, according to a cognitive paradigm that Kant had made famous in 1781, when he wrote in his *Critique of Pure Reason*:

> Our age is the age of criticism, to which everything must be subjected. The sacredness of religion, and the authority of legislation, are by many regarded as grounds of exemption from the examination of this tribunal. But, if they are exempted, they become the subjects of just suspicion, and cannot lay claim to sincere respect, which reason accords only that which has stood the test of a free and public examination.[48]

In his works, Voltaire shows a keen understanding of the way in which times had changed, and of the potentialities this opened. The new system of cultural production and communication that had come into being with the invention of the printing press was causing a radical redefinition of the identity and task of the eighteenth-century man of letters compared to his predecessors in the recent past. In his youth Voltaire had visited London. There, to his admiration and bewilderment, he had witnessed the tumultuous birth of what has been defined as modern cultural consumerism, which came about with the progressive expansion of the English publishing industry in the course of the eighteenth century. A steady production of books, newspapers, gazettes, and great collective works sustained a healthy marketplace that soon would be able to support not only writers like Samuel Richardson, author of the bestseller *Pamela*, but also the many unfortunate Grub Street hacks, so that it became imperative to find a speedy solution to the problem of copyright and intellectual property.[49]

At the time of Voltaire's visit, London was teeming with publishers, impresarios, art merchants, and collectors. It also boasted a thriving theater culture, and aristocrats and bourgeois alike keenly sought out the best music and visited picture galleries and reading rooms. All of this cultural activity clearly fascinated Voltaire and persuaded him that the future now lay with men of letters: it was up to them to make history and create new élites based on talent. Hence his tongue-in-cheek remark in the twelfth of his *Lettres philosophiques*: "Since [. . .] you desire me to give you an account of the famous personages which *England* has given birth to, I shall begin with Lord *Bacon*, Mr. *Locke*, Sir *Isaac Newton*, &c. [and] afterwards the warriors and ministers of state shall come in their order."[50]

Voltaire saw perfectly well, and often underlined, the fact that civic society in London was already showing marked differences compared to *Ancient Régime* society on the Continent. And yet there was no shortage of similarities. For instance, the sudden rise of public opinion, and of a widening "pubblic" (thanks also to the progressive replacement of Latin by national languages), which delivered a powerful weapon into the hands of the new Enlightenment man of letters on both sides of the Channel.[51]

This was a fundamental aspect in the politicization of the *philosophes* in the course of the eighteenth century. Jacques Necker was not at all exaggerating in 1784 when he wrote with admiration of how foreigners found it hard to conceive of exactly how strong public opinion was in France: how it was "an invisible power that, without treasure, guard, or army, gives its laws to the city, the court, and even the palaces of kings."[52]

Of course, it would be impossible to explain the huge popularity of the Enlightenment style of thought without taking in account the results of research that has been carried out on the rise of public opinion in the Western world, and on the emergence of modern cultural consumer society, or without considering the institutional and cultural history of eighteenth-century social behavior. Some of this research, especially on the sociability issue, is still subject to a major historical misunderstanding: that of hastily identifying the Freemasons, the academic movement, the Republic of Letters, and the salons with the cultural system of the Enlightenment. In fact, we now know that these were different phenomena, each with a course, origins, and modalities of its own, even though they were destined to intersect and overlap and even, sometimes, to cover much the same ground. Historical research must therefore consider each case on its own terms and try to reconstruct the individual instances when, in various contexts, the values, language, and representations of the Enlightenment affected the cultural practices of specific forms of sociability, and were in turn influenced by them.[53]

These developments were already obvious to contemporary observers, who began to investigate such matters as the autonomy, identity, and function of men of letters and their relationship to various kinds of public and private cultural institutions, to political power, and to the vertiginous growth in the publishing market and in the number of writers. In France, for instance, between 1750 and 1789 the number of authors doubled compared to the previous period, reaching three thousand.[54]

In his 1753 *Essai sur la société des gens de lettres et des grands*, D'Alembert was among the first to set the *philosophes* movement the task of asserting their ideas by breaking into the royal system of venerable academies and starting a dialogue with the monarchy and the aristocracy. To preserve the autonomy, dignity, and liberty of the philosophical spirit of the man of letters, as well as his emancipatory function, Voltaire did not hesitate to denounce those professional writers who were being produced in increasing numbers in the major European cities by the modern cultural consumer society and its market.

Voltaire unleashed a fierce attack on the new figure of the "author," and especially against those "writers" who were in the hands of professional communities, booksellers, and the powerful, and who catered to the needs and tastes of the "public." He branded them "riff-raff" and "hacks," purveyors of "low literature," who were ready to sell themselves and to commit any kind of treason for a few cents. To the kind of living provided by the publishing market, as well as to the protection afforded by the Renaissance mechanism of patronage, Voltaire went so far as to prefer the absolutist cultural model of the *Ancien Régime*: a corporative model, based on the so-called *corps savants* at the service of the monarchy, which had been created in France by Richelieu and by Louis XIV. For this he was harshly criticized by those writers who adhered to the newly reborn "republican spirit," Rousseau and Diderot among them, and later especially by Brissot, Marat, Alfieri, and many other exponents of late eighteenth-century Enlightenment. These figures were now fiercely opposed to the paradoxical changes undergone by the former egalitarian and libertarian ideals of the old Republic of Letters. In many parts of Europe, this group had now effectively turned into a hateful *Ancien Régime*-style corporation, complete with privileges, rites, and ostentatious hierarchies of talent, which, though royally-approved, were no less odious than those of the old aristocracy of blood.

As has been rightly observed, Jean-Baptiste Pigalle's 1776 statue of the nude Voltaire, who was represented holding a scroll in one hand and a pen in the other, must have seemed to contemporaries as the perfect incarnation of the "contradictions that permeated both the definition and the status of the man of letters in the age of the Enlightenment: privilege and equality, protection and independence, prudent reformism and utopian aspiration."[55] In fact, the *Ancien Régime* had its own corporative logics, its values, beliefs, practices, and representations, which brought its centuries-old culture into being in concrete terms. This caused serious problems for the ideals and transformation projects that were linked to the Enlightenment way of thinking, as well as for the activities of those who were hoping to draw on that specific cultural system in order to create a new civilization.

This was a historical context that was common to the whole of Europe, one founded on the imposition of inequality and on the primacy of hierarchical structures, of tradition, and of hereditary rights. It was a system based on an ironclad pact between a Monarchy and a Church determined to legitimize the principle of authority and the sacrality of power. This system, however, influenced the history of the Enlightenment at every stage and determined its original characteristics, the actual objects of its critical spirit, and its evolution in different national contexts.

Let us take for instance this concise definition from the 1694 *Dictionnaire de l'Académie française*: "Under the name 'Republic of Letters' we mean figuratively men of letters in general, considered as if they formed a single body." This was an element that, paradoxically, would significantly aid the ascendancy of the new social élite, as one powerful corporation among others. In short, the Enlightenment was also, and far more than we have hitherto realized, a legitimate child of the *Ancien Régime*. Failure to recognize this would be a serious historical error.[56] In fact, as has been rightly pointed out, the Republic of Letters, with its cosmopolitan and libertarian character, was one of the social structures of reference for the Enlightenment, together with Freemasonry.[57] However, that structure itself was torn apart by furious internecine struggles in its attempt to escape the logic of domination and the culture of privilege that ruled within the *corps savants*. There is no doubt, therefore, that, from a historical point of view, any attempt to understand the great cultural transformation of the Western world that we now call the Enlightenment will meet its greatest challenge and most important task in the analysis of historical contexts and of the close dialectical relationship between the Enlightenment itself and the prerevolutionary world of the *Ancien Régime*.

13

||||||||||||||||||||||||

THE CHRONOLOGY AND GEOGRAPHY
OF A CULTURAL REVOLUTION

In the *Lit de Justice* held before the Paris Parliament on March 12, 1776, at the behest of Louis XVI, the *avocat du roi*, Antoine-Louis Séguier, synthesized in the following terms the social situation of the Kingdom of France as it appeared to contemporaries:

> Your subjects, Sire, are divided into as many different bodies as there are different States within your realm: the clergy, the nobility, sovereign courts, lower tribunals, the officers attached to those tribunals, universities, academies, financial companies, trade companies—every one of these, in every part of the State, contain bodies that can be regarded as the rings of an enormous chain. And the first of those rings is in Your Majesty's hands, as the Head and sovereign administrator of everything that constitutes the body of the nation.[1]

In fact, a corporative structure was dominant in every part of European society. Tocqueville used to discuss the constitution of "the old regime" in terms of "the old European constitution." He noted:

> I have had occasion to study the political institutions which flourished in England, France, and Germany during the Middle Ages. As I advanced in the work, I have been filled with amazement at the wonderful similarity of the laws established by races so far apart and so widely different. They vary constantly and infinitely, it is true, in matters of detail, but in the main they are identical every where. [...] From the confines of Poland to the Irish Sea we can trace the same seigniories, seigniors' courts, feuds, rents, feudal services, feudal rights, corporate bodies.[2]

In the course of the eighteenth century, as evidenced by Tocqueville, this world, whose origins obviously reached far into the Middle Ages, seemed to be "falling to pieces."[3] It was in an evident state of ruin and moving towards an irreversible final crisis. The drive towards centralization and absolutism on the part of all European monarchies, both large and small, had long since undermined the ancient political society based on a feudal and aristocratic system. This set in motion a large-scale historical process that resulted in the creation of new élites, such as the intellectuals or service nobility, which in turn led to the overall rise of modern civil society—a society that focused more and more on individuals rather than on social groupings, and which was independent of that absolute State that had inadvertently and dialectically nurtured it at its bosom. And yet, despite all the radical changes that were under way, this final phase still appeared to French revolutionaries as a world that was not at all dead. They were the first who in arguing against it invented the phrase, and consequently the historical category, of an *Ancien Régime*.[4] Now, they were solemnly and vigorously demanding its demise. In the famous preamble to the French Constitution of 1791, they announced that the National Assembly would finally abolish all institutions detrimental to man's liberty and equality of rights:

> There is no longer either a nobility or a peerage, or hereditary distinctions, or distinctions of orders, or a feudal regime, or private justice, or any of the titles, denominations or prerogatives deriving from them, or any order of chivalry, or any of the corporations or decorations for which proofs of nobility were required, or which implied distinctions of birth, or any other superiority but that of public officials in the exercise of their duties.
>
> There is no longer venality or heredity of public office.
>
> There is no longer for any part of the nation or for any individual any privilege or exception to the common law of all the French.
>
> There are no longer either guilds, or corporations of professions, arts and crafts.
>
> The law no longer recognizes either religious vows or any other engagement contrary to natural rights and the constitution.[5]

In fact, historical research has only partly validated the compact and clear-cut picture of the *Ancien Régime* that would seem to emerge from the denunciations of the American Founding Fathers. Studies are still being carried out on its genesis, as well as on its geography and its chronology in a European context, as opposed to an exclusively French one, and on the modes and timescale of its final crisis.[6] So-called original qualities of the *Ancien Régime* include the nobility, fiefdoms, "seigniories," ecclesiastical tithes, and the venal and hereditary character of offices, all of which were generically mentioned in late eighteenth-century documents as elements of a common "feudal regime" that should be suppressed once and for all. In this way enemies of the *Régime* grouped together very different institutions that had come into being at different times, producing what seemed like a confused mass of privileges, juridical ordinances founded on distinction and inequality, community institutions, and sometimes contradictory customs and practices, all superimposed one on top of the other, creating a system characterized by favoritism and the fragmentation of sovereign power. To Pierre Goubert, for instance, this resembled an overflowing river, full of murky water and detritus: a reality that was magmatic, unstable, and confused.[7] Others, however, have seen in the *Ancien Régime* a way of life that was naturally and organically structured around shared principles of authority granted sanction through the mechanism of titles and honors. According to this view, it was a system that hinged on forms of social organization and power that were justified by religious faith, by specific and widely-accepted hierarchies of values that originated from centuries-old traditions, and by a courtly society that was the source of civilization and good manners.[8]

It is important to remember that in the eighteenth century Europe underwent significant transformations that changed the course of Western history and lent further complexity, in our view, to the link between the crisis of the *Ancien Régime* and Enlightenment critique. In the space of only a hundred years the population in Europe grew by over 60 percent, from 118 to 193 million. The populations of London and Paris topped half a million. There were 400,000 inhabitants in Naples, and 200,000 in Vienna and St. Petersburg.[9] It would perhaps be an exaggeration to speak of an agrarian revolution, in view of the persistence of servitude on the other side of the Elbe, and of heavy seigneurial rights over lands and farmers and hateful forms of baronial feudality in the judicial and economic field pretty much everywhere in Europe. However, it is undeniable that there was considerable improvement in productivity and that modern economic structures were gaining increasing importance. This was the case, for instance, of the *fermiers*, the rich leaseholders beloved of the physiocrats and praised in the 1756 *Encyclopédie*, who would engineer a slow but constant development of the countryside in capitalistic terms. If, on the one hand, it was only in England that industry really took off at the end of the century, on the other hand many European States saw the establishment of mechanized factories and workshops in the production of metal and textiles, in which production benefited from technological innovations and labor practices inspired by the so-called "factory system." Albeit with regional variations in terms of modalities and timescale, the significant growth in overall production led to clashes between the proponents of economic liberalism, that is to say of a free labor market, and supporters of a system based on corporations and protectionism.[10]

The consequence of progress in the fields of economy, technology, and science was not always an immediate increase in "public happiness," as Rousseau noted in his reflections on inequality. In fact, the growing numbers of paupers, beggars and the unemployed in Paris led Linguet to formulate his famous bitter comparison between the slaves of the ancient world, whose masters at least fed them and put a roof over their heads, and modern salaried workers, who were constantly threatened by unemployment and tormented by hunger.

And yet, from the point of view of the history of the Enlightenment and of the crisis of the *Ancien Régime*, not enough attention has been devoted to what happened outside Europe. The eighteenth century was, first and foremost, the era of the sudden expansion of colonial empires, i.e., of what we might anachronistically call the first great modern "globalization," with significant consequences for material and intellectual life. This commercial expansion, which left Europe alone controlling two thirds of world trade, developed with unprecedented speed and to an astonishing extent, as the volume of trade rose from 62 million pounds in 1720 to 137 million in 1780.

The vigorous growth in transoceanic traffic between Europe, Asia, Africa, and America benefited from significant capital investment and from the construction of huge fleets of ships in France, Holland, and Russia. Between 1689 and 1786, the English navy alone went from 350,000 to 881,000 tonnes. Conflict broke out at every level between the English East India Company, the Dutch Vereenigde Oostindische Compagnie, and the French Compagnie des Indes over control of the lucrative commerce with India, which provided silk and cotton materials, spices and dyes. The struggle expanded to colonial trade with North and South America, Indonesia, and China. England and France fought over sugar from the Antilles and for control over harbors in India and China, while the slave trade mainly saw England opposed to Spain and Portugal.

There were, clearly, concrete reasons behind the eighteenth-century explosion in the publishing industry's output of travel literature and books about the "other," i.e., about all kinds of savages, barbarians, and non-European civilizations, which was balanced by a move to reassert national identities in face of this irruption of alterity and difference. Those reasons can only be properly understood if we consider the huge expansion of trade in the eighteenth century, the growth of colonial empires, and the amazing geographical discoveries of those years on the part of explorers such as Cook and Bougainville, who in 1771 wrote a celebrated *Voyage autour du monde*. India, China, Africa, America, and Oceania became objects of curiosity and of significant interest not only from a commercial and political point of view, but also and especially in cultural terms.[11] Readers also became more interested in great universal histories, which were seen as accounts of man's history around the globe, and in the science of man, which comprised the study of the customs, religions, and the physiology of different ethnical groups.

The publication between 1754 and 1758 of Voltaire's seven-volume *Essai sur les moeurs et l'esprit des nations* tied in with the renewed cosmopolitanism and universalism of the Enlightenment, which was a result of eighteenth-century globalization, as opposed to the similar positions developed by the ancient tradition of Stoic universalism. On the other hand, Raynal's 1770 bestseller, *Histoire philosophique et politique des établissements et du commerce des Européens dans les deux Indes*, reflected the importance of colonial wars and the huge dimensions of the slave trade, around which revolved vast financial and commercial interests. Of the nearly ten million Africans who were shipped to America in the three and a half centuries of the slave trade, the greatest portion were transported during the age of Enlightenment: over six million between 1701 and 1810, or about 63 percent. That cruel traffic sparked many a debate among Enlightenment thinkers at the turn of the century on the phenomenon of modern slavery and consequently on the idea of equality and of the universality of the rights of man. First place in this form of commerce was held by England, followed by Portugal, and in third place came the *philosophes'* own France.

The Seven Years' War, which was fought by land and by sea from 1756 to 1763 and involved every major European country, confirms without any doubt the importance of what we have defined as eighteenth-century globalization. It is rightly defined by historians as the first real world war, because not only did Russia, Austria, Prussia, and Sweden face one another on battlefields across the whole of Europe, but the war also involved the French, the Spaniards, and the English fighting against one another in every corner of the world.

Great Britain's victory in the war laid the foundations for one of the greatest empires in history. Britain defeated the French in Africa, in India, in the Antilles, and in the whole of North America, where it completed its conquest of Canada. It humiliated Spain with the conquest of the Philippines and of Cuba. However, Britain also left itself open to its opponents' desire for revenge, thus helping to create an unstable and volatile international situation and ushering in an era of transition and profound transformation.

In fact, this first world war represented a decisive stage in the periodization of the Enlightenment, bringing about radical change in many areas. It opened the way to the prolonged final crisis of the *Ancien Régime*, and initiated a period in which national monarchies reformed themselves from above: an era of enlightened despotism in the wake of the successes of Frederick II, of Catherine the Great, of Joseph II, and also an era of democratic revolution as the response from down below. In short, the Seven Years' War transformed almost every aspect of Enlightenment culture. Thus, in the last quarter of the century, intellectual debate and political action by governments and élites were forced to address such issues as the obvious anachronism of a system based on feudalism and seigneurial privileges; the liberalization of commerce and of the labor market (which inflicted the first major blow to the system of corporations); the rights of man, patriotism, constitutionalism, republicanism; the legitimacy of governments and of power in the light of the principle of equality and of popular sovereignty; the social and political function of religions; and public opinion. The list could be expanded to include yet other issues: the sociability of the moderns and the construction of a civil society and a European civilization on new and different bases; and the creation of a modern economy where virtue could coexist with wealth, and development go hand in hand with a concern for fair dealing. One issue in particular that took center stage and redefined almost everything else was the new view of nature and of the task of the natural sciences.

In this regard, the context of the *Ancien Régime* remains an essential reference point for historical analysis, despite the profound changes and the crisis accentuated by eighteenth-century globalization, because without an understanding of that element it will be impossible to comprehend the sudden politicization of the Enlightenment at the end of the century, or its specific transformations. Our main historical problem remains how we are to picture the shock and concerned amazement of their contemporaries when faced with the statements put forward by supporters of the Enlightenment throughout the eighteenth century, according to which all men are born and remain free and equal in their rights. Three centuries have since gone by, which is a very long time. This forces us to underscore the elements of discontinuity, the differences in mentality, and to reflect on that distant past *iuxta propria principia*. We should keep in mind that in the world of the *Ancien Régime*, with its feudal lords, corporations, and "Estates," the individual as a holder of rights was an unknown concept, so that the Enlightenment's bold statements about "equality" risked being seen as entirely meaningless. They could perhaps be perceived as belonging to the realm of utopia and social dreams—but they were the dreams of a new élite that turned out to be terribly effective in bringing about change. And yet, precisely because of this, from a historical point of view we cannot understand the huge success of Enlightenment culture in the final quarter of the century if we do not take into account its dialectical relationship with the *Ancien Régime* and its final crisis.

In this context, it will prove useful to look at the rise of public opinion. There is not much to be gained here by applying Marx's version of the Centaur, or the theory of a link between the social and economic structure and the ideological superstructure. The hypothesis of the rise of a bourgeois public sphere in the eighteenth century as a result of capitalism and absolutism also seems unlikely to yield any useful results. In fact, the society of the time seems completely to lack that frank and open debate between free and equal participants that identifies public opinion in the definition given by Jürgen Habermas.[12] The rise of the public arena is far easier to understand if we study elements of the context, such as the exponential growth of the new publishing industry and the effects of reading practices and of the circulation of printed texts. But what is likely to yield the most fruitful results is a study of the ability of Enlightenment élites to discover, promote, and plant in the collective consciousness a conceptual and social entity such as public opinion, which established itself alongside and against all inequalities, all hierarchies based on wealth, against privileges and the domination of ecclesiastical and royal censorship.

By public opinion we mean a collective and anonymous conceptual entity, which was both abstract and homogeneous, and which gathered together individual opinions formed in the course of private reading. In the Enlightenment period, this entity was mainly a happy discovery on the part of the new intellectual élites, who derived from it a useful tool for their political struggle and for increasing their own social prestige. The riddle of its sudden appearance is well described by Kant in his essay "Was ist Aufklärung?" in which he describes the population under the *Ancien Régime* as a fragmented community, in which the individual was subsumed by his function, occupation, and, more generally, by the social class to which he belonged. Such an individual could make *private use* of reason within his community. To this picture Kant opposed the myth of the Republic of Letters, and the ideal of a new and universal civil society of readers and writers, all of whom are free and equal and able to make *public use* of reason by communicating their thought to everyone. In actual fact, the prevailing view of the world was split in two by the realization that written communication, together with the cultural practice of the free and public use of critique advocated by Enlightenment thinkers, miraculously made everyone equal with respect to the circulation of ideas, regardless of what might be happening in the "real world" outside. This important dichotomy accelerated the crisis of the *Ancien Régime* and created the premises for the cultural transformation of the Western world.

Something similar happened also in the case of other aspects of eighteenth-century European society: for instance, in salons, where the aristocrats' smart social life continued alongside the personal ambitions and the circulation of the emancipatory values of the new élites of "enlightened" men of letters.[13] This phenomenon can also be observed in the academies, which were subject to both the hierarchical logics of the *corps savant* and the new categories of merit and talent.[14] Not to mention the Freemasons: with the massive entry of enlightened brothers into their extensive circuit of European lodges in the last quarter of the century, the contradictions between the world of Freemasonry and the world outside were felt ever more keenly, and became capable of influencing the rest of society and its institutions. The Lodges practiced constitutional self-government, conducted egalitarian and republican discourses, and promoted cosmopolitanism and propaganda in favor of the rights of man and universal brotherhood. How could they then accept that the world outside should be based on privilege and inequality, on favoritism, on patriotism, on the rights of blood, and on the slave trade?

Long before the complex philosophical theorization of Kant's "having to be," Gaetano Filangieri understood the extent of this gap between the way of living and the way of representing reality. He also recognized the early signs of the gradual dialectical split between the *Ancien Régime* and the new society advocated by the Enlightenment at the end of the century, i.e., a more equitable and just civil society. Hence the distinction he made between reflection on reality as it is and another form of reflection, the form that in fact oriented his entire intellectual activity; namely, a critical, working reflection on reality as it could be and ought to be. Filangieri's conclusions applied especially to the constitution of modern law and a new science of legislation.[15] However, analogous conclusions were reached by other authors in relation to other disciplines that were being established or reformed at the time, such as politics and economics, or in fields such as religion, which many major Enlightenment figures wanted to transform into a civil religion in the service of values that had nothing to do with the centuries-old beliefs that sustained the culture and anthropology of the *Ancien Régime*.

Once again, Franco Venturi was in the forefront. He was among the first to feel the need to build a sort of new "chronology and geography of the Enlightenment" based on the context of eighteenth-century Europe, this in an attempt to break free of the historiographical logics of the philosophers' Centaur. In the fourth of his 1969 Trevelyan Lectures, Venturi addressed the research carried out by Lefebvre and by Labrousse in the field of social and economic history, synthesizing decades of intellectual history represented by the work of Hazard and Cassirer, down to the more recent contributions by Cobban, Gay, and a then young and unknown Robert Darnton. To finally pinpoint the rhythms and boundaries of the "movement of the Enlightenment," the only effective gauge would be the economic trend described by the great Labrousse in relation to the French economy:

> Every time one looks at Labrousse's price curve for wheat in France; every time one notes the increase in the population of eighteenth-century Europe, it is clear that all society, and not just the movement of ideas and politics, is expanding at the beginning of the century, reaches a crisis in the thirties and reaches its peak

in the fifties and sixties, while the last twenty-five years of the century witness a period of profound disturbance. It is the curve of the eighteenth century, and also of the Enlightenment.[16]

Going beyond obvious national differences, Venturi described the rise of the first forms of culture that would blossom into the Enlightenment-inspired rationalism of Augustan England, which was home to Freethinkers and Commonwealth men such as Collins and Toland. In this respect, Venturi reprised Hazard's thesis according to which European consciousness had undergone a period of crisis between 1685 and 1725. He further underlined how the resolution of the economic and civil crisis of the 1730s had been accompanied by the tumultuous rise of a new era in intellectual life, marked by a series of shifts, including that from *Frühaufklärung* to *Aufklärung*. The religious and moral problems that arose following Louis XIV's momentous revocation of the edict of Nantes and in the aftermath of the English Revolution gave way to political and social problems. Deism and regalism were superseded by juridical and economic issues, such as those addressed in Montesquieu's 1748 *De l'Esprit des lois* and Ferdinando Galiani's *Della moneta* (1751).

This led to the rise of what Venturi always considered the true great Enlightenment, the movement most deserving to be carefully studied by historians. Its heart was in Paris, the city that created the *Encyclopédie*, with its determination to change the way people thought, and which nurtured the generation of Diderot and Rousseau ("people making a living with their pen and existing for their own ideas. [. . .] They did not depend on the state. They were not an academy. They were a group of free philosophers," 120–21). That small isolated world, which constituted a minority even in France, had grown fast in the midst of struggles and repression, and within a decade it was influencing intellectual circles in every European capital through translations of their books and, above all, through their ideas. In the decade between 1760 and 1770, the mid-century "spring of the Enlightenment" had reached its triumphant peak. It was a direct influence on the process of political reform.

In those years, in Italy, Corsica was fighting for independence, a struggle that occupied much space in the pages devoted to political and constitutional debate in the gazettes. In Milan, Cesare Beccaria and the Verri brothers were publishing the periodical *Il Caffè*, while in Naples Antonio Genovesi brought out his *Lezioni di commercio*, which gave rise to a school that was like a modern political party of men of letters. In Austria, Sonnenfels was writing his *Mann ohne Vorurteil*, which supported the Habsburgs' reformist drive with the impetus of Enlightenment ideas. In Russia, the 1767 *Nakaz* addressed by Catherine II to the members of the Legislative Commission translated some of the fundamental ideas of Montesquieu and Beccaria into actual acts of government. In Prussia, too, Frederick II was often, though not consistently, under the spell of the *philosophes'* pronouncements. Finally, in Spain, Charles III put considerable power into the hands of Enlightenment figures such as Aranda, Campomanes, Olavide, and Jovelanos.

Thus, according to Venturi, England was the only great country that did not respond to the triumphant call of the Enlightenment in those years. The most advanced country in the Western world seemed to proceed at a different pace: "English radicalism, too, was born around 1764, but it exhibited very different characteristics from the philosophy of the continent. One has to wait until the eighties and nineties to find men such as Bentham, Price, Godwin, and Paine. In England the rhythm was different." Such unequivocal statements are less surprising if we keep in mind that for Venturi the circulation of Enlightenment ideas was one thing, but quite another thing was the actual "organization of the Enlightenment" as a movement consciously led by a kind of *parti des philosophes* (132). The latter was to be found in Scotland, Naples, Paris, and Berlin—but not in London or Venice. In those great urban conglomerates, the ideas and writings of the *philosophes* were in fact very popular and supported a strong publishing industry based on what we would now call the cultural consumption of the Enlightenment by the élites. What we do not find there, however, are authoritative writers professing their adherence to the Enlightenment, great protagonists capable of creating an autonomous group and giving rise to a conscious political movement like the movements that had arisen in Paris, or around the *Caffè* in Milan. Thus, the lives of men, self-conscious groups, guiding principles, contexts, and political action are all considered together in Franco Venturi's intellectual history, and together determine its evaluation criteria.

Considered on this basis, the chronology and geography of the Enlightenment were bound to change considerably in the period of decline that began in the 1770s. This decade saw the demise of the great Enlightenment generation of Voltaire (1694–1778), Rousseau (1712–1778), and Diderot (1713–1784). The inevitable result was the end of the Enlightenment as a movement, and then the end of Enlightenment itself, i.e., of the real, politically significant Enlightenment, that had been created at the same time as the *Encyclopédie*. In the last quarter of the century, Europe as a whole entered "the age of great reforms, and of the reactions they aroused. The age of Turgot and Joseph II also witnessed three decades of economic expansion replaced by a period of uncertainty and of abrupt fluctuations" (135). This ushered in social and political conflict in Russia, the United Provinces, Austrian Bohemia, and then on the other side of the Atlantic, which culminated with the great Revolution. Venturi, then, enthusiastically concurred with the conclusions set out in Robert Darnton's early work, *Mesmerism and the End of the Enlightenment in France* (1968), which investigated the rise of a prerevolutionary mentality far-removed from the rationalistic certainties of thinkers like d'Alembert and Condorcet. For Venturi, too, figures such as Marat, Brissot, and Carra, together with their Mesmerian and Rousseauian emulators from all over Europe, now belonged to a different era from the Great Enlightenment of the *Encyclopédie* years.

The last quarter of the eighteenth century seemed dominated by a new generation of mostly "not very nice" intellectuals: strange characters who promoted weird languages and ideas that had nothing to do with the old and glorious world of Enlightenment rationalism. In their political projects and pronouncements, "the yearning for a new world took on aberrant and pathological forms" (ibid.). Although Venturi does not say this, those "forms" prefigured the anguish and violent folly of a Reign of Terror in which the sleep of reason had generated the worst possible monsters.

The chronology and geography of the Enlightenment authoritatively outlined by Venturi remain valid today. No substantial qualifications are needed. We should not be distracted by the sensation that the crypto-nationalistic theses put forward in a work like *Enlightenment in National Context* caused. In trustworthy scholarship the European dimension and cosmopolitan nature of the Enlightenment have never really been in doubt. There are certainly no changes in the geographical or national landscape. If anything, some new elements of chronology have been added, coming from the new English intellectual history practiced by Jonathan Israel and John Robertson.

Jonathan Israel's imposing two-volume work offers a drastically modified picture from that painted by Venturi. The volume titles are significant in themselves: *Radical Enlightenment: Philosophy and the Making of Modernity, 1650–1750* (Oxford: Oxford University Press, 2001) and *Enlightenment Contested: Philosophy, Modernity and the Emancipation of Man, 1670–1752* (ibid., 2006). In Israel's discussion, the fundamental core and the apex of the Enlightenment in its initial phase as a historical phenomenon are no longer to be found in Freethinker England, or, in its later phase, in the *Encyclopédie* and the Paris of the *philosophes* in the 1760s and 1770s. Israel instead shifts the focus onto the Dutch Republic and the intellectual controversies that arose throughout Europe in the seventeenth and eighteenth century around Spinoza and his materialistic philosophy. This philosophy is credited by Israel with providing the theoretical basis for all those elements that distinctively characterize the Enlightenment: secularization, toleration, democracy, the liberty of the individual, emancipation, equality, and modernity.

The framework of Israel's work is largely indebted to the inspiring and pioneering work carried out by Margaret Candee Jacob on this subject in her 1981

The Radical Enlightenment: Pantheists, Freemasons and Republicans. According to this scheme, eighteenth-century Spinozism and its multifarious interpretations down to the French Revolution become the foundation of the Radical Enlightenment. By reaction this in turn generates a more minor Moderate Enlightenment, based on principles derived from Locke and Newton. However, the fundamental ideas and the definitive picture of the decisive radical component had already been completed by the middle of the century, with the publication of the works of La Mettrie and of the young Diderot. As Israel writes: "In the 1740s, the real business was already over" (I, 6).

In fact, Israel's radical revision involves more than just a few modifications of the chronology, locations, and protagonists of the Enlightenment. Venturi's intellectual history had focused primarily on ideas, especially those concerning politics and economics, whose historical function he studied in relation to their context. However, his starting point had always been the human beings and the politically self-conscious groups involved, in relation to which he had studied things like the various rebellions, reforms, conquests, boundaries, markets, roads, currencies, and laws. Israel, on the other hand, prioritizes the study of "philosophical ideas." He sometimes seems to take seriously the paradoxical theses of French and Italian reactionaries, who blamed the legacy of Spinoza's *esprit philosophique* for the rise of the modern Enlightenment world and consequently for the French Revolution. Israel's work is effectively a valuable and well-informed synthesis of "history of philosophy." It focuses on elements such as the great debate on miracles in modern Europe, Bayle's theory of the virtuous atheist, Deism and Cartesianism, and it is built on the methodical application of a "controversialist technique in opposition to the claims of the 'new social history', focused on the broad mass of Early Enlightenment controversies—French, German, British, Italian and Dutch" (II, 26).[17]

In fact Israel's substantial and well-crafted work risks causing a sudden and unexpected deviation towards idealism, which would nullify the work done by the most creative research of recent years in establishing a mutually beneficial dialogue among different approaches and techniques. One case in point, in the Anglo-Saxon world, is Margaret Jacob's 1991 work, *Living the Enlightenment: Freemasonry and Politics in Eighteenth-Century Europe*, which identifies the hidden origins of the modern political and constitutional language of the Enlightenment in Masonic social practices and in the cultural practices of the European lodges. Another instance of this type of research is Robert Darnton's work on men of letters and book circulation in prerevolutionary France. It is to Darnton's chronology and to the hugely valuable results of his research that we must refer in future if we want to get back on the right track of historiographical innovation.

It is ironic that, despite his international reputation in this respect, Darnton has never claimed to be a historian of the Enlightenment. He was never really interested in Kant's famous question, *Was ist Aufklärung?* From the early days, his declared objective was never to contribute something original in this field, but rather to analyze the forms and character of French prerevolutionary culture in the last quarter of the eighteenth century. He was concerned with studying the relevant books and authors and, if anything, with helping to further clarify the traditional link between the Enlightenment and the Revolution. Recently, critics of Darnton's work have given rise to what has been termed an actual "Darnton debate." In reply to their sometimes rather unfocused and poisonous accusations, Darnton has often and firmly stressed this precise aspect of his intellectual experience, i.e., that he was never interested in defining the Enlightenment in relation to Venturi's or Cassirer's theses: "I derived my idea of the Enlightenment from my tutor at Oxford, Robert Shackleton, and the scholars I met there from 1960 to 1964, notably Franco Venturi, Ralph Leigh, and Isaiah Berlin. Ever since I myself began to teach, I have assigned Cassirer's *The Philosophy of the Enlightenment* and Mornet's *Les Origines intellectuelles de la Révolution française* to my graduate students."[18] While there is much that is true in these assertions, Darnton's historiographical discoveries, which were always based on solid archival work, are still today absolutely fundamental to our understanding of the nature, geography, and chronology of the Enlightenment, whether or not we share his interpretations, his point of view, or even his intentions.

For instance, Darnton's famous 1971 essay, "The High Enlightenment and the Low-Life of Literature in Pre-Revolutionary France,"[19] made known the deep split and fierce disagreements that erupted within the new social class of men of letters at the end of the century. On one side of the divide were the heirs to the first Enlightenment generation, the generation of Fontenelle and of Voltaire, and then later of the so-called High Enlightenment of Suard, Marmontel, La Harpe, and Chamfort. On the other side, were the poor and desperate hacks of Paris's Grub Street, who were excluded from the system of State patronage, as well as from the alliance that d'Alembert and Voltaire had aspired to in the years after 1752, i.e., the co-operation between *gens de lettres* and the *grands seigneurs* who were part of the French *monde* of the salons and of the court, an alliance that aimed at bringing about the triumph of the culture of the Enlightenment in the Republic of Letters. The existence of this dynamic has been known at least since the time of Taine's *Origines de la France contemporaine*. What is new is that Darnton interprets it solely from the point of view of the causes of the Revolution, such as the rise of prerevolutionary propaganda and of a prerevolutionary climate precisely because of this clash between the heirs of Voltaire—who by now ruled the academies and the salons and were perfectly integrated into the *Ancien Régime*'s system of privileges and pensions—and all those who were excluded from that system: charlatans, Mesmerists, and literary hacks who would do anything in order to survive. It was among these marginal figures that Darnton detected the first restless stirrings of the revolutionary spirit and of what was to be the Jacobin version of Rousseau's followers. He saw nothing of the kind among the main protagonists of the High Enlightenment, with their moderate, rationalist, and conservative stance. Darnton went on to apply the same methodology in his more recent and foundational work on the history of the book. Essentially sociological and economic in its method, it focuses on the study of professional careers rather than on the ideas and writings of the main figures, and for the most part still takes a teleological approach to the Enlightenment-Revolution paradigm.

In *The Business of Enlightenment* Darnton had explained why the *Encyclopédie* had been such a success in commercial terms. In subsequent years, he described the precipitous increase in the number of writers and in book production, attempting to answer the question first posed by Daniel Mornet in 1910 of what it was that the French public was actually reading in the eighteenth century, and how their reading habits may have determined the intellectual causes of the Revolution. Once again Darnton was able to make an important contribution to the discussion of traditional themes thanks to brilliant and fortunate archival discoveries. In this case, he discovered the *livres philosophiques* (as they were called at the time),[20] a myriad of seditious booklets and pamphlets—sensational and pornographic in nature—in which philosophical ideas and reflections on the right to happiness were presented side by side with erotic messages and a denunciation of the immorality of the powerful.

These widely popular and irreverent publications disclosed the human feelings and sexual habits of kings and queens, priests and aristocrats, servants and masters alike, with total disregard for the hierarchical logic of the *Ancien Régime*, and exposed public opinion to a propagandistic message that amounted to a clear and definitive desacralization of power and contributed to a general feeling of disenchantment. Thus, these otherwise trivial publications helped bring about the assumption of responsibility by a mankind finally liberated from divine tutelage—in short, they helped create the indispensable premises for the unleashing of revolutionary fervor. Darnton had made a truly important discovery about the 1780s, a fundamentally important period that had been unaccountably neglected by Mornet and all previous historians. Alongside the acknowledged canon of Enlightenment literature that includes writers such as Voltaire, Diderot, and Rousseau, Darnton had found a cache of new and significantly interesting books that were also directly connected to the conflict and surprising rift within the new class of the men of letters, thus highlighting a social and cultural phenomenon that had had a major effect on life in Paris in the last quarter of the eighteenth century. However, Darnton's interpretation of this phenomenon in historiographical terms did not live up to the importance of the discovery itself.

This is due to the fact that Darnton allowed himself to be influenced by the Enlightenment-Revolution paradigm and was, thus, entirely dependent on Cassirer and Venturi for his view of the Enlightenment. He uncritically accepted Venturi's chronology and geography, according to which the demise of Voltaire and Diderot's generation also signaled the end of the peak phase of the Enlightenment itself. In his view, while the representatives of low literature, the so-called *libellistes*, were doing nothing more than expressing their social rage and their irrational revolutionary spirit, the major figures of the High Enlightenment, i.e., the new generation of conservative and moderate *philosophes*, were not worth much more from an intellectual point of view, since all they really cared about was defending their pensions and privileges: "Suard's generation of *philosophes* had remarkably little to say. They argued over Gluck and Piccinni, dabbled in preromanticism, chanted the old litanies about legal reform and the *infâme*, and collected their tithes."[21] One is tempted to sum up Darnton's contribution by saying that, despite what he may have believed himself, he really did discover a new and unexpected aspect of Enlightenment culture, something that came close to being an actual historical period that was autonomous and "original" in Dilthey's sense of the term, and which from now on we shall call the late Enlightenment.[22] However, he gave a sadly reductive interpretation of this period, which he misunderstood and misrepresented as a period of crisis that saw the decline and even the death of the Enlightenment. Applying the usual literary categories, Darnton described this period as "preromanticism," a rather confused phase of transition towards the Romantic era, thus proposing yet another theory of the intellectual origins of the great Revolution, albeit an evocative and little-known one.

This erroneous reading was in any case in line with traditionally accepted chronology, from Mornet to Venturi. In fact, Darnton had been following this line from his very first book, *Mesmerism and the End of the Enlightenment in France* (1968). That pioneering study described both the "golden age of popular science" and the definitive and momentous triumph of science as the main category of knowledge available to man in the Republic of Letters and among the Parisian élites. Finally, historians were looking beyond the scientific conquests achieved by the great academies, or by the powerful community of professionals that now existed from Saint Petersburg to Philadelphia, from Edinburgh to Naples. Historians were also studying the social dimension of this phenomenon, that is to say the extraordinary interest that the public was now showing in everything that pertained to the new world of science, as manifested in specialist periodicals and in the gazettes, in aristocratic salons and among the common people. Indeed, this period saw thousands of Parisians greet the first hot-air balloons with amazement and enthusiasm, not to mention Franklin's experiments with electricity, and the prestigious and lucrative academy competitions won by Lavoisier and Lagrange.

Louis-Sébastien Mercier gave the perfect account of that important turning point in his *Tableau de Paris*. The reign of letters is over, he says, speaking ironically: poetry and the novel have been replaced by the physical sciences, and electric machines have taken the place of drama.[23] With reference to the controversies caused by Mesmerism, Mercier goes on to describe a kind of new chronological succession in eighteenth-century French intellectual life: "Autrefois Moliniste—Ensuite Janséniste—Puis Encyclopédiste—Et puis Economiste—A présent Mesmériste."[24]

It is on this explosion of the controversy over Mesmerism that Darnton founded his thesis, according to which in the last few decades of the century the Enlightenment experienced a sort of natural death. And indeed Mesmerism was debated by every part of the nation: the court, eminent scholars, l'Académie des Sciences, the Société Royale de Médecine, periodicals and gazettes, any number of people of every social rank, plus the government and the political class. To this effect, the extraordinary success of Mesmer and his followers and of their alternative to official medicine is presented as giving rise to a clash between two irreconcilable positions. On one side there was a group of irrationalist charlatans, who cynically tried to effect an unexpected return to magic and the supernatural, and whose belief in the existence of a magnetized fluid, in Darnton's view, marked the definitive "end of the Enlightenment."[25] On the other side there was official science, staunchly defending Newton's physical-mathematical mechanism and Galileo's epistemological model based on experimental verification. Darnton does not address the specifically scientific and philosophical aspects of this question. He focuses on the furious arguments between Mesmerists like Marat, Carra, and Brissot on the one hand, and the proponents of Newton's mechanistic universe on the other, who were derided in the ironic battle cry of the Mesmerist *prophètes philosophes*: "Hors de Newton point de salut."[26] Darnton discusses those controversies primarily as revealing the existence of a socially and politically prerevolutionary stance that was strongly critical of the oligarchies and despotism of the academics, who for their part were bent on defending their *Ancien-Régime* privileges in the name of true scientific knowledge.

In fact, a little more attention should have been paid to the writings of those eminent figures who did admire the work of Austrian doctor Anton Mesmer, and who tried to find plausible and rational explanations for the strange effects produced during sessions where the practitioner attempted to treat all kinds of diseases and social discomforts by placing his hands over the patient like two magnetic poles. This action was purported to restore universal harmony by ensuring the correct flow of a vital magnetic fluid, which in turn would restore a balanced relationship between man and nature and between body and mind. But instead of reading the practice in this light, Darnton mostly reiterated Cassirer's theses, according to which the philosophy of the Enlightenment originated and drew its substance from the paradigm of Newtonian physics. Consequently, he presented an abstract vision of a simple contest between irrationalist charlatans on one side and eminent men of science devoted to the idea of a mechanistic universe on the other. He was therefore unable to see how blurred the demarcation really was, and still is today, between opposing armies at a time of great transformations within the Republic of Sciences. To find the truth, one probably need only look at what was happening in the rest of the continent. It was not in Paris only that Mesmer and his followers were stirring up problems: the controversy produced clashes and aroused vigorous debates between academics in the universities and in the public opinion of all the great European capitals, where it became intertwined with other debates that were just as important and heated, such as those over the increasing success of rhabdomancy and physiognomy.[27]

All this happened because in the second half of the century the idea of nature and the way in which men perceived themselves and the world around them began to undergo a radical change. This affected both the collective mind of the intellectual élites and important sectors of the scientific community. Something like a new philosophical and scientific *Gestalt* began to emerge, and soon became the prevailing outlook. Thus the old concept of a mechanistic nature that was static, immutable in time, and preformed gave way to a view of nature as a dynamic, vitalistic, temporalized, and protean entity.[28] A new and powerful epistemological transformation was taking place in the sciences of man and life in general, following on the first revolution brought about by Descartes, Galileo, and Newton. This "second scientific revolution" saw breakthroughs in the fields of electricity, chemistry, medicine, and meteorology. It gave rise to new and discordant paradigms, contrasting and evocative representations of the great chain of being, which were necessarily associated with different forms of professionalization and institutionalization within the practice of science. As mentioned above, this raised for the first time the question of what could be legitimately considered to be science, and of who scientists really were.

Denis Diderot was among the first to understand and to let the Republic of Letters know about the extraordinary process that was then taking place. As early as 1754, in his *De l'interprétation de la nature*, he wrote of a "big revolution" that was about to happen in the field of science, because of the new representation of nature. In his work Diderot announced the end of that reign of physics and mathematics that had arisen in the seventeenth century. He also saw the imminent demise of the *philosophie rationnelle* and of the mechanistic model that had been adopted by Newton's followers, among them d'Alembert, Clairaut, and Euler, a model that explained reality by means of formulae so abstract and incomprehensible that they almost made it inhuman. "L'homme n'est pas une machine," Diderot was wont to say: "La région des mathématiciens est un monde intellectuel." That world was now in terminal decline. In its place, a new "physique expérimentale" was arising: a more democratic and popular kind of physics, which, in the wake of Francis Bacon, privileged instead aspects like observation, experience, and the simple qualitative evaluation of phenomena on the basis of their usefulness and of the morphology of signs.

In his *Lettre sur les aveugles* (1749), as well as in his unpublished *Rêve de d'Alembert* and in the 1770 *Pensées philosophiques sur la matière et le mouvement*, Diderot gave a passionate account of the rapid decline of the image of a mechanistic universe, which was to be superseded by the representation of nature as a "grand animal": as *natura naturans*, constantly changing habit and forms, like "une femme qui aime à se travestir."[29] Diderot also attacked Réaumur and Linnaeus's idea of the fixity of species on the basis of the theories of transformation put forward by Maupertuis and by Benoît de Maillet and of Buffon's considerations on the need to think of nature in time. It was a view that focused on the whirlwind of history, whose millions of years of catastrophic discontinuities and probable evolutions were undermining the bases of Biblical creationism. Diderot's somewhat materialistic stance revived ancient concepts such as epigenesis and spontaneous generation. He believed in the need to go finally beyond Descartes's dualism and to reconcile man and nature, microcosm and macrocosm, mind and body, consciousness and matter. The research carried out by important scholars such as Wolff, Needham, Robinet, Blumenbach, Bichat, and Bonnet gave credibility and appeal to the views that Diderot was addressing a larger audience.

European intellectual life in the last quarter of the century was strongly affected by this contest between the supporters of a mechanistic and physical-mathematical view of the great chain of being and those who believed in a Renaissance-style *natura naturans*. There were important scientists and Enlightenment figures on both sides of the divide, and Diderot was only one of the protagonists of this harsh debate. From Saint Petersburg to London, from Paris to Pavia, and from Turin to Berlin, Galileo and Newton's followers rebutted their adversaries' arguments blow by blow. Lagrange took up d'Alembert's legacy and continued undaunted to transform mechanics into a branch of mathematics. This provided scientists like Monge and Laplace with increasingly sophisticated algorithms, and inspired the quantitative model that

Lavoisier applied to the new chemistry, and Daniel Bernoulli and Condorcet to social mathematics. Some scholars, including Spallanzani, Coulomb, Bézout, and Cavendish, were quite suspicious and critical of the new image of nature. In fact, most of the time the boundaries between the two contrasting positions were far from clear-cut. A case in point is Carlo Amoretti, an important expert on electrochemical phenomena and the author of a voluminous tract entitled *Della raddomanzia ossia elettrometria animale*. Amoretti showed no hesitation in embarking on a frank and learned discussion with Alessandro Volta in order to establish whether there could be any links between Volta's research on the production and conduction of electricity through metals and Thouvenel's study of fluids as a possible explanation for rhabdomancy and for the "animal electric fluid" discovered by Luigi Galvani in frogs.[30]

The rise of modern clinical medicine itself profited greatly from the vitalistic model of a *natura naturans*. One need only read the works of Diderot's great friend, Théophile de Bordeu, who was head of the *École de Montpellier*, or the entry for *"Influence"* written for the *Encyclopédie* by a pupil of the latter, Jean-Jacques Ménuret: these writings display a brand of medical science light years in advance of the old "iatromechanical" paradigm that explained physiology and pathology with physics. The new *médecine pratique* was founded on experimental empiricism, on semiotics, and on the neo-Hippocratic clinical medicine revived by the eminent English physician Thomas Sydenham at the end of the seventeenth century. This new medicine eschewed intellectual constructions, and what we would now call reductionist and mechanistic views of diseases. Instead, it examined the patient's body looking for relevant signs and symptoms, took note of valuable clues and signs to be examined comparatively, and then boldly experimented with remedies and treatments, which were finally evaluated only on the basis of their results. *Sensibilité*, a term used to indicate a newly-discovered faculty of nervous fibers in the human body, became a magic word that opened the way to the interpretation of a variety of things: for instance, it relaunched disciplines like astrological medicine, which sought to provide a rational explanation for epidemics by resorting to the influence of the stars, and magnetic and natural medicine, which treated nervous disorders with electric shock, the objective being to restore the overall cosmic balance. With this concept of sensibility and influence, the followers of the *École de Montpellier* finally did away with Descartes's old dualism between the *physique* and the *morale*, thus inaugurating a series of studies that would be taken further by the *idéologues* in the course of the following decades.

In his 1775 *De l'homme, ou des principes et des loix de l'influence de l'âme sur le corps et du corps sur l'âme*, Marat gives a good account of the new chain of being, a vitalistic and interactive concept whose ultimate meaning he finds in the key shift from the *homme machine* to the *homme sensible*. Together with Brissot, Marat led the Mesmerists' rebellion against the power of the academics. Their revolt was based on these peculiar scientific theories, which had nothing to do with magic and irrationality. Thus, they reacted indignantly to the accusation of being charlatans, levied against them because of their passionate argument with the followers of Newton and Voltaire.

The Mesmerists did have a point. In the general confusion created by the fierce clashes that divided the international scientific community, they were afraid of being lumped together with the numerous actual charlatans, fake healers, and quack magicians operating at the time. These dubious figures were taking advantage of the successes of contemporary science and of the increasing public interest in a truly baroque cosmos, with its variety of fluids—electric and igneous, as well as magnetic—and other entities that appeared mysterious and undefined even when their origins lay in the academic world, such as the force of gravity, phlogiston, and caloric. One could well be forgiven for seeing these conflicts as the death certificate of the Enlightenment. But in fact, things like natural medicine and the popular sciences of the turn of the century, from Mesmerism to physiognomy, were legitimate offspring of the Enlightenment, just as much as the forms of scientific rationalization that were governed by the much more celebrated and powerful Newtonian paradigm. As has been pointed out at every possible opportunity, the apparently bizarre and irrational world of Mesmerism in fact had illustrious spiritual ancestors of the caliber of Diderot and Rousseau. Moreover, in every part of Europe there were numerous other famous figures of the Enlightenment (for instance, the Baron d'Holbach and the Abbé Raynal) who were not great admirers of Newton's mechanistic universe, but had no qualms about taking part in rhabdomancy experiments. Above all, these popular sciences openly aimed at fulfilling man's free and autonomous need for happiness and knowledge, and at the emancipation of man through man, that is to say those pursuits that constituted the very essence and the main original qualities of Enlightenment humanism. Hence the necessity to finally question the traditional twentieth-century chronology and geography of the Enlightenment. It is time to file away the obsolete aspects of past research hypotheses and methods of analysis, and to move on from our obsession with understanding European history in the final quarter of the eighteenth century solely in terms of the causes of the French Revolution, with the attendant ideological and political celebration or demonization of its forebears. It is only by doing so that we will finally be able to give due importance to the question of the *Late Enlightenment* as a self-contained period and original cultural system: a global historical event whose specific characteristics deserve to be studied in their own right.

14

||||||||||||||||||||||||

POLITICIZATION AND *NATURA NATURANS*

The Late Enlightenment Question
and the Crisis of the Ancien Régime

FROM THE POINT OF view of cultural history, the Late Enlightenment certainly represents the historical moment of hegemony. Over the course of more than a century, the Enlightenment had developed as a cultural revolution directed against the *Ancien Régime*, and the final decades of the eighteenth century saw the culmination of that profound transformation of Western identity, the legacy of which lasts to this day, albeit amidst fierce debates and controversies.

The crisis of the *Ancien Régime* proceeded step by step with the late Enlightenment, which therefore had a profound impact on Western identity, because it involved the governments and the élites of all the great European cities and directly influenced every form of knowledge, effectively setting off a process of cultural hegemony such as has rarely been seen in any other time or place.[1] This was a historical and cultural phenomenon of great importance, in that it affected virtually everyone who was able to read and write, regardless of class or social standing. In the 1770s and 1780s many of the values, ideas, practices, and specialized vocabularies that had been developed in small intellectual circles in the first part of the century became objects of large-scale cultural consumption in salons, Masonic lodges, universities, academies, and in the courts. These cultural products spread everywhere through gazettes, periodicals, and popular almanacs, and also thanks to the publishing industry, the theatre, literature, painting, music, and the sciences. Although the most innovative elements of this cultural system were often misunderstood, manipulated, argued against, and rejected, they continued to be at the center of every discussion, and were the object of cultural enjoyment and of creative consumption—as Michel de Certeau would put it—to the point of affecting even the way of being and of acting of those who opposed the cultural system itself.[2]

A case in point is the changed attitude on the part of the Catholic Church at the end of the century when faced with the triumph of the Enlightenment. The Church was forced to acknowledge the growing importance of the public sphere, of book circulation, and of the new means of social and political communication that had been developed by the *philosophes* in their fight for hegemony. Accepting the challenge, the Church denounced admirers of the *Encyclopédie* as heretics and dangerous. However, it was itself affected by the new cultural practices and subversive ideas, so that it updated its methods in order to have a better chance of success in the fight against modernity. For instance, it decided to "govern" the practice of reading *ad maiorem Dei gloriam* rather than forbidding it.[3] And indeed it was in those frenzied and fascinating years, and in part due to the Enlightenment's increasing cultural hegemony, that the Republic of Letters and the new social class of the men of letters became a powerful and influential *Ancien Régime* corporation. In this regard, we might look at a striking event that took place in Paris on March 30, 1778, in front of the *Comédie française*. The *Comédie* had solemnly gathered together *en corps* and, after a performance of the tragedy *Irène*, proceeded to publicly and with great fanfare "crown" the writer Voltaire.

Newspaper accounts of the time turned this into a symbolic event of unprecedented magnitude and, by means of detailed articles and well-crafted etchings, ensured that it would become known throughout Europe. In his *Mémoires*, Fleury describes Voltaire's return to Paris, at the age of eighty-four and after a twenty-seven-year absence caused by his having suffered persecutions and threats. In Fleury's account this becomes a *triomphe*, a true *apothéose*, which went well beyond the person of Voltaire, being a salute to his work and ideas and to his standing as the recognized head of the *philosophes*.

> I doubt whether the arrival of a king, a hero, or a prophet would have excited greater enthusiasm, than was felt on the appearance of Voltaire in Paris; every other subject of interest was for a time forgotten. Court intrigues, and even the great musical war between the Gluckists and the Picenists, were suspended. The Sorbonne trembled, the parliament observed silence, excitement pervaded the literary circles, and Paris proudly rendered homage to the nation's idol.[4]

That March 30th, after receiving "des honneurs inusités" at the Académie Française, Voltaire went to see a repeat performance of his *Irène*, at which he was acclaimed by the public and by the most important members of the Parisian aristocracy, the government, and the royal family.

At the conclusion of the play, his bust was brought to the front of the stage, and crowned by the actors amidst transports of admiration. Some verses, written for the occasion by M. de Saint Mare, were recited by Madame Vestris. The performers then advanced one by one, and each laid a wreath of flowers beside the bust. Mademoiselle Funier, seized with a fit of ecstasy, threw her arms round the bust and kissed it. So contagious is enthusiasm that we all followed her example, and several persons in the pit climbed on the stage for the purpose of saluting it.[5]

And it was not over yet. Voltaire's triumph and symbolic coronation continued, significantly, outside the theatre, with a parade through the streets of Paris, which now saw the population walking beside his carriage:

A vast concourse of persons who had collected in the street, wished to take the horses from his carriage and draw him home. It was with great difficulty they were prevented from doing so, but they followed him to his place of residence, making the air resound with his name and the titles of his principal works; nothing was heard as he passed through the streets, but shouts of *Vive Voltaire! vive l'auteur Zaire!* [sic] *vive l'auteur de l'Henriade!* &c.[6]

Thus, thirteen years before his *panthéonisation* at the hands of the revolutionaries in 1791, Voltaire, and with him, indirectly, all his comrades in arms were crowned and carried in triumph through the streets of Paris. The same *Ancien Régime* that had unhesitatingly sent them to the *Bastille* a few decades earlier had now unexpectedly and at a very early stage turned them into national heroes and fathers of the nation. This was a true *sacre de l'écrivain*, to rival the celebration of Louis XVI that had taken place in Rheims three years earlier, where among other things the King had solemnly sworn to defend the Catholic Church and destroy all heretics. There could be no better proof of the hegemony achieved by the culture of the Enlightenment at the end of the century. However, the peculiar forms and characteristics of this hegemony still need to be thoroughly investigated.

For instance, it would be a mistake to think of the Late Enlightenment as a tired repetition of ideas, values, and practices developed in a more glorious past. Or as a hegemonic phase built mainly on the publishing, social, and institutional success of a bygone era, like a wave formed in a time long past, whose creative impetus was by now pretty much spent. In fact, according to our chronology, the real apex of the Enlightenment was not reached until the French Revolution. Thus the last few decades of the eighteenth century, and especially the years between the American Revolution in 1776 and the year 1789, were marked by the rise of a generation of brilliant new Enlightenment personalities in every corner of Europe: from Raynal to Condorcet, from Beaumarchais to Mozart, and on to David, Goya, Filangieri, Pagano, Jefferson, Franklin, Lessing, Goethe, Paine, Jovellanos, and Radishchev. Many of them embraced this Late Enlightenment period with passion and great hopes that would be dashed by the tumult and violence of the Revolution and of the Reign of Terror. The work that this generation produced, mostly in the ten years leading up to the Revolution, gave rise to original debates and innovative political theories and solutions. It developed vocabularies and images never before seen or even thought of, whose real meaning was mostly overshadowed by the glaring light of the Revolution itself. And so it will remain, unless we begin seeing it in relation to that precise end-of-the-century cultural context and the two major phenomena that characterized it: the sudden and momentous politicization of the Republic of Letters, and the gradual move towards neonaturalism in every field of knowledge.

These two elements had a huge influence over the Late Enlightenment and thus deserve to be studied closely. As far as neonaturalism is concerned, we should note that the mechanistic universe and physical and mathematical empiricism of Newton, and the deterministic view of the relationship between man and nature within the great chain of being continued to dominate in the scientific academies and universities. However, the view of *natura naturans* embraced by Enlightenment figures such as Diderot rapidly prevailed in the Republic of Letters and among the artists, men of letters, architects, painters, and musicians. This view became the ideal frame of reference for intellectual life in a large part of Europe. It was a dynamic concept of a nature that existed firmly anchored in time and overflowing with vital energy, and it led everywhere to new reflections and new ways of seeing man's limits, functions, and potentialities.

In Naples, for instance, this view led to the rise of an evocative philosophy of history as a series of cycles, and of the social development of mankind as subject to a succession of huge natural catastrophes. It was a view that revived principles and images of the Renaissance Hermetic tradition, albeit in new and intriguing forms.[7]

In Germany this view is found in Lessing and, especially, in the young Goethe.[8] Both of these writers were quick to embrace the new concept of a living nature that was finally autonomous, free from under God's thumb, and in harmony with a pantheistic view that stressed the eternal sacrality and sovereignty of nature as it attempted to redefine aesthetic principles and the artist's task. Lessing and Goethe were not alone in this. Boileau, a follower of Descartes, had begun his own movement denouncing classical aesthetics as early as the first decades of the century. However, after Burke's *Philosophical Inquiry into the Origin of Our Ideas of the Sublime and Beautiful* (1756), Diderot's *Salons* and *Essai sur la peinture* (1765), and Lessing's *Laocoon* (1766), the widespread acceptance of the concept of *natura naturans* certainly acted as a strong catalyst in bringing about the definitive success of the new concepts of art. It was in just this period of the Late Enlightenment with its radical humanism that a thorough-going renewal of aesthetic theories finally came into its own and began to produce its best results. This encouraged the formation of a modern and cosmopolitan republic of artists and European talents. Evidence is found in Canova's masterpieces, as well as in works painted before the Revolution by Fuseli, such as the famous 1781 *Nightmare*, or by Fragonard, Piranesi, Blake, David, and Goya.[9] Or it may be gleaned by listening to Mozart, focusing more however on the contents and meanings of Masonic music and on the end-of-century debate about the theatre and opera of the *Ancien Régime* that engaged Enlightenment circles.[10]

Nicolas Boileau's eighteenth-century classicist model had been rigid. The great "législateur du Parnasse" still saw the artistic phenomenon in mechanistic terms, as an objective fact governed by rules that were rational, universal, and above all timeless. The new esthetic theories were now finally taking into account values of an opposite aspect, such as empiricism, experience, and the relativity of taste throughout history. The centrality, or rather the actual enthronement of man and all his faculties as preached by the *Encyclopédie* and by Enlightenment humanism went hand in hand with the circulation of the new paradigm of a *natura naturans*. Together, these elements once and for all focused on the subject, the I, and on the individual and particular in human existence, as well as on universal and communal aspects. Feelings, sensibility, and man's anxieties took their place next to the cult of reason, and deductive and inductive reasoning learnt to coexist with intuition, imagination, and reason of a poetic stamp.

The overall intellectual background rested on a dynamic view of the great chain of being and of a living nature that was full of expanding energy.[11] Lessing found the very essence of poetry in movement, action, and life. Diderot looked to the disciplines of psychology and physiognomy when judging the artistic value of the new eighteenth-century portrait painting, which sought to convey the depth of its subjects' feelings. From now on, the artist's task was no longer limited to the simple and objective imitation of nature according to merely rationalistic criteria: it was not imitation but, on the contrary, an act of creation itself, an act of man's intimate and free participation in the development of natural forms and in their powerful and constant change. Hence the amazing vogue for formulations of the theory of genius, and the avid interest in Enlightenment circles in the various interpretations of the concept of the sublime. The latter was most often seen as a breakdown of the deterministic barriers of the finite: a powerful and unstoppable feeling that was capable of fully expressing man's intimate freedom in relation to destiny and to the objects of nature, and a form of complete and authentic emancipation, and of man's universal right to the pursuit of happiness. This brought to fruition the most important legacy of the Enlightenment cultural revolution to Western identity; namely, the invention of the modern concept of man's liberty.[12]

This modern understanding of liberty did not consist simply in the political acknowledgment of a natural right inherent in man's very way of being. Liberty was also an attempt to enfranchise oneself from the fixity of species and the Aristotelian-Ptolemaic cosmos in general and, above all, from immovable Biblical creationism. This kind of liberty was nothing less than the very definition of the humanity of man, a liberty seen as the common destiny of the free man and of a living nature. And the latter was conceived, in a pantheistic sense, as a being in constant and autonomous transformation, along the lines of a model that reprised and reinforced Rousseau's famous pronouncement, in his *Social Contract*, against the Aristotelian theory of the natural slave, which was being revived in the course of the eighteenth century: "To renounce liberty is to renounce being a man, to surrender the rights of humanity and even its duties. For him who renounces everything no indemnity is possible. Such a renunciation is incompatible with man's nature; to remove all liberty from his will is to remove all morality from his acts."[13] The politicization of the Republic of Letters took place within this evocative frame of reference and especially against the background of the Late Enlightenment, so that it became one of the period's specific distinguishing traits as compared to previous phases.

But what do we mean by "politicization"?

As we have already seen, the phenomenon was nothing new for historians. It was denounced both by Burke in his *Reflections on the Revolution in France* and by Tocqueville in his volume on *L'Ancien Régime et la Révolution*, not to mention Barruel's farnetications about the political conspiracy supposedly organized by Masonic and Enlightenment figures against the altar and the throne. In this regard, we should also mention Burke's comments on politicized men of letters in France, and Tocqueville's remarks on the politicization of literature and its equally dire consequence: the literarization of politics. But these observations, however important, were rather generic with regard to content, to geography (were they really limited to France?) and to the chronology of events (did they embrace the entire eighteenth century?). And they were always arrived at from the perspective of an obsessive search for the ideological causes of the Revolution. It is only recently that we have started to investigate the originality and novelty of this phenomenon, as well as its nature, causes, and above all its vast scale. We have thus been able to pinpoint its precise and autonomous place in Western life in the last quarter of the century, the crucial moment in time that saw the dramatic and momentous explosion of the crisis of the *Ancien Régime*.[14]

It all began with the Seven Years' War; that is, with the start of a major period of reforms from above, which were matched by violent reactions from below on the part of the people—the farmers' rebellions, the Catalan Revolt, and a series of revolutions from both the liberal and the conservative side.[15] These reforms were the brainchildren of sovereigns and princes such as Catherine the Great, Frederick II, Gustav III, and above all Joseph II, rulers determined to assert their power once and for all over the old representative assemblies, over all kinds of parliaments and senates, over farm and urban communities, feudal and aristocratic privileges, corporations and favors, and ecclesiastical demands. Their reforms effectively set in motion the definitive crisis of the *Ancien Régime* and of the old political order internationally.

The pace of change in this case was quite different from the traditional rhythms that had applied, from the fifteenth century onwards, to that central-ization process on the part of monarchical power that had led to the rise of the modern nation-states in Europe under the aegis of absolutism. The end of the Seven Years' War, which can be considered the first great world war, and the ensuing problems abruptly accelerated the process. An urgent need for change at the political, social, and institutional level was everywhere apparent. On the one hand it was necessary to repair the devastation caused by the war. On the other, the global dimension of future contests for control over international trade and the building of new colonial empires in Asia, Africa, and America demanded the construction of huge fleets and powerful arsenals of technolog-ically advanced weapons. Any nation that wanted to play a primary role in the looming wars was forced to spend astronomical amounts of money on equip-ping increasingly huge and menacing armies.

In this regard, Gaetano Filangieri was certainly right in denouncing the "mil-itary mania" of his time. In the opening lines of his 1780 *Scienza della legisla-zione*, he laments, "What are the sole objects that have hitherto engaged the at-tention of the Sovereigns of Europe? A formidable arsenal, a numerous artillery, a well-disciplined army. All the propositions that have been investigated before Princes, have been merely preparatory to the solution of a single problem: To find the method of killing the greatest number of men in the least time possi-ble."[16] To all this were added the social effects of the rapid economic growth that took place in the course of the century, which caused an urgent need for the State to rationalize and modernize the way in which it governed its territory, by harmonizing and strengthening control of the periphery by the center.

To that end, these reforms from above took a multiplicity of forms, which unleashed angry reactions and responses. For instance, under the Portuguese prime minister Pombal, the process of secularization of the modern State led to the great Catholic monarchies driving the Jesuits away from their territory. This happened, in succession, in Portugal, France, and Spain, and finally led to the order being disbanded. In 1773, by explicit request of the Spanish ambassador, José Moniño, count of Floridablanca, Clement XIV dissolved the Jesuits with the brief encyclical *Dominus ac redemptor*. After the Seven Years' War, this reform process underwent an important change in terms of jurisdictional politics.[17] Crucial questions that now took center stage included that of the temporal goods of the Church, the autonomy of religious orders, the status of the clergy, and religious toleration. The first to take action was the Republic of Lucca, which in 1764 issued a decree that restricted ecclesiastical mortmain. Other interventions followed across the continent, culminating in Joseph II's radical reforms of the 1780s, which included the emancipation of Jews, publication of the general Patent of Toleration in favor of Protestants and the Greek Orthodox, the suppression of several religious orders and finally, in 1783, the introduction of civil marriage, and the change of status of parish priests and bishops into salaried officials. It could almost be said that if ever there was a public figure who more or less consciously undermined the very foundations of the religious *Ancien Régime*, it was Joseph II.

However, the destabilizing and subversive effect of these reforms from above was not limited to the field of religion. The radical version of absolutism, or rather—as contemporaries put it—the "despotic face" of a sovereign right that aimed at leveling everyone before the king, regardless of hierarchies, first developed at the institutional and administrative level, and took mainly the form of an attack on late-medieval particularisms and against the powers and privileges of intermediate bodies and corporations in general. Feudalism was suddenly seen everywhere in Europe as a great problem, mostly from an economic and juridical point of view. It was an obstacle to progress and economic development in the first instance, which inevitably also became a political and constitutional issue.

There were many attempts at reforming peripheral bureaucracies with the aim of finally taking power away from local aristocratic potentates and reasserting the administrative and political primacy of the crown. In France in 1770, Chancellor Maupeou's absolutist "coup d'état" restored the appointment of members of parliament as a royal prerogative and abolished the sale of titles, which led to a fierce clash between the monarchy and the houses of parliament. Equally dramatic struggles broke out in Denmark following the reforms of Prussian Count Johann Struensee, and in the Sweden of Gustav III, who was determined to thwart any aristocratic claims within the system of representation. In Russia in 1773, the immediate social import of the administrative reform of the empire that had begun with the *Nakaz* became apparent to all with the peasant uprising led by the Cossack Pugachev and the ensuing bloodbath.

Those communities that were seeing their vital interests jeopardized reacted by claiming back ancient identities and privileges, in the face of an uncertain future and of abstract measures that showed little regard for history and traditions. A few years later the same would happen to Joseph II, who was forced to face what amounted to actual reactionary revolutions in response to his measures that abolished serfdom in Bohemia, Moravia, and Sudetenland. In the first few months of 1789, his final decrees, which suppressed ecclesiastical tithes and the so-called *robot* (peasants' *corvées*) caused widespread malcontent. The *Ancien Régime* seemed entirely unwilling to accept any variant of even a partial reform: its crisis now appeared irreversible. No appreciable results were achieved by international debates on the liberalization of the wheat trade or on the creation of a modern labor market by doing away with the system of guilds. Equally fruitless were the various calls for the liberalization of the land market and the anti-famine measures applied by governments in Italy, England, and Germany. If anything, these efforts exacerbated feelings and led to uprisings in places such as Paris and Madrid.

What was taking place was nothing less than a profound crisis of a structural, political, and constitutional nature. Its resolution would require an overall cultural transformation capable of redefining the very foundations of the old state order, and the creation of a new civic society based on a new secularized humanism, the emancipation of man through man, and the acknowledgment of man's natural rights. With events like Pasquale Paoli's rebellion in Corsica, quashed by France in 1769, and the revolution started in 1776 by American settlers against the British Empire, in this case successfully, the demise of the *Ancien Régime* was now well and truly underway. None of its protagonists was any longer able to prevent the politicization of the crisis, as the rapid pace of changes provoked unmanageable violence.

It is no longer profitable to ask whether these radical reforms from above were inspired by the ideas of the Enlightenment, or were instead results of a long-term strategy of dominion and modernization by the absolute monarchies. Whether or not this historical period should be called an era of enlightened despotism is no longer a useful question, and is more likely to confuse the issue.[18] It is true that many of those great sovereigns were personal friends of Diderot and Voltaire, and had read and taken on board the works of Montesquieu, Beccaria, Lessing and Campomanes. However, this does not authorize us to confuse the rise of the new political culture *ex parte civium*, i.e., that republican and constitutional culture advocated in European Enlightenment circles between 1776 and 1789, with the traditional politics *ex parte principis* that was practiced at court and in the chanceries.

Despite its being part of this wider crisis, the politicization of the Late Enlightenment was a peculiar phenomenon, which had well-defined contours. To a large extent, it was characterized by more than the mere determination to go beyond the organic society of the *Ancien Régime*. Its main trait was the originality of the solutions deployed in the process that was to lead to the transformation of the cultural politics of the time. In fact, the Enlightenment's vocation to political action was inscribed in its DNA, and especially in its programmatic development of the new sciences of man as applied to reality. There is no need to resort to Michel Foucault or to the usual considerations on the link between power and the different forms of knowledge in order to trace the rise of the eighteenth-century intellectual as protagonist in the political struggle. If anything, we should make a greater effort at reconstructing the crucial phases and precise modalities that brought the denizens of the Republic of Letters to this stage.

In this respect, there is no doubt that, within the Republic of Letters, it was the proponents of Enlightenment who assigned a political, moral, and social function to the modern "philosopher." They were thus defining themselves as a "universal class"—as we would say today, in the wake of Marx—and as natural and legitimate representatives of the rights of the whole of mankind. In 1780, Gaetano Filangieri, a major exponent of the European Late Enlightenment, wrote a short appeal that gives us a good illustration of the cosmopolitan vocation and political purposes of philosophers, who were now conscious of their roles. It highlights the profound renewal that had taken place within political language, with the rise of new keywords such as "rights of man," "liberty," "happiness," "citizenship," "the struggle against tyranny," against "fanaticism" and against "imposture":

> Sages of the earth, Philosophers of every nation,—O all ye to whom the sacred deposit of knowledge is intrusted, if ye would live, if ye would that your names should remain engraven in the temple of memory, if ye would that immortality should crown your labours, employ yourselves on these subjets, which, over two thousand leagues of space, and after twenty centuries, continue to be interesting! Never write for a man, but for mankind: unite your glory with the eternal interests of the human race [. . .] despite the vain applause of the vulgar, and the mercenary gratitude of the great, the threats of persecution, and the derision of ignorance: boldly instruct your brethren and freely defend their rights. Then shall mankind, interested in the hopes of happiness to which you point the road, hear you with transport; then shall posterity, grateful to your labours, in public

repositories distinguish your writings: then, neither the impotent rage of tyranny, nor the interested clamours of fanaticism, nor the sophisms of imposture [. . .] shall avail to bring them into disrepute, or bury them in oblivion: they will pass from generation to generation with the glory of your name; they will be read, and perhaps washed with the tears of those who would never have otherwise known you; and your genius, always useful, will then be the contemporary of every age, and the citizen of every State.[19]

Current research has shown that the struggle for hegemony on the part of Enlightenment culture took root first within the Republic of Letters and then spread to other sectors—to governments, sovereigns, élites, and finally, directly and as a priority, to international public opinion. The movement used all means at its disposal. It occupied and influenced the life of lodges, academies, and salons. It renewed social communication. It created modern political culture by means of new discourses and theories, and of practices, representations, and vocabularies that were more and more alien and hostile to the *Ancien Régime*.

In 1760, in the introductory letter to his comedy *Les Philosophes*, Charles Palissot gave a useful description of the beginning of the process of politicization of the Enlightenment in France. Palissot describes a "secte impériose," which had formed under the aegis of a work, i.e., the *Encyclopédie*, and which had extended its dominion to encompass all of the sciences, as well as literature, the arts, and custom. In Palissot's view, the religious skepticism and anti-religious stance of adherents to the Enlightenment qualified them as a form of *tyrannie universelle*.[20] Those were terrible war years, uncertain times in which, because of their cosmopolitism and their appreciation for enlightened rulers such as Frederick II, the *philosophes* were being publically accused of betraying their country and of being in collusion with the enemy.[21] This led to the need to redefine the very concept of patriotism by giving it new meanings. One's home country was no longer defined as the land of one's fathers, an ethnic and historical reality: it was now, instead, a political community of men who were free, equal, and bent on self-government, and on breaking free from the centuries-old dominion exercised by the alliance between the altar and the throne.

Inevitably, this movement was on a collision course with the old *Ancien Régime* politics of nation-states. Everywhere in Europe, Enlightenment circles were called upon to define their engagement. They reasserted their determination to relaunch the concept of the political that prevailed in classical antiquity, which saw politics as striving towards the common good and a life well lived. Their goal was to reinvigorate this concept on the basis of new ideals and original perspectives, which could be summarized in the apt eighteenth-century formula of a "pursuit of happiness" in both the public and the private spheres.[22]

Given the challenges posed by absolutism in the second half of the eighteenth century, an appeal to the *libertas philosophandi* and to the philosopher's generic moral superiority was no longer enough. Having unmasked the imposture of religions and having reflected on the necessity to build a rational form of morality, it was now necessary to move on to concrete political action, to the reform of laws and institutions, and to the search for a government based on laws. In short, the search was on for a different kind of State, in terms both of its nature and its purposes: a State that respected the autonomy achieved by the modern civil society that the Enlightenment had sought to bring about.

This change of perspective could be summarized as follows. Montesquieu's objective had been above all to guarantee the freedom of the Estates and to hem in the sovereign's despotism through intermediate bodies and respect for the principle of legality. As positive models, he pointed to the French administrative monarchy before Louis XIV and the English mixed constitution. However, his overall logic was still that of the *Ancien Régime*. The international uproar caused by Pasquale Paoli's anticolonial and republican revolution, and Rousseau's social contract and reflections on the legitimacy of power opened a new era characterized by the revival of the "republican spirit," which this time was seen as a rejection of monarchic despotism and an attempt to secure the widest possible participation to the exercise of power and sovereignty. This was a necessary premise for a union between the virtue of the ancients and the richness of the moderns. It was important to maintain strong social and community ties through the exercise of public republican virtues and to achieve different objectives from those that guided the recent past, objectives such as the freedom of the individual and his right to the pursuit of happiness, and equality of rights for all.

The invention and use of the language of the rights of man in the second half of the eighteenth century was certainly a turning point. It constituted a powerful instrument for both the politicization of the Late Enlightenment and for the creation of a modern politics for the emancipation of man such as had never before been seen in the Western world. This language was a result of the translation of the old objective "natural right" into a subjective "political right" within the framework of a thorough-going postmechanistic and neonaturalistic shift that impacted the sciences of man. It allowed the discussion of the future of mankind in universal terms, and made it possible to think finally of politics, religion, morality, and economics from the standpoint of man, seen as the ultimate endpoint rather than simply as a means within a wider eschatological scheme. This language was a hugely effective instrument for bringing together utopia and reform, and it soon came to be used by the Enlightenment in order to intervene in a new and original way in the political debate on contractualism, sovereignty, and representation, and in deliberations on how best to conceive a constitution and a republicanism suited to the conditions of the moderns. All this, coupled with the steady intent of achieving an overall cultural system and civil society openly critical of the *Ancien Régime* and thus effectively working towards its demise.

Voltaire was among the first to realize the potential of this language for communication and propaganda in the struggle against intolerance and fanaticism that he undertook in his defense of Calas. However, the great European debate on the right to punish that developed after the publication in 1764 of Beccaria's *On Crimes and Punishments* was the beginning of a long process that eventually shifted the focus from the struggle for civil rights to that for political and social rights. In this way the crisis of the *Ancien Régime* and the attendant politicization of the Late Enlightenment became a powerful laboratory of modernity.

The American colonies' 1776 Declaration of Independence was a milestone in this process. The open acknowledgment of the natural rights of man on which this text was based became the core of all debate in European Enlightenment circles. American independence asserted, and defended with weapons, the principle that a government could only be considered legitimate if it was born in order to guarantee the inalienable rights of individuals—the rights to life, liberty, and the pursuit of happiness. This inevitably revolutionized the political culture of the Enlightenment, both from the point of view of discourse and theory and in terms of its vocabularies, representations, practices and symbolism. Far from being an issue confined to dusty and little-read works by political theoreticians, the question of rights was communicated to public opinion at an international level through novels and literature in general, and through theater and other arts, such as painting and music. No form of knowledge or artistic expression remained exempt from it. The new republicanism of rights spread to all sectors, unleashing passions and giving rise to new and original social utopias. The major European gazettes, for example, launched a heated political debate on the issue of representative government and on the need to follow the American example and achieve the constitutionalization of rights within the framework of a new science of legislation. This debate represented the most original theoretical victory of the Enlightenment, and the one that would prove richest in political consequences.

Finally, in a historical context that saw problems acquiring worldwide dimensions and the rise of modern empires, the politicization of Late Enlightenment was profoundly affected by issues such as the legitimacy of colonialism, the slave trade, the universality of rights, and the on-going development of European civilization vs. the lack of development among savage nations. In discussions of these issues, neonaturalism was of course a constant underlying theme. There were constant references to precipitous advances in the sciences of man, which were now set to explore every aspect of the human species—physiological, psychological, social, and political. The traditional horizons of politics were changing. It was no longer enough to accept the concept of equality as a moral postulate, without further discussion, as had the members of early eighteenth-century Enlightenment circles, including Rousseau. New and important works of reference had come into being, alongside those by Cook, Bouganville, Forster, and Raynal's famous *Histoire philosophique et politique des établissements et du commerce des européens dans les deux Indes*. These new works included studies in medicine, comparative anatomy and zoology, which compared and contrasted monogenetic and polygenetic theories of the origin of human populations. The struggle against slavery and colonialism, based on the thesis of the universal equality of rights for all human beings, had to confront results of research carried out within the Enlightenment environment itself that demonstrated, with uncompromising rationality, the irreducible peculiarities and differences among the peoples of the earth.

Above and beyond important innovations in the field of social communications and in its position in the historical context of the end of the century, Late Enlightenment politics seemed designed to provoke clashes and increasingly clear-cut rifts between moderates and radicals within the Republic of Letters. Was man really free within the great chain of being? Who was actually right: those Enlightenment figures who adhered to Helvetius' theories on human perfectibility and thus advocated reforms to bring about equality of rights, or those who still believed in the fixity of species, and thus preferred a more limited program of reform, just enough to modernize the *Ancien Régime*? Was it right to follow a politics based on "having to be" and on reasonable utopia? Or should one rather revisit Machiavelli's political realism, and examine man scientifically as he actually was, in the light of obvious human inequalities that could at best be minimized, but without entertaining too many hopes of social justice and palingenesis? Hopefully these reflections will suffice to make us realize why it is now more than ever necessary to study the European Late Enlightenment in its autonomy as historical era that was grappling with the crisis of the *Ancien Régime*. In this way, it may finally emerge from the shadow cast by the French Revolution, which deserves itself to be studied *per se* rather than as a chapter in certain philosophies of history that were too strongly affected by nineteenth- and twentieth-century ideologies.

AFTERWORD

||||||||||||||||||||||

The Enlightenment: A Revolution of the Mind
or the Ancien Régime's Cultural Revolution?

IT IS A PLEASURE AND an honor to accept the invitation by this volume's publishers to write an afterword placing these lectures, that were originally given at the Collège de France and that embody and synthesize thirty years of research on the Enlightenment, within the current debate in English-speaking countries. This request is entirely justified. In recent years, colleagues in Britain and America have made truly important contributions, effectively relaunching the debate on an international level and attracting the attention not only of subject specialists but also of a larger audience, made up of all those who are interested in the definition and origins of modernity, and in the continuing relevance of the call for freedom and emancipation that is associated with it.

As I will try to explain below, the point of view that I put forward, the issues that I address, and the methodological considerations and conclusions that I formulate here will hopefully provide a useful tool for furthering those important debates that will form future generations of Enlightenment scholars. It is not an easy task. Compared to the lively arguments generated, for instance, by the publication of Jonathan Israel's monumental works on the "radical Enlightenment," these contributions of mine may appear at first glance to be unrelated to the most sensitive problems and issues of the present day—they may seem, in a word, *unzeitgemässig*, "out of season," to adopt the famous Nietzschean expression. In fact, that is far from being the case.

Conceived as an attempt to take stock of our knowledge of the Enlightenment and to point towards new research perspectives, these essays can undoubtedly be read as the expression of a very specific point of view. In fact that point of view has a long history behind it, deriving not only from my own original research on this topic,[1] but also from a specific Italian tradition that arose in the course of the twentieth century through the work of eminent scholars such as Arnaldo Momigliano, Eugenio Garin, Paolo Rossi, Franco Venturi, and others. This tradition was characterized by a steady awareness of the fundamental distinction between history and historiography, between *Res gestae* (the events themselves) and *Historia rerum gestarum* (the narrative relating those events); in other words between on the one hand a view of history as essentially a question to be addressed in philological and epistemological terms, and on the other a methodology-driven view based on various intriguing but misleading forms of the philosophy of history.[2] I must also point out that the present essays have their origins in an important collaborative project that in the late 1990s involved more than forty distinguished scholars from several countries, who analyzed the historical world of the Enlightenment on the basis of the latest research trends. A volume in the form of a "dictionary" was subsequently published in several languages presenting the results of this research,[3] which had arisen to a great extent from the realization that we had finally come to the end of the fierce and inconclusive debate between a social history in the *Annales* tradition and a history of Enlightenment ideas as represented at the highest level by the work of Paul Hazard, Peter Gay and Franco Venturi.

In the *Trevelyan Lectures* that he gave in Cambridge in 1969, Venturi severely criticized the quantitative methods and history of mentalities popular at the time, which in his view severely underplayed the importance of ideas and failed to consider either their role in bringing about historical developments and advances, or their importance within the fundamental sphere of individual creativity. In consequence the centrality of the individual in history yielded ground to the kind of Marxist structural determinism that informed the fashionable historiography of the day. However, the Italian scholar denounced, just as soundly, the survival of the old and hackneyed history of Enlightenment ideas, an approach still based on Ernst Cassirer's seminal 1932 work, *Die Philosophie der Aufklärung*, and more generally on an exclusively philosophical way of reading intellectual history that had prevailed from Kant onwards. This way of thinking was shackled by its need for strong conceptualization, and it had, moreover, its logical foundation in the history of Western rationality, which meant that any attempt at achieving a general historical overview of the Enlightenment was necessarily subject to a search for unified criteria, and to the need for a consistent and systematic approach. All of which reduced the Enlightenment to just one more chapter—however important—in the history of Western philosophy.

In fact—Venturi pointed out—the reality of history hardly ever fits into the rigid reconstructions created by philosophers. It is wrong to think of ideas as separate from human beings, and even worse to isolate an idea and study its manifestations from its origins to our times, as if it were an immutable entity with its own fixed structure and autonomy. It is far more useful to study an idea's function, how its form and meaning changed in different contexts, how it could generate events and political action on the part of figures like the militant intellectual, a latter-day *philosophe* who eschews any kind of metaphysical construction and concentrates on real life instead.

Clearly we must not follow ideas back to their origins, but rather examine their function in the history of the eighteenth century. Philosophers are tempted to push upstream until they arrive at the source. Historians must tell us how the river made its way, among what obstacles and difficulties it made its course.[4]

Later on Venturi asks:

> Wouldn't it be better to return to the interpretation of the encyclopaedists as *philosophers* and reformers, as people who lived for their ideas, and who found a way of changing the reality which surrounded them?[5]

The history of the Enlightenment is the history of its goals and its struggles. This is at the basis of Venturi's entirely personal and original reply to Kant's famous question, *Was ist Aufklärung?* It was a reply that yoked together utopia and reform, thought and action, ideas and a political program that sought to change the *Ancien Régime's* society, institutions, and way of thinking. And it led to the European notion of the eighteenth century as the "century of reforms," this being the only Ariadne's thread that guided the seeker to a unified historical idea of the Enlightenment's modern political character, because reform was seen as the truly innovative and distinguishing characteristic of the Enlightenment experience.[6]

Venturi was among the first to realize that all purely intellectual syntheses based on the idea of a logically consistent philosophical system, and all grand narratives that artificially attempted to encompass the whole history of the Enlightenment were a thing of the past. Why should historians be so bent on finding that mythical unity, that single magical thread that could explain every aspect of the actual development of ideas in relation to the context? Had not the *philosophes* themselves been opposed to the old philosophy's strictly ordered metaphysical character? In the same way, the new history of ideas must take into account the inevitable fragmentariness of any discourse that ventures to look at actual reality. The crucial task of tracking the rise of a new social and political movement led by militant intellectuals, who were the real political and social protagonists of the Enlightenment, must go hand in hand with a realization of the fragmentary and contradictory character of their ideas and programs of action. The history of the Enlightenment should then be studied as a series of key issues, looking, for instance, at the impact and transformations of the republican tradition in the eighteenth century, or at the revolutionary implications of the debate started by Cesare Beccaria on the right to punish in a fair and reasonable manner, all along taking into account the chronological and geographical differences within the scope of the European Enlightenment.[7]

Also in the 1980s and 1990s, at the same time as Franco Venturi was attempting to revise the way we looked at the history of ideas, an analogous change was taking place in the field of *Annales*-type social history. Eminent scholars such as Roger Chartier severely critiqued practices such as the history of mentalities, quantitative methods, and serial analysis, while at the same time recognizing the importance of ideas as concrete means of change, of the cultural and creative consumption of texts, of a new intellectual history that was aware of the mechanisms pertaining to the sociology of knowledge, as well as the importance of social communication and of the rise of public opinion. Finally, in the past twenty years, international historiography has been transformed and enriched by important research that has taken place in several areas. Among them: the history of the book, freemasonry, the academies, utopian literature, and above all the history of science, with its pioneering interest in new representations of nature in the eighteenth century, and its redefinition of institutions and the figure of the scientist. The research that resulted in our *Dictionary* (see n. 3, p. 200) arose precisely from an awareness of the limits and inadequacy of either tradition and in open opposition to the practice of placing the emphasis on research methods rather than issues. The same is true of the essays in the present volume, which seek to address the centuries-old division between the methods and objectives of philosophers and those of historians.

Part I in this volume examines the philosophers' point of view and tries to uncover and document the existence of an "original sin" in the modern conception of the Enlightenment as it was created—by philosophers—in Germany at the end of the eighteenth century. The question *Was ist Aufklärung?* had been posed with renewed critical spirit by Kant who, as a militant intellectual with a keen eye for the contemporary world, had wanted to investigate the forms and nature of a cultural phenomenon that was radically transforming the present all around him. On the other hand, Hegel had redrafted the logical and dialectical basis of that phenomenon by blending together history and philosophy, and projecting it back into the past life of the phenomenology of spirit. He then left it to his many followers to unravel and rebuild the concept of the Enlightenment as a major and fundamental philosophical problem in modernity's search for the ultimate foundation of the very nature of man, of the subject looking at itself in the mirror.

For historians, on the other hand, the Enlightenment was a completely different entity, something dependent on context, on individual events, and above all on the rigorous application of a critical and philological methodology. That notwithstanding, even historical research—and especially those studies devoted mainly to intellectual history—has continued to be more or less consciously influenced by the powerful interpretative paradigm of the Centaur—or, according to the tongue-in-cheek definition we used in the original Italian, of the *ircocervo*, the mythical goat-stag—created by Hegel's genius through a blending together of philosophy and history, dialectic and reality, the spirit's rational unity and the irrational discontinuity of events, which was then successfully applied to the modern conceptualization of the Enlightenment. Maybe it took the dramatic rift caused by the events of 1989, with the fall of the Berlin Wall and the dream of philosophically inspired revolutionary palingenesis, to wean us from facile recourse to the shortcuts provided by the many philosophies of history that had been devised in the past. This allowed us to embrace again the historians' discontinuist point of view and confront anew the problem of understanding and explaining what the world of the Enlightenment *really was*, in its specific autonomy and with all its various original characteristics.

In the latter sense, Part II in this volume postulates a new history of the Enlightenment as an epochal rift and cultural revolution of the *Ancien Régime*. This section highlights the way in which discontinuity and profound change affected all reference values, all ideas pertaining to a centuries-old European society, its intellectual horizons and style of thought, but also the until then dominant representations of a natural, social, and political order founded on the fixity not only of species but also of social and political hierarchies, cultural practices, institutions, and the languages in use. This is a cultural history of the Enlightenment as a work in progress: open to new issues and contextual differences, ready to accommodate changes in our knowledge and ideas and in their process of appropriation, as well as economic and social transformations. But first and foremost it is a history that is ready to embrace a new, extraordinary and original form of humanism, a bold project for the emancipation of man by man, scientifically investigating himself. It is a cultural history that leads to the emergence of a new and very different critical spirit, capable of refreshing the legacy of past figures while serving at the same time as the real Ariadne's thread that leads through the Enlightenment identity of the modern. It is a history that, once it has finally broken free of the teleological obsession with explaining at all costs how the French Revolution came to pass, may finally be capable of entirely redefining the specific and autonomous identity of the Enlightenment, tracing its geography and chronology in cosmopolitan and universalistic terms. Its aim is to resolve the main issues by resorting in each case to the most appropriate tools, whether from the history of ideas or social history, from the study of cultural consumption or of political and artistic communication, so as to throw light, for instance, on the reasons for the unprecedented success of the powerful new corporation of intellectuals and ideas at the end of the eighteenth century. It is a history that is capable of accounting for phenomena like the resounding rise of new representations of nature in science and art, and for a different style of social and political ties, based on the newly emergent relationship between the natural rights of individuals and their duties to the community. In sum, it is a history that goes well beyond the tiresome methodological controversies of the past few decades.

Jonathan Israel's three substantial volumes are clearly informed by an entirely different strategy and modality. They represent a conscious attack on a kind of social and cultural history of the Enlightenment that has long since ceased to exist in the form in which he still appears to conceive of it: it is no accident that he refers to old debates that took place in the 1970s and 1980s, while ignoring all subsequent developments and revisionisms, as described in our *Dictionary*. Indeed Israel's brand of intellectual history is an attempt to reinstate the old primacy of "philosophical ideas," and of a method based on the study of the great intellectual debates initiated by the great figures of philosophical thought. Rather than describing the transformations, appropriations, and different historical functions of ideas, it aims to document only their presence and circulation in the course of the seventeenth and eighteenth centuries as a cohesive doctrinal *corpus*, a "radical 'package' of ideas,"[8] as molded once and for all into a consistent philosophical system by Spinoza.[9] Through this successful yoking together of a historical category (such as the Radical Enlightenment) with a typical category within the history of philosophy (such as Spinozism— now once again the focus of much post-Marxist and revolutionary left-wing philosophy in Europe),[10] Israel is for the first time in many years recreating a suggestive and powerful unified picture of the Enlightenment. His 2010 synthesis, *A Revolution of The Mind*, clearly outlines this attempt at reviving something methodologically akin to the old *Centaur* (with Spinoza now seen as the true father of modernity, democracy, and the rights of man, and with his atheist materialism taking the place of Cassirer's Newton-Kant paradigm or Koselleck's Hegelian dialectic). Moreover, by acknowledging (in his preface) Isaiah Berlin as an important source of inspiration for his enterprise, Israel expresses his hope "that what follows will stand as a small tribute to his memory and achievements, especially by again attempting to draw philosophy and history into a closer, more meaningful partnership" (xiv).

Indeed, in recent years the wished-for return to a holy alliance of philosophers and historians aimed at reviving the fortunes of intellectual history has already produced its first ambiguous fruits, bringing back to life, especially in Israel's work, the danger of anachronism and of a problematic use of sources, which in turn risks transforming as important an element in the history of Western philosophy as Spinozism into yet another dubious philosophy of history, speculating on the genesis and the materialistic and secular character of a modernity based on the Enlightenment. This becomes apparent if we move from the open declaration and acknowledgement of the historical and philosophical method that Israel is following to a consideration of the actual contents and results of this type of research. We will then see how, via this tight narrative, sustained with undoubted erudition through volumes bristling with names and quotations from texts gathered from every corner of the world, Israel has arrived at the dubious and controversial interpretation of this complex historical phenomenon mainly as a Radical Enlightenment, as the concrete realization of a philosophical system, of a specific and consistent *Spinozistic ideology* founded on materialistic monism and on atheism, and also on the circulation and diffusion of a system of subversive ideas. Those ideas include: the recourse to reason as the sole and indisputable criterion of truth, the rejection of miracles and of the supernatural, a secularized and universal ethics, racial and sexual equality, tolerance and freedom of thought, sexual freedom, freedom of expression, democratic republicanism in its version of representative government—in short, all the greatest achievements of so-called Western modernity.

With the force of a real *tsunami* of printed matter—thousands of pages that cannot but engender a feeling of true admiration and appreciation for the sheer intellectual courage they betoken—Israel has redirected the focus of research towards Spinozistic secularization and philosophical materialism as the authentic source and original character of our modernity. Through his stubborn persistence, figures such as Voltaire, Montesquieu, Rousseau, Locke, Newton, and Hume been cast out of the traditional Enlightenment *pantheon* of our textbooks, or at least relegated to the wings. Their crime: under-appreciation of the materialistic ideas and political radicalism of Spinoza. In their place, we find the latter's real or supposed followers, among them Helvetius, Diderot, and the Baron d'Holbach. From a chronological point of view, he has also relocated the origin of the ideological nucleus of the Enlightenment from Paris and the *Encyclopédie* to the crucial decades between 1660 and 1740, identifying the Dutch Republic as its true land of origin. Then, in his final volume, *Democratic Enlightenment. Philosophy, Revolution, and Human Rights, 1750–1790*, with incredible boldness Israel has thrown down his Spinozistic gauntlet in the very epicenter of the traditional historiographic paradigm of the Enlightenment, claiming for the Radical Enlightenment the role of true and long-unrecognized intellectual father of the French Revolution.

No wonder the subject's specialists were incensed, as Israel's stance triggered a prickly debate among the international scholarly community. All previous books on the Enlightenment and the French Revolution seemed destined for the pulp mill as this scholar put forward his shattering new thesis, one with a directness and simplicity that fitted it well to the public arena. Israel argued his thesis of the centrality of the Radical Enlightenment in an unflinching and inflexible style, selectively ignoring some of the documentation that contradicted it to the point that it seems biased in the eyes of many scholars. In fact, the virulence of the debate in itself shows that these are far from foregone conclusions. If anything, the main problem, which is being neglected, is that of the modalities of the debate itself. How can one critique and evaluate such a gigantic body of work, which requires, among other things, uncommonly vast linguistic abilities? But above all how can one apply objective true and false judgment criteria to a body of research that has been carefully built specifically on the amphibious character and ambiguous duality of the concept of Enlightenment itself? The Enlightenment's double nature as both a historical and philosophical entity, which Israel cleverly reproduces at the methodological level, has given rise to controversy and misunderstandings, and will continue to do so until we become fully conscious of its importance as a theoretical premise. It is not by chance that Israel's three volumes have been praised by philosophers, with their love for synthetic and incisive conceptualizations, while at the same time being fiercely criticized by historians, who appreciate how complex and contradictory reality can be, and the importance of providing stringent documentary evidence.

Israel sought to uphold at all costs the philosophically consistent and unified narrative of a neo-Spinozistic interpretation that identified the Radical Enlightenment as the source of modernity. However, that effort has undoubtedly caused serious problems in philological terms and from the point of view of his use of sources. For instance, no historian will take kindly to having his archival research used simply as a container from which to extract second-hand quotations with which to prove the diffusion of Spinoza's ideas, and this with total disregard for the accompanying interpretative hypotheses and for the essential role of context in determining their real meaning. Israel's selective use of sources, and the way in which at times he misunderstood or overinterpreted the nature and meaning of those sources, also inevitably attracted criticism. Should those three volumes, then, be discussed, and if necessary refuted, at the level of their methodology—that is to say, with respect to Israel's handling of specific issues and individual contexts and his erroneous interpretations of individual figures and misuse of their ideas? Or should they be trusted as basically truthful in terms of the general historical and philosophical picture they delineate, admitting that that picture may be possible?

Reactions to the first volume were significant in this respect. *Radical Enlight-enment: Philosophy and the Making of Modernity, 1650–1750* is undoubtedly the most important of the three volumes. In it, Israel highlights the cosmopolitan character of the Radical Enlightenment and its importance for the rise of modernity, while at the same time attempting to provide a philosophically consistent representation of the influence exercised over it by Spinoza, with results that have seemed questionable particularly to historians of ideas.[11] How can one possibly simplify to such an extent the rich philosophical pluralism of something as fluid as the clandestine and materialistic literature at the cusp of the seventeenth- and the eighteenth centuries? How can it be encompassed within Spinozism, especially when it is far from clear that the latter even existed as a consistent philosophical and above all philosophical system throughout the centuries? How can one force into this mold the whole tradition of libertinism, including the Italian debate on the mortality of the soul from Pomponazzi to Cremonini and Vanini, Giordano Bruno's anti-Christian heresy, and the concept of the imposture of religions as theorized by Machiavelli and then by Charron, Naudé, and Hobbes? And what about Deism, the new republicanism of freethinkers from Collins to Toland, Toland's pantheism and the way in which it redescribed the properties of matter in a modern Newtonian context, thus influencing European debates on this subject all the way down to Diderot and d'Holbach. Are these really marginal elements in the rise of the Radical Enlightenment compared to Spinozism? Above all, how can Spinoza's rationalistic fundamentalism be reconciled with the success of the powerful philosophical currents of Pyrrhonism and philosophical skepticism in undermining established Churches and religions and fostering unbelief? Moreover, we should keep in mind also that the inflexible truth claims of the geometrical-deductive method applied by Spinoza in his *Ethica more geometrico demonstrata* were criticized by Pierre Bayle, the founder of the Enlightenment's skeptical current, who was much loved by Voltaire and who envisioned a society of virtuous atheists. Finally, having studied these topics for many years, I find it extremely difficult to stretch Israel's Radical Enlightenment to include such figures as, for instance, Giovan Battista Vico and Paolo Mattia Doria, to mention only the Italian context.

Above and beyond any concerns caused by a process of oversimplification aimed at bringing a vast number of thinkers and ideas back within the fold of a materialistic and secularized Spinozism, however, Israel's first volume has the great merit of focusing our gaze on the Radical Enlightenment, which until now, although it has attracted some attention (as in Margaret Candee Jacob's pioneering study), has undoubtedly been seen as rather marginal and of secondary importance. When all is considered, the real question raised by Israel is this: Assuming that there was indeed a Radical Enlightenment characterized by Spinoza's materialistic monism along the lines that Israel describes, what role did it actually play in the history of the Western world? Did it really provide the fundamental theoretical bases for the rights of man, democracy, emancipation, and modernity itself? Above all, what was the relationship between that philosophical and ideological system and the revolutionary wave of the late eighteenth century, and in particular the French Revolution? Like others before him, Israel was unable to resist the powerful draw of the teleological Enlightenment-Revolution paradigm, and so offered yet another solution to the myth of the intellectual origins of the French Revolution, this time under the banner of Spinozism and the Radical Enlightenment: "The Radical Enlightenment [. . .] is the only important direct cause of the French Revolution" (*Democratic Enlightenment*, 16). Such a conclusion, however, had major consequences, for it forced Israel into an even more rigid and simplified formulation of his theses. This resulted in an extreme philosophical reductionism that forced people and ideas into a sort of cage, thus further reducing the legitimacy and reliability of the whole construct.

The purpose of the first volume had been to define the Spinozian bases of the Radical Enlightenment's ideological system, situating it at the center of a process of intellectual renewal and identifying within it the element that triggered both the traditionalists' reaction and, especially, the birth of the so-called Moderate Enlightenment, a movement that arose throughout Europe to defend the role of divine Providence in history, a form of Newtonian and Lockian rationalism for the preservation of Christianity and monarchy. The second volume, *Enlightenment Contested: Philosophy, Modernity and the Emancipation of Man, 1670–1752*, sought to explain in what ways and for what reasons the ideology created by the followers of Spinoza had become the main cause of the revolutionary movements that took place throughout the Western world.

Once again, Israel forcefully insisted that the Enlightenment was essentially an intellectual rather than a social phenomenon. By placing stress on the intellectual, he intended to open the way to a study of the Enlightenment's contents within a new history of philosophy, emphasizing the capacity of ideas to create a revolutionary consciousness and, by their very existence, to give rise to a "revolution of the mind" capable of triggering political action through major debates and controversies. To this end, Israel did not find his main sources in the texts themselves and their circulation, in socialization processes and contexts, or in the ways in which the main players in history appropriated and used certain ideas. Instead, he relied solely on the recriminations of the Enlightenment's enemies, those clergymen and reactionary thinkers who believed that the devil was constantly busy setting up philosophical conspiracies inspired by the ideas of Hobbes, Bayle, and, above all, Spinoza.[12] In fact, Israel's faith in the capacity of philosophy to change reality, even through the presumed truthfulness of these accusations, borders on fideism. He begins to sound uncomfortably like Hegel and his view of the Enlightenment and the French Revolution as the artwork purely of thought, or of the *esprit philosophique*; i.e., as stages and phases in the dialectic of the phenomenology of spirit.

The most innovative aspect of Israel's thesis of the role of the Radical Enlightenment in unleashing revolutionary processes throughout Western civilization is undoubtedly his formulation, from the second volume onwards, of the theory of the *two* Enlightenments, each of them autonomous, strongly determined, and destined to clash incessantly one against the other, thus giving rise to the "revolution of the mind" of the final quarter of the eighteenth century. On one side there was the Radical Enlightenment, represented first and foremost by Helvetius, Diderot, and d'Holbach—thinkers who subscribed to Spinoza's theory of one substance, atheistic and anticlerical in outlook, politically moving towards modernity, in that they were supporters of republicanism, human rights, equality, and representative democracy. On the other side stood the Moderate Enlightenment of figures such as Locke, Hume, Montesquieu, Voltaire, Turgot, and Rousseau, who supported the idea of a natural religion and deist Providentialism, believed in substance dualism, and were associated with political stances that were either conservative, such as monarchical absolutism, or dangerous—like Rousseau's direct democracy, which is said to have inspired Robespierre and thus to have been at the root of the Reign of Terror.

Despite the wealth of knowledge displayed by Israel in the hundreds of pages he devotes to these great philosophical debates, his positions have been severely criticized from both a philological and interpretative point of view. This is hardly surprising, given the peremptoriness with which Israel defends his theses, determined as he is to uphold his conviction that there are clear-cut differences between his two Enlightenments on such fundamental issues as religious tolerance, equality, freedom of conscience, the relationship between religion and science, republicanism and the idea of democracy, the right of resistance, popular sovereignty, slavery, and the new colonialism of modern empires.

As a matter of fact, most of the time Israel simply propounds his main thesis—that of a strong organic connection within the Radical Enlightenment between atheist materialism, Spinoza's rationalistic monism, and political radicalism—rather than actually demonstrating it (even assuming that it might indeed be demonstrable).[13] As is usually the case, things are far more complex. Many of the major players in these controversies combine political radicalism with a desire for religious reform, with a deistic stance, and with support for the new idea, soon to gain more and more favor, of a civil religion without churches or priests but devoted to the defense of the rights of man and emancipation. We see this, for example, clearly and for the first time, in the famous eighth chapter of *The Social Contract*. And indeed, one is particularly taken aback by the treatment meted out to poor Rousseau, a champion of modern forms of civil religion, undoubtedly a believer, but also, from a political point of view, strongly opposed to the *Ancien Régime* in his writings, impassioned, in fact, in his appeals for freedom and equality against any form of tyranny. For here he is now, summarily grouped together with the fathers of the reactionary Counter-Enlightenment (no less!) One could multiply the examples of famous figures similarly treated and of perplexing representations of philosophical debates in historical contexts, such as the Italian example Israel conjures of a clash in the public arena between the exponents of a hypothetical politically moderate Catholic Enlightenment under the leadership of the Neapolitan reformer Antonio Genovesi on the one hand and, on the other, the adherents of a Spinozistic monism characterized by republican and democratic tendencies that dates back to Vico, Doria, Giannone, and Radicati di Passerano. And what about Beccaria and Filangieri? Which side are they supposed to be on?

Neither Venturi nor Ricuperati, nor any other eminent Italian historiographer had become aware, in the course of their extensive archival research, of this mighty intellectual struggle between materialists and believers, or indeed of the existence of a specific "Catholic Enlightenment"—though the latter seems to matter a lot, not just to Israel's thesis, but also to Joseph Ratzinger and the exponents of the new international Catholic historiography that came into being in the aftermath of the Second Vatican Council and whose intent was to create the image of a Christianized modernity by blithely manipulating historical memory.[14]

Despite all this, the effort to clearly demarcate the differences and contradictions between the two Enlightenments from the philosophical, moral, economic, and political point of view, even at the cost of gross oversimplifications, does not in itself explain how the Radical Enlightenment succeeded in sparking revolutionary processes on a scale that engulfed all of Europe and the whole of the American continent. Israel is, in fact, entirely conscious of the fact that historical events of this magnitude cannot be explained solely as the products of a "revolution of the mind" brought about by philosophical debates. He therefore elaborates his thesis (again, rather more by proclamation than demonstration) that the Radical Enlightenment gained the upper hand at the end of the century precisely because of the failure of the reforms advocated by supporters of the moderate Enlightenment and enlightened absolutism. This then led to the advent of the political radicalism of figures like Helvetius and d'Holbach, following in the footsteps of Spinoza; but also of Socinianism and Unitarian-ism, as represented by Thomas Paine and Joseph Priestley, and the leader of the Bavarian Illuminati, Adam Weishaupt. All of these Israel summarily enrolls under the banner of the Radical Enlightenment.

To be sure, the reader feels some dizziness at being transported nonstop from Paris to Berlin, to China, India, and the American colonies, as well as across Germany, France, and Holland in order to delve into the complex phil-osophical debate between Voltaire, Lessing, and Kant, but there is one motif that persists throughout: Israel's assertion of the extraordinary role played by Spinoza. In a kind of political and philosophical manifesto that summarizes the entire work, he writes:

> In the longer perspective, Spinoza's role as a key progenitor of the Radical En-lightenment was unparalleled. He was the only seventeenth-century philosopher to remain a prominent and constant presence in the philosophical debates of the later eighteenth and nineteenth centuries. After 1750 Bayle receded gradually into the background. Spinoza, by contrast, remained at the forefront and was regarded throughout the later Enlightenment era by many intellectuals—and later by nineteenth-century freethinkers and creative minds, ranging from Heine to George Eliot—as the philosopher who, more than any other, forged the basic metaphysical ground-plan, exclusively secular moral values, and culture of in-dividual liberty, democratic politics, and freedom of thought and the press that embody today the defining core values of modern secular egalitarianism: that is to say, of Radical Enlightenment. (*A Revolution of the Mind*, Princeton: Princeton University Press, 2010, 240–241).

It is indeed true that Israel's passion for classification, especially as de-ployed in his third volume, *Democratic Enlightenment: Philosophy, Revolution, and Human Rights, 1750–1790* (Oxford: Oxford University Press, 2011), aims at separating the followers of Spinoza from his detractors, the good from the bad, the atheist materialists from the believers, the radical from the moderate, and even the intellectual forebears of the modern left from those of the right (19). However, this does not, in the end, remove our distinct impression that the promising initial project of writing a new *history of philosophy* as regards the Enlightenment has turned, page after page, into yet another *philosophy of the history* of modernity, not dissimilar from the old Hegelian Centaur.

As we have already mentioned, the interpretation of the Enlightenment as a historical phenomenon that we are offering here is radically different from Israel's, in terms both of its research methodology and its conclusions. Our po-sition also differs in what we consider to be the original characteristics of the Enlightenment. Above and beyond aspects like the exponential growth of the

publishing industry, or the rise of important social subjects such as the powerful new conglomerates of literati or the Masonic societies, the specific trait that
in our view gives the Enlightenment its own original intellectual profile is not
to be found in the philosophy of Spinoza, but rather in the creation of a humanism of the "Moderns."[15]

Indeed, the enigma of the Enlightenment lies to a great extent in the way in
which it consistently placed man and his constant striving towards happiness
and emancipation at the center of everything, at the very heart of a new culture alternative to that of medieval Christianity and the *Ancien Régime*. This
was lucidly explained by Voltaire in his witty pamphlets, as well as in Diderot's
Encyclopédie, whose philosophical and epistemological program, with its em-
piricist bias, placed equal emphasis on reason, imagination, and memory. In
so far as it explored from a critical and unbiased perspective the human condition and the capabilities and limitations of the subject, both in its individual and its collective identity, the Enlightenment's ambitious and necessarily
eclectic and polysemic project clearly had received a formidable boost from
the so-called "second scientific revolution." This modern-humanist Enlightenment was shaped and informed by a new science devoted to the improvement
of the human condition and by the updating of the first scientific revolution
in the light of new perspectives and new methodologies inspired by critical
empiricism. This new science in the service of man played a far more influential role than did a philosophy viewed mainly as an ancient discipline and
a coherent way of thinking, along the lines of the seventeenth-century spirit
of systematization—a philosophy whose purposes and epistemological profile
had in any case been scaled down and largely redefined by the *philosophes* in
the course of the eighteenth century itself.[16] The increasing progress achieved
by research in the fields of medicine, zoology, physiology, chemistry, electricity,
and magnetism—thanks to the speed with which results reached the general
public via the burgeoning number of journals and other periodicals written for
the public at large—joined with literature, music, and the visual arts to expose
man's lowly position within the chain of being.[17] Notwithstanding the Enlightenment's renewed will to power, enhanced by the rise of public opinion, man
appeared as a mere reed in the wind—to borrow Voltaire's famous image—a
prisoner of his own finitude and historicity, free to strive after happiness but
at the same time a hostage to the fatality of evil and answerable to the Other.

In the course of the eighteenth century, the Enlightenment's myth of a new
"Science of Man" gave way to the rise or redefinition of individual human sciences such as history, anthropology, and political economy. This created several
new disciplines that are still today an integral and active part of our modernity. And all of this led to widespread controversy and dissention. As has been

extensively documented, in the second half of the eighteenth century fierce scientific debates took place in major European cities that would enflame people's minds and souls far more than the learned philosophical and metaphysical disputes carried out within restricted circles. These controversies were mostly the result of a radical change in the representation of nature and the scientific image that would eventually reshape the whole of human knowledge: a change that created deep rifts in the corporative structure of the scientific community and therefore within the social and political order of the *Ancien Régime* in general. This entailed a move from the fixism beloved of Newton and Linnaeus to Diderot's transformism of species, and to the temporalization and dynamization of matter according to a pattern that was a far cry from Spinoza's philosophical theories. The increasingly important results achieved by the study of animal magnetism and electricity undermined the primacy of the mechanistic universe and the geometric-deductive method; and Galileo and Newton's *numero pondere et mensura* gave way to the new empirical and qualitative views of matter beloved of the followers of Rousseau. With the rise of *neonaturalism*—whose renaissance origins are revealed in its many points of contact with the concept of a *natura naturans*—the precarious process that since the seventeenth century had slowly established the scientist as a professional and institutional figure had suffered a decline. The intellectual world was presented now for the first time with the modern epistemological issue of demarcation: What is science? Who decides what scientific truth is, and on what basis?[18]

It was the decades just before the French Revolution in particular—a time of fierce polemics and clashes between various factions within the international Enlightenment community—that saw the rise of the modern discourse on the "rights of man" as we now understand it, thanks to inquiry into what constitutes an individual's humanity and to the emancipation of man through scientific knowledge. In this way the medieval concept of man's natural rights was transformed into that of "droits politiques," as expounded by Condorcet in his *Esquisse d'un tableau historique des progrès de l'esprit humain*.

It is important to keep this in mind in order to evaluate further not only the overall solidity of Israel's work, but especially any future research perspectives that it might inspire—or, as the case may be, that it might close off through the rigidity and peremptoriness of his theses. This is because Israel links the Radical Enlightenment directly to modern rights politics, without feeling the need to spend too much time demonstrating what he deems to be entirely obvious. Justly considered "as corner-stones of 'modernity'" (*Democratic Enlightenment*, 33), those rights are defined as "inextricably linked to radically monist philosophical positions during the Enlightenment era" (21).[19] In fact this is far from being the case. The early studies that have appeared so far already show how complicated it is to trace the genealogy of that discourse, which goes back to the various permutations of the concept of natural right that have arisen across the centuries.

The idea of natural rights is not philosophical in origin. It is an extraordinarily important moral idea,[20] an ethical postulate that derives first and foremost from the concept of the dignity of the human being, according to a concept that is frequently encountered in Cicero, Pico della Mirandola, and Voltaire, and that in the course of the eighteenth century became a powerful new political and juridical discourse of the moderns through its use in the fight for reform, emancipation, and the recognition of the autonomy of the individual. This happened step by step, and it involved Locke, Barbeyrac, Burlamaqui, Rousseau, Genovesi, Beccaria, Filangieri, and many others.[21] If we are really intent on discovering its intellectual roots, we should not look to Spinoza's monism or Spinoza's philosophy, but rather to the advent of the new science of man, and to the Enlightenment's ambitious project, clearly outlined in the *Encyclopédie*, of a new humanism capable of placing the individual above everything. Indeed, how could one invent "the rights of man" without first creating a new idea of man? Without first redefining the relationship between the subject and its community, between its freedom and responsibilities; without finding in history, if anywhere, rather than within philosophy, the ultimate legitimation, basis, and civilization value of those rights that shook the very foundations of the *Ancien Régime*?

It should be noted, however, that the most powerful and irreconcilable way in which Israel's synthesis diverges from the view I am presenting in this volume is in his putting forward once again the old teleological paradigm of the intellectual origins of the French Revolution. This is a view that originated in English-speaking cultural areas, and its being advanced here once more under the banner of the Radical Enlightenment seems yet again to ignore the efforts of those branches of European historiography that have been battling for years against the many negative consequences of precisely that paradigm. It was created and has been shared since the early nineteenth century by both revolutionaries and reactionaries as an ideological battleground on which to enact their clashes. It soon became an unassailable political myth and now risks putting an end to current efforts to leave behind certain antiquated and benighted aspects of individual European national historiographies, forever obsessed with the centrality of Revolutionary and Napoleonic France in their reconstruction of their own cosmopolitan and Enlightenment past. It is also in danger of becoming an actual epistemological stumbling block in the study of the specific characteristics of the Enlightenment. An exemplary case in point is that of Filangieri and the European legacy of his *Science of Legislation*, which was left incomplete at the author's death before 1789. In fact, it was only thanks to the search for the specific characteristics of the Late Enlightenment, and the refusal to fall into the trap of a teleological and revolutionary narrative, that it was possible to trace the main features of a specific European Enlightenment politics, based on a constitutional plan and a new legal system founded on the rights of man, something quite far from the revolutionary culture's intentions and outcomes.[22]

Thus, whereas recent discoveries in the history of science have enabled us to break free of a myopic view that denied any measure of autonomy or creativity to the *Late Enlightenment* (known variously as the *Tardo Illuminismo*, *Lumière tardive*, or *Spätaufklärung*), the resurrection now of the controversy over the true or supposed *pères de la Révolution* in fact represents an abrupt (however legitimate) return to the past. This late eighteenth-century epoch has been generally considered, even by figures such as Venturi and Darnton, as the period that saw the terminal decline of the Enlightenment, a time characterized by a pathological irrationalism that ushered in the imminent revolutionary excesses through the challenges posed by Mesmerism and the new science of physiognomy to mechanicism and Newtonian physics. It is my belief, however, that those years deserve instead to be studied with the utmost attention by future generations of scholars. It is not by chance that that suddenly politicized world, which saw the definitive rise of the discourse on the rights of man, was so fiercely attacked in the following decades by the so-called *Counter-Enlightenment*, a movement that rightly detected in that period many of the principal traits of our disturbing political modernity founded on man's arrogant claim to autonomy and freedom.

The problem is that, beyond the undoubtedly positive fact of having brought the Enlightenment to the forefront of international debate, Israel's uncompromising and biased pronouncements risk returning us to the old ways again, while precluding the future exploration of new paths. He makes too many concessions to philosophy. Identifying the Enlightenment's supposed land of origin as the Dutch Republic, and not the more commonly cited England or France, is a sure way to set off a competition for that title within other historical contexts as well. Why, for example, could we not credit the intellectual genesis of the Enlightenment to the Italian Renaissance, to the ideas of Machiavelli, Bruno, and Galileo, as is maintained with no paucity of arguments by the great historian of philosophy Eugenio Garin? Finally, the most disconcerting and perplexing aspect of Israel's theses is his view of the Enlightenment as a closed world, collectively defined once and for all by its intellectual bias, a claustrophobic world built entirely on philosophical controversies, as though it consisted only in a scintillating insight on the part of one lone philosopher, Baruch Spinoza, whose ideas single-handedly produced what we now call modernity.

Luckily, decades of research and the work of many scholars have taught us that the Enlightenment was not like that at all. On the contrary, it was open, empirical and based on experimentation, eclectic, polysemic, cosmopolitan, and ready to embody contributions from the natural sciences, from the arts such as music and painting, and from political science. It was sustained in its fight against the *Ancien Régime* by new cultural and linguistic practices, as well as by a renewed critical spirit that had its basis and legitimation in the study of mankind and mankind's limitations, and in the search for happiness through the exercise of the rights of man. Far from being a project single-mindedly aimed at the goal of modernity, entirely encompassed and accomplished under the banner of Spinoza's monism, the Enlightenment is more accurately understood as a cultural experience defined first and foremost (and this probably remains so to this day) by the values it has bequeathed us. It is a *laboratory of modernity*, a process that may have stalled at times but that was never entirely suppressed, nor ever brought to a conclusion once and for all.

Despite all this, we salute the intellectual courage shown by Jonathan Israel and with him by those young scholars who, in the English-speaking world, are achieving important results in their remapping of the Enlightenment. Their work poses an intellectual challenge to which our new European historians must rise, always genially keeping in mind an old Italian proverb: "He who has the most yarn will weave the most cloth."

Turin, July 2013

NOTES

‖‖‖‖‖‖‖‖‖‖‖‖‖‖‖‖‖‖‖‖‖‖

INTRODUCTION

1. "On a dit l'*Europe sauvage*, l'*Europe payenne*, on a dit l'*Europe chrétienne*, peut être dirait-on encore pis, mais il faut qu'on dise enfin l'*Europe raisonnable.*" Translations of quotations that are not otherwise attributed are due to the present translator.

2. B. Croce, *History as the Story of Liberty*, tr. Sylvia Saunders Sprigge (New York: Norton, 1941), 194. The literal translation of the book's Italian title is "History as Thought and Action."

3. For the lecture on human rights, see now V. Ferrone, *Storia dei diritti dell'uomo. L'Illuminismo e la costruzione del linguaggio politico dei moderni* (Rome-Bari: Laterza, 2014).

CHAPTER 1
HISTORIANS AND PHILOSOPHERS

1. Cf. A. Trampus, "Orientamenti bibliografici," in *L'Illuminismo. Dizionario storico*, ed. V. Ferrone and D. Roche (Rome-Bari: Laterza, 1997), 593ff.

2. In the original Italian version of these lectures the term used to describe the Enlightenment's double nature is *ircocervo*, i.e., the Aristotelian "goat-stag." In Italian, this word is glossed as "a fabulous animal, half goat, half stag; idea or thing that is intrinsically contradictory, impossible and therefore inexistent" (T. De Mauro, *Dizionario della lingua italiana*, Turin: Paravia, 2000), but in this study it refers rather to the way in which the Enlightenment is vividly present in our social imaginary and our mode of thinking. We believe that "Centaur" brings this across more clearly to an English-speaking audience, as long as no "hierarchical" or "qualitative" difference is inferred between the two aspects of the "animal."

3. The same applies to historical categories such as the Middle Ages, on which see G. Sergi, *L'idea di medioevo. Fra storia e senso comune* (Rome: Donzelli, 2005).

4. On Western historical consciousness as distinct from that which developed in Islamic countries, see J. Le Goff, *History and Memory*, tr. Steven Rendall and Elizabeth Claman (New York: Columbia University Press, 1992), 156ff.

5. On these very common theses, see the entry for "Aufklärung" in *Geschichtliche Grundbegriffe. Historisches Lexikon zur politisch-sozialen Sprache in Deutschland*, ed. O. Brunner, W. Conze, and R. Koselleck, vol. 1 (Stuttgart: Klett-Cotta, 1972), 240ff.

6. Cf. W. Dilthey, *Einleitung in die Geisteswissenschaften. Versuch einer Grundlegung für das Studium der Gesellschaft und der Geschichte* [1883] (Leipzig, n.d.). For an English translation, see *Selected Works*, vol. 1, ed. R. A. Makkreel and F. Rodi (Princeton,

NJ: Princeton University Press, 1985. See also Dilthey, *Gesammelte Schriften*, vol. 3, *Studien zur Geschichte des deutschen Geistes: Leibniz und sein Zeitalter. Friedrich der grosse und die deutsche Aufklärung. Das achtzehnte Jahrhundert und die geschichtliche Welt* (Stuttgart & Göttingen: B. G. Teubner; Vandenhoeck & Ruprecht, 1962).

7. Cf. R. Koselleck, *Futures Past: On the Semantics of Historical Time* (Cambridge, MA: MIT Press, 1985), xxiv (original: *Vergangene Zukunft. Zur Semantik geschichtlicher Zeiten*, Frankfurt am Main, 1979).

8. Ibid., 203ff.

9. Cf. Voltaire, *Essai sur les moeurs et l'esprit des nations* (Geneva, 1765). On Voltaire being the first to speak as a "historian" and "philosopher," rather than from a theological view of history, see K. Löwith, *Meaning in History: The Theological Implications of the Philosophy of History* (Chicago: University of Chicago Press, 1949), ch. 5, esp. 107.

10. Cf. Koselleck, *Futures Past*, where this process is usefully summarized as follows:

. . . our current idea of history arose in Western culture only around the end of the eighteenth century.

It is an outcome of the lengthy theoretical reflections of the Enlightenment. Formerly there had existed, for instance, the history that God had set in motion with humanity. But there was no history for which humanity might have been the subject or which could be thought of as its own subject. Previously, histories had existed in the plural—all sorts of histories which had occurred and which might be used as exempla in teachings on ethics and religion, and in law and philosophy. [. . .] If anyone had said before 1780 that he studied history, he would have at once been asked by his interlocutor: Which history? History of what? Imperial history, or the history of theological doctrine, or perhaps the history of France? [. . .] [H]istory could only be conceived together with an associated subject that underwent change or upon which change occurred (200–201).

11. We shall return to this subject in the second part of this book. For the moment, we will simply refer to A. Momigliano's pages on the inevitable relativism of modern historicism, and therefore on how historical knowledge today must embrace the idea of "studying change from a changeable point of view," even while the task of the historian remains "to distinguish true from false." Cf. Momigliano, *Sui fondamenti della storia antica* (Turin: Einaudi, 1984), 460, but see also especially 297ff. and 455ff. It should be noted that, for Momigliano, Gibbon was the prototype of the modern historian in that he was capable of applying both the critical and philological method and that of philosophical conceptualization.

12. See the quotations and comments in Koselleck, *Futures Past*, 145 and 148.

13. See H. Blumenberg, *The Legitimacy of the Modern Age*, tr. Robert M. Wallace (Cambridge, MA: MIT Press, 1983; original: *Legitimität der Neuzeit* [Frankfurt am Main, 1974]) on how only the modern age has been capable, through the secularization of time, to reflect on itself and on its entitlement to feel different from the past and from tradition, thus opening up to the future.

Chapter 2
Kant: *Was ist Aufklärung?*

1. Kant, "Idea for a Universal History from a Cosmopolitan Point of View," tr. Lewis White Beck, in *On History*, ed. Lewis White Beck (Indianapolis: Bobbs-Merrill, 1963), 11–26 (25). On this topic, cf. M. Riedel, "Historie oder Geschichte? Sprachkritik

und Begriffsbildung in Kants Theorie der historischen Erkenntnis," in *Vernünftiges Denken*, ed. J. Mittelstraß and M. Riedel (Berlin-New York: De Gruyter, 1978).

2. Kant, "An Old Question Raised Again: Is the Human Race Constantly Progressing?" tr. Robert E. Anchor, in *On History*, 137–154 (147).

3. Kant, "Idea for a Universal History," 23.

4. Ibid., 13.

5. Ibid., 25.

6. Kant, "What Is Enlightenment?" in *On History*, 3–10 (3).

7. "What Is Enlightenment?" 9.

8. "What Is Enlightenment?" 8–9.

9. For example, a form of twentieth-century militant neo-Enlightenment in the Italian context is described in *Il neoilluminismo italiano. Cronache di filosofia (1953–1962)*, ed. M. Pasini and D. Rolando (Milan: Il Saggiatore, 1991). Further instances could be adduced for different periods and countries. But see Marx's ironic treatment of Bruno Bauer and other Young Hegelian liberals in his 1843–44 essay "On *The Jewish Question*."

10. Kant, "On a Pure Mysticism in Religion," appended to "The Philosophy Faculty versus the Theology Faculty," in *The Conflict of the Faculties*, tr. with an intro. by Mary J. Gregor (New York: Abaris, 1979), 127.

CHAPTER 3
HEGEL

1. Cf. E. Tortarolo, *La ragione sulla Sprea. Coscienza storica e cultura politica nell'illuminismo berlinese* (Bologna: Il Mulino, 1989), 261ff. An Italian collection usefully gathers together several key texts: I. Kant, *Che cos'è l'Illuminismo? Con altri testi e risposte di Erhard, Forster, Hamann, Herder, Laukhard, Lessing, Mendelssohn, Riem, Schiller, Wedekind, Wieland* (Rome: Editori Riuniti, 1987).

2. Cf. A. Trampus, *I gesuiti e l'Illuminismo. Politica e religione in Austria e nell'Europa centrale (1773–1798)* (Florence: Olschki, 2000), 252ff.

3. J. Habermas rightly stresses Hegel's role as founder of the philosophical discourse of modernity. See his *Der philosophische Diskurs der Moderne. Zwölf Vorlesungen* (Frankfurt: Suhrkamp, 1985; Engl. tr.: *The Philosophical Discourse of Modernity: Twelve Lectures*, Cambridge, MA: MIT Press, 1990).

4. Cf. G.W.F. Hegel, *The Difference Between Fichte's and Schelling's System of Philosophy*, tr. H. S. Harris and W. Cerf (Albany: State University of New York Press, 1977), 93–94. These remarks are still relevant today. In 1962 Gadamer expressed his interest in Hegel's choices by discussing how the very concept of spirit is still at the basis of all that critique of the subjective spirit that has become our task in the post-Hegelian era. Gadamer further stressed how this concept of spirit, which transcends the ego's subjectivity, finds its real corresponding phenomenon in language, a phenomenon that today is coming more and more to the fore in contemporary philosophy. On this, cf. *Filosofia '86*, ed. G. Vattimo (Rome-Bari: Laterza, 1987), 89.

5. Hegel, *Phenomenology of Spirit*, tr. A. V. Miller (Oxford: Oxford University Press, 1977), 296.

6. Ibid., 340. Subsequent page references to this work are in parentheses within the text.

7. See also ibid., 349: "Faith has, in fact, become the same as Enlightenment, viz. the consciousness of the relation of what is in itself finite to an Absolute without predicates, an Absolute unknown and unknowable; but there is this difference, the latter is *satisfied* Enlightenment, but faith is *unsatisfied* Enlightenment."

8. Hegel, *The Philosophy of History*, tr. J. Sibree (New York: Dover, 1956), 412. Subsequent page references to this work are in parentheses within the text.

9. On the Romantic condemnation of the *Aufklärung*, especially in works by Herder, Novalis, Görres, Hölderlin, and others, see V. Ferrone and D. Roche, *L'Illuminismo nella cultura contemporanea. Storia e storiografia* (Rome-Bari: Laterza, 2002), 30ff.

10. See, for instance, Hegel's denunciation of the inadequacy of mathematical knowledge in the *Phenomenology of Spirit*: "With non-actual things like the objects of mathematics, neither concrete sense-intuition nor philosophy has the least concern" (26). On Hegel's polemic against the rights of man, cf. V. Verra, *Introduzione a Hegel* (Rome-Bari: Laterza, 1992[4]), 30.

11. Hegel, *Philosophy of History*, "Introduction," 11. Subsequent page references to this work are in parentheses within the text.

CHAPTER 4
MARX AND NIETZSCHE

1. On the rise of the concept of civil society, cf. N. Bobbio, *Democracy and Dictatorship: the Nature and Limits of State Power*, tr. Peter Kennealy (Oxford: Polity, 1989), 22–43.

2. K. Marx and F. Engels, *The Holy Family*, tr. Richard Dixon and Clemens Dutt, in *Collected Works*, vol. 4 (London: Lawrence & Wishart, 1975), ch. 6, paragraph c, "Critical Battle against the French Revolution," 122–123.

3. For Marx's stern critique of the rights of man as class instrument and bourgeois ideology, cf. especially his 1843–44 work, "On *The Jewish Question*."

4. On the typically nineteenth-century invention of a hegemonic tradition of individualism, supposedly created by the eighteenth-century Enlightenment, cf. P. Costa, *Civitas. Storia della cittadinanza in Europa*, vol. 2, *L'età delle rivoluzioni* (Rome-Bari: Laterza, 2000), 630ff.

5. Marx's source here is Hegel's *Elements of the Philosophy of Right*, where the philosopher discusses the Enlightenment's bourgeois "individuality," and how the idea that communities "can be split up again into a collection of individuals [. . .] involves separating civil and political life from each other and leaves political life hanging, so to speak, in the air; for its basis is then merely the abstract individuality of arbitrary will and opinion, and is thus grounded only on contingency rather than on a foundation which is *stable* and *legitimate* in and for itself" (G.W.F. Hegel, *Elements of the Philosophy of Right*, ed. Allen W. Wood, tr. H. B. Nisbet [Cambridge: Cambridge University Press, 1991], § 303, p. 344).

6. Marx, "On *The Jewish Question*," tr. Clemens Dutt, in *Collected Works*, vol. 3, 168.

7. Cf. what is also known as Engels's "Antidühring," later reissued as "Socialism: Utopian and Scientific," in *Collected Works*, vol. 24, 287.

8. On the "trial" to which European culture subjected the Enlightenment and its values in the years between 1890 and 1930, cf. H. Stuart Hughes, *Consciousness and*

Society: The Reorientation of European Social Thought, 1890–1930 (New York: Knopf, 1958), 33ff.; and especially Zeev Sternhell, *The Anti-Enlightenment Tradition*, tr. David Maisel (New Haven, CT: Yale University Press, 2010), though the latter's approach may be a little schematic.

9. F. Nietzsche, *The Birth of Tragedy and Other Writings*, ed. Raymond Geuss and Ronald Speirs, tr. Ronald Speirs (Cambridge: Cambridge University Press, 1999), ch. 17, 82.

10. Ibid., ch. 15, 72. For Nietzsche the demise of Dionysiac, i.e., mythical and tragical, thinking was due to the rise of three forms of optimism: "'Virtue is knowledge; sin is only committed out of ignorance; the virtuous man is a happy man'" (ch. 14, 70).

11. Cf. E. Fink, *Nietzsche's Philosophy*, tr. G. Richter (London-New York: Continuum, 2003; original: *Nietzsches Philosophie* [Stuttgart, 1960]). For a different view on this aspect, cf. G. Colli, *Scritti su Nietzsche* (Milan: Adelphi, 1980), 94.

12. Nietzsche, *Human, All Too Human*, tr. R. J. Hollingdale (Cambridge: Cambridge University Press, 1986), vol. 1, § 237: "Renaissance and Reformation," 114.

13. Nietzsche, *Daybreak*, ed. Maudemarie Clark and Brian Leiter, tr. R. J. Hollingdale (Cambridge: Cambridge University Press, 1997), § 197: "German Hostility to the Enlightenment," 117.

14. Nietzsche, *Human, All Too Human*, vol. 2, part 2, § 221: "The Perilousness of the Enlightenment," 367.

15. Ibid., vol. 1, § 463: "A Delusion in the Theory of Revolution," 169.

16. Ibid., vol. 1, § 26: "Reaction as Progress," 26.

17. See Nietzsche, *On the Genealogy of Morality*, ed. Keith Ansell-Pearson, tr. Carol Diethe (Cambridge: Cambridge University Press, 1994), 128.

CHAPTER 5
HORKHEIMER AND ADORNO

1. Max Horkheimer and Theodor W. Adorno, *Dialectic of Enlightenment*, ed. Gunzelin Schmid Noerr, tr. Edmund Jephcott (Stanford, CA: Stanford University Press, 2002). Subsequent page references to this work are in parentheses within the text.

2. For an insightful review of the vast literature on these themes, cf. P. Rossi, *Paragone degli ingegni moderni e postmoderni* (Bologna: Il Mulino, 1989).

3. Cf. Horkheimer's *Eclipse of Reason* (1947), which valuably reprises Horkheimer and Adorno's larger work that we are discussing here.

CHAPTER 6
FOUCAULT

1. For M. Foucault, "'Dialectic' is a way of evading the always open and hazardous reality of conflict by reducing it to a Hegelian skeleton"—from an interview with Alessandro Fontana and Pasquale Pasquino, first published in F. Foucault, *Microfisica del potere* (Turin: Einaudi, 1977). Now chapter 6, "Truth and Power," tr. C. Gordon, in Foucault, *Power/Knowledge: Selected Interviews and Other Writings, 1972–1977*, ed. Colin Gordon (New York: Vintage, 1980), 109–133 (114–115).

2. Cf. Foucault, *The Order of Things: An Archaeology of the Human Sciences* (London: Routledge, 1974), 342 (original: *Les Mots et les choses. Une archéologie des sciences humaines* [Paris, 1966]).

3. From an interview first published in the *Magazine littéraire* in June 1975. Now chapter 2, "Prison Talk," tr. Colin Gordon, in Foucault, *Power/Knowledge*, 37–54 (52).

4. Foucault, "Truth and Power," 117. The key text of Foucault's genealogy is "Nietzsche, la généalogie, l'histoire", published in his 1971 *Hommage à Jean Hyppolite*. This text is available in English as "Nietzsche, Genealogy, History," tr. Donald F. Brouchard and Sherry Simon, in Foucault, *Aesthetics, Method, and Epistemology*, ed. James D. Faubion (London: Allen Lane, 1998), 369–391.

5. Engl. ed.: *Madness and Civilization: A History of Insanity in the Age of Reason*, tr. Richard Howard (London and Sydney: Tavistock, 1967). Now also available as *History of Madness*, ed. Jean Khalfa, tr. Jonathan Murphy and Jean Khalfa (London and New York: Routledge, 2006).

6. Engl. ed.: *The Birth of the Clinic*, tr. A. M. Sheridan Smith (New York: Pantheon, 1973).

7. Cf. Foucault, *Discipline and Punish: The Birth of the Prison*, tr. Alan Sheridan (London: Allen Lane, 1977), Pt. 2, ch. 2, "The Gentle Way in Punishment," 104–131 (original: *Surveiller et punir. Naissance de la prison* [Paris, 1975]).

8. Ibid., 222.

9. On historians' fierce criticism of many of Foucault's (at times rather strained) interpretations, cf. J. G. Merquior, *Foucault*, 2nd ed. (London: Fontana, 1991). Of particular interest is the parallel between the research that was simultaneously carried out by Franco Venturi and by Foucault on Beccaria and the right to punish in eighteenth-century Europe (cf. 104–105).

10. Cf. the epigraph to Foucault, *Fearless Speech*, ed. Joseph Pearson (Los Angeles, CA: Semiotext(e), 2001). See also "Concluding Remarks," 167–173 (169–170).

11. Foucault's polemics were probably directed against Reinhart Koselleck, who in his *Critique and Crisis: Enlightenment and the Pathogenesis of Modern Society* (Oxford: Berg, 1988; original: *Kritik und Krise. Ein Beitrag zur Pathogenese der bürgerlichen Welt* [Freiburg, 1959]) completely equated the history of critique with Enlightenment rationalism.

12. Foucault, "What Is Critique?" tr. Lysa Hochroth, in *The Politics of Truth*, ed. Sylvère Lotringer (Los Angeles, CA: Semiotext(e), 1997), 41–82 (43).

13. Ibid., 45. Cf. also the extensive bibliography on these topics in Foucault, *Qu'est-ce que les Lumières?* ed. O. Dekens (Paris: Bréal, 2004).

14. Foucault, "What Is Critique?" 47.

15. Ibid., 48.

16. Ibid., 49.

17. Ibid., 52.

18. Cf. Foucault, "What Is Revolution?" tr. Lysa Hochroth, in *The Politics of Truth*, 83–95 (93). An insightful analysis of Foucault's attack against teleological readings of the eighteenth century and the Enlightenment-Revolution link can be found in Roger Chartier, *Au bord de la falaise. L'histoire entre certitudes et inquiétude* (Paris: Albin Michel, 1998), 145ff. On the distance between Foucault's position and that of the *Annales* school, and of historians in general, cf. G. Noirel, "Foucault and History: The Lessons of a Disillusion," *Journal of Modern History* 66 (1994), 547–568.

19. Foucault, "What Is Critique?" 55. Subsequent page references to this work are in parentheses within the text.

20. Foucault, "What Is Revolution?" 83–84. Subsequent page references to this work are in parentheses within the text.

21. Cf. Hilary Putnam, *Pragmatism: An Open Question* (Oxford: Blackwell, 1995), 2. On the growing interest among philosophers in the so-called "Enlightenment project," see also *What Is Enlightenment? Eighteenth-Century Answers and Twentieth-Century Questions*, ed. J. Schmidt (Berkeley: University of California Press, 1996).

22. See, for instance, Gianni Vattimo, *The End of Modernity: Nihilism and Hermeneutics in Post-Modern Culture*, tr. with an introduction by Jon R. Snyder (Cambridge: Polity, 1988; original: *La fine della modernità. Nichilismo ed ermeneutica nella cultura post-moderna* [Milan, 1985]).

CHAPTER 7

POSTMODERN ANTI-ENLIGHTENMENT POSITIONS

1. Cf. R. Rorty, "The Continuity between the Enlightenment and 'Postmodernism'," in *What's Left of Enlightenment? A Postmodern Question*, ed. K. M. Baker and P. H. Reill (Stanford, CA: Stanford University Press, 2001), 18ff.

2. Cf. Ernst Cassirer and Martin Heidegger, *Débat sur le kantisme et la philosophie (Davos, mars 1929) et autres textes de 1929–1931*, ed. P. Aubenque (Paris: Beauchesne, 1972). See also the text appended to M. Heidegger, *Kant and the Problem of Metaphysics*, tr. Richard Taft (Bloomington: Indiana University Press, 1990; original: *Kant und das Problem der Metaphysik* [Bonn, 1929]).

3. Berlin, 1923–1929. Engl. ed.: *The Philosophy of Symbolic Forms*, 4 vols. (New Haven, CT: Yale University Press, 1953–1996).

4. "Of course man is finite, but he is also a finite being who is aware of his finitude, and rises above it precisely within that knowledge, which in itself is not finite." Cf. Cassirer and Heidegger, *Débat sur le kantisme*, 27.

5. ". . . destruction of what until now have been the foundations of Western metaphysics (Spirit, Logos, Reason)." Ibid., p. 24.

6. The most famous synthesis of Heidegger's thought on this subject is no doubt his 1946 "Brief über den 'Humanismus'", in Heidegger, *Platons Lehre von der Wahrheit* (Bern, 1947); cf. the English version, "Letter on Humanism," tr. Frank A. Capuzzi with J. Glenn Gray, in Heidegger, *Basic Writings*, ed. David Farrell Krell (London: Routledge & Kegan Paul, 1978), 193–242.

7. Ibid., 221–222.

8. Ibid., 226.

9. Heidegger, *The Essence of Truth*, tr. Ted Sadler (London and New York: Continuum, 2002), 47ff. (original: *Vom Wesen der Wahrheit* [Frankfurt am Main, 1943]).

10. Cf. Heidegger, *Kant and the Problem of Metaphysics*, tr. Richard Taft, 4th ed. (Bloomington and Indianapolis: Indiana University Press, 1990), § 31, "The Originality of the Previously Laid Ground and Kant's Shrinking-Back from the Transcendental Power of Imagination," 110–117.

11. Cf. Cassirer's review of Heidegger's book on Kant, "Kant und das Problem der Metaphysik. Bemerkungen zu Martin Heideggers Kant-Interpretation," *Kantstudien* 36

(1931), 1–26 (14). Cf. Peter E. Gordon, *Continental Divide. Heidegger, Cassirer, Davos* (Cambridge, MA: Harvard University Press, 2010), 268–281. Where available, we have taken quotations in English from Gordon's study. The numbers in parentheses refer to the page numbers of the *Kantstudien* article, as given by Gordon.

12. Cf. Gilles Kepel, *The Revenge of God: the Resurgence of Islam, Christianity, and Judaism in the Modern World*, tr. Alan Braley (Cambridge: Polity, 1994; original: *La Revanche de Dieu. Chrétiens, juifs et musulmans à la reconquête du monde* [Paris, 1991]); José Casanova, *Public Religions in the Modern World* (Chicago: University of Chicago Press, 1994); Enzo Pace, *Perché le religioni scendono in guerra?* (Rome-Bari: Laterza, 2004).

13. Cf. J. Habermas and J. Ratzinger, *The Dialectics of Secularization: On Reason and Religion*, ed. Florian Schuller, tr. Brian McNeil (San Francisco: Ignatius, 2006). The original debate took place in Munich in January 2004 under the aegis of the Catholic Academy in Bavaria, but it does not seem to have produced anything significantly new. The two participants acknowledged that both modernity and the organized religions are subject to aberrations and pathological manifestations and that, therefore, in a post-secular context such as the present seems to be, it is necessary to keep the dialogue open and strive towards toleration. Habermas certainly continued to uphold the principle of the lay State, simply acknowledging that the continued strength of religion posed a "cognitive challenge" to lay thought. Ratzinger, for his part, chose to insist on the need to analyze the double identity of European culture, which is informed by both Christianity and the Enlightenment. What seems to be particularly interesting, on the other hand, are Habermas's considerations on the need to question the excesses of scientism, which has forgotten that its ultimate end should be the centrality of man (cf. Habermas, *The Future of Human Nature*, tr. Hella Beister [Oxford: Polity, 2002]).

14. Cf. Ferrone, "Le radici illuministiche della libertà religiosa," in *Le ragioni dei laici*, ed. G. Preterossi (Rome-Bari: Laterza, 2005), 57ff. on the centuries-old, difficult relationship between theology and history, and especially on the meaning of the 2000 Apostolic Letter *Tertio millennio adveniente*, on the "purification of memory."

15. See, on these issues, the debate on Cardinal K. Lehmann's theses organized by the journal *Il Regno*: E.-W. Böckenförde, "Verità e libertà. Sulla responsabilità della Chiesa nel mondo di oggi," *Il Regno* 9 n. 49 (2004), 716ff.; Ferrone, "La laicità spazio di valori," *Il Regno* 9 n. 50 (2005), 282ff. A position of great interest is that expressed by Cardinal Carlo Maria Martini in a sermon delivered in Milan Cathedral, on the issue of truth and the need for a form of Christian relativism. For an account, see the *Corriere della Sera*, Monday, May 9, 2005.

16. Cf. Ferrone, "Chiesa cattolica e modernità. La scoperta dei diritti dell'uomo dopo l'esperienza dei totalitarismi," in *Chiesa cattolica e modernità*, ed. Bolgiani, Ferrone, and Margiotta Broglio (Bologna: Il Mulino, 2004), 17ff. Unsurprisingly, few scholars, especially in Italy, are willing to address the delicate issue of the responsibilities of the Catholic Church in relation to twentieth-century totalitarianism. For an attempt in this direction by eminent scholars such as Luisa Mangoni, Giovanni Miccoli, Lutz Klinkhammer, Andrea Riccardi, Guido Verucci, and others, cf. *La Chiesa cattolica e il totalitarismo*, Proceedings of the conference held at the Fondazione Firpo in Turin on October 25–26, 2001, ed. Ferrone (Florence: Olschki, 2004).

17. Cf. J. Maritain, "Integral Humanism," tr. Joseph W. Evans, in Maritain, *Integral Humanism; Freedom in the Modern World; and, A Letter on Independence*, ed. Otto Bird

(Notre Dame, IN: University of Notre Dame Press, 1996), 169 (original: *Humanisme intégral. Problèmes temporels et spirituels d'une nouvelle chrétienté* [Paris, 1936]).

18. Ibid., 210.

19. The future John Paul II's reaction is reported in E.-W. Böckenförde, "Verità e libertà," 721. An insightful reconstruction of these events can be found in G. Miccoli, "Due nodi. La libertà religiosa e le relazioni con gli ebrei," in *Storia del Concilio Vaticano II*, ed. A. Melloni, gen. ed. Giuseppe Alberigo (Bologna: Il Mulino, 1995–2001), vol. 4, 119ff.

20. Cf. the evaluations in this sense by H. Jedin, M.-D. Chenu, H.-I. Marrou, and K. Rahner. In the context of his discussion of the new departure embodied in the definition of the Church as "God's people" and in the new strategy of "friendship" with mankind, Rahner compared Vatican II to the moment in which Paul moved the epicenter of Christianity from Jerusalem to Rome. On the other hand, according to French Dominican Chenu, there were four innovative pivotal points in the Council's theology: the primacy of the mystery over the institution; the acknowledgement of the fundamental value of the human subject within the framework and dynamics of salvation; the Church's awareness of the fact that it exists within history; and the acknowledgement of the value of earthly reality. Cf. G. Alberigo, "Transizione epocale?" in *Storia del Concilio Vaticano II*, vol. 5, 628ff.

21. Already before the rise of the *nouvelle théologie*, at the beginning of the twentieth century, theologians had started to reconsider the historicity of Christianity and the importance to be attributed to the link between history and theology. In the 1930s, for instance, Chenu reevaluated the studies in biblical exegesis by Father Lagrange, founder of the prestigious École biblique de Jérusalem, and launched a vast program of research into Christianity "as history and theology of confession." He thus gave rise to a strong movement destined to influence the course of the Church. Cf. G. Alberigo's introductory note to M.-D. Chenu, *Le Saulchoir. Una scuola di teologia* (Casale Monferrato: Marietti, 1982), ixff. (original: *Le Saulchoir: une école de théologie*, [n.p., 1937]). In the Italian reissue of his old essays, which had provoked so much scandal and condemnation in Rome when they were first published, Chenu expresses his satisfaction at how one of the main merits of Vatican II was that it took stock of the historical dimension of the Church. The very term *historia* had been missing from the vocabulary of the Church, while here it occurred sixty-three times. The method of *Le Saulchoir* introduced history within the framework of theology, just as forty years previously, and battling against the same opposition, Father Lagrange had introduced the "historical method" for the understanding of Scripture. Vatican II had validated both enterprises (cf. xxxiv). For an overview of these issues, cf. Étienne Fouilloux, "Il cattolicesimo," in *Storia del cristianesimo*, ed. J.-M. Mayeur, Ch. Pietri, A. Vauchez, and M. Venard, vol. 11 (Rome: Borla/Città Nuova, 1997), 159ff.

22. Thus reads the English version of the encyclical found on the Vatican website at www.vatican.va/archive/hist_councils/ii_vatican_council/documents/vat-ii_cons_19651207_gaudium-et-spes_en.html (accessed January 26, 2014), paragraph 10. Cf. the Latin version (also accessible from www.vatican.va/archive/hist_councils/ii_vatican_council/index_it.htm): "Quid est homo? Quinam est sensus doloris, mali, mortis, quae, quamquam tantus progressus factus est, subsistere pergunt?" See also *Conciliorum Oecumenorum Decreta*, ed. G. Alberigo et al. (Bologna: Istituto per le Scienze Religiose, 1973), 1074.

23. R. Guardini, *The End of the Modern World*, tr. J. Theman and H. Burke, ed. F. D. Wilhelmsen (London: Sheed & Ward, 1957; original: *Das Ende der Neuzeit. Ein Versuch zur Orientierung* [Wurzburg, 1951]), 106–107. Subsequent page references, to the English translation of this work, are in parentheses within the text.

24. Cf. Ferrone, "Chiesa cattolica e modernità," 122ff.

25. Cf. *Aufklärung Heute. Castel Gandolfo-Gespräche (1996)*, ed. K. Michalski (Stuttgart: Klett-Cotta, 1997). Page references to this work are in parentheses within the text.

26. Cf. Ratzinger, *Church, Ecumenism and Politics: New Essays in Ecclesiology*, tr. Robert Nowell (New York: Crossroad, 1988), 160 (original: *Kirche, Ökumene und Politik* [Cinisello Balsamo, 1987]).

27. Ibid., 154. In an interview with the *Repubblica* newspaper (Monday, August 12, 1996), then Cardinal Ratzinger gave the following, rather irenicist, reply to a question on the conflict between the Church and the Enlightenment: "It is only natural that that should happen. In the sense that the century of the *Lumières* was one thing, and the actual Enlightenment was another. There was also such a thing as a Christian Enlightenment." This long-overdue reappraisal of the issue of the "katholische Aufklärung" had in fact already begun independently several years earlier, with the conference on comparative ecclesiastical history that was held in Warsaw in June 1978, with the intention of taking up the Council's invitation to set up a closer debate with the ways of modernity. Since then, Catholic historians have devoted ample space to Christian currents of the European *Aufklärung* between the end of the seventeenth century and the late Restoration. The historiographical premises of this question were lucidly analyzed in a volume edited by Mario Rosa, *Cattolicesimo e Lumi nel Settecento italiano* (Rome: Herder, 1981). Rosa is also the author of several articles on the so-called "Catholic Enlightenment" in Italy, now collected in M. Rosa, *Settecento religioso. Politica della ragione e religione del cuore* (Venice: Marsilio, 1999). A particularly important contribution on this topic is the article by B. Plongeron, "Les Églises au défi de la modernité à la charnière des 18e et 19e siècles," in *Deux mille ans d'histoire de l'Église*, special issue of the *Revue d'histoire ecclésiastique* 95 (2000), 613–633. I myself have strong reservations about the use of this historiographical category, which in my opinion is liable to cause confusion in several respects. This issue deserves far more in-depth consideration than it is possible to give here. However, one should recall in this context an already-mentioned pioneering study by A. Trampus, *I gesuiti e l'Illuminismo*, which traces the origins of the concept of a "Catholic Enlightenment" as far back as the late eighteenth century, and highlights its Jesuit connections and obviously apologetic intent (cf., in particular, 145ff.).

28. Cf. Pera and Ratzinger, *Without Roots: The West, Relativism, Christianity, Islam*, tr. Michael F. Moore (New York: Basic Books, 2006), 115–116 (original: *Senza radici. Europa, Relativismo, Cristianesimo, Islam* [Milan, 2004]). It is from the eighteenth century that "the new 'denomination' of *laici* (secular people) was born" (115), together with the peremptory claim to "free thinking and freedom from religious constrictions" (116).

29. Kant's text to which Ratzinger is referring is his 1794 "Das Ende aller Dinge," where, according to Ratzinger, Kant acknowledged that "in a moral respect, this could lead to the (perverted) end of all things" (see Encyclical *Spe Salvi*, end of § 19, http://www.vatican.va/holy_father/benedict_xvi/encyclicals/documents/hf_ben-xvi

NOTES TO CHAPTER 8 • 183

_enc_20071130_spe-salvi_en.html, accessed 1.30.14). However, one should compare this with the overall meaning of Kant's passage; see "The End of All Things," tr. Allen W. Wood, in I. Kant, *Religion and Rational Theology*, tr. and ed. A. W. Wood and G. Di Giovanni (Cambridge: Cambridge University Press, 1996), 217–31 (226). An eminent example of these peculiarly oscillating opinions on the Enlightenment can be seen in Mario Pendinelli's comments on the *Spe Salvi* encyclical in the *Osservatore Romano* of November 13–14, 2007. Pendinelli defines Neo-Enlightenment as

> a defeated subculture. [. . .] Already in the past the Enlightenment turned into a livid and supercilious atheism that had meant to regenerate Europe's features, but only succeeded in turning them into a wrinkled, ugly face. In reality, the eclipse of Christian humanism brought about by the Enlightenment dramatically resulted in the rise of Nazism and Stalinism. Today's Neo-Enlightenment carries along in its wake a nihilism by which it is eventually overcome.

30. Cf. Ratzinger, "Un secondo Illuminismo," *Il Regno, Documenti* 19 (2001), 650ff. For a useful synthesis of Ratzinger's thought on the Enlightenment, see E. Jüngel, "J. Ratzinger: Illuminismo alla luce del Vangelo," *Il Regno* 10, n. 50 (2005), 301ff.

31. Cf. Ferrone, "La 'sana laicità' della Chiesa bellarminiana di Benedetto XVI tra 'potestas indirecta' e 'parresia'," *Passato e Presente* 26 (2008), 21–40.

CHAPTER 8
FOR A DEFENSE OF HISTORICAL KNOWLEDGE

1. For a different view on this matter, see ed. Schmidt, *What Is Enlightenment?*

2. On Momigliano's interest in the so-called "Greek Enlightenment," cf. G. Giarrizzo, "Storia sacra, storia profana: la tradizione come unità vissuta," in the special issue of the *Rivista Storica Italiana* dedicated to Arnaldo Momigliano: *Rivista Storica Italiana* 100 (1988), 382. On the concept of "Greek Enlightenment" and that of "Roman Enlightenment," see also P. Gay, *The Enlightenment: An Interpretation* (New York: Knopf, 1996[3]), 94ff. In the preface to his history of Hellenism (originally published in 1836–77), Droysen defined that era as "the modern age of pagan antiquity" (cf. *Geschichte des Hellenismus*, 3 vols, ed. E. Bayer [Darmstadt: Wissenschaftliche Buchgesellschaft, 1998]).

3. For a review of international historical scholarship on the Enlightenment, see *Historiographie et usage des lumières*, ed. Giuseppe Ricuperati (Berlin: Arno Spitz, 2002).

4. Cf. L. G. Crocker, *An Age of Crisis: Man and World in Eighteenth-Century French Thought* (Baltimore: Johns Hopkins, 1959) and Koselleck, *Critique and Crisis*.

5. Koselleck, *Critique and Crisis*, p. 122.

6. Cf. P. Gay, *The Enlightenment: An Interpretation*, 8. See also xiii, where Gay refers to a course of lectures that he gave at Columbia University in the early 1960s: "I presented . . . the central argument of these two volumes—the dialectic of the Enlightenment—and had that argument examined, criticized, modified, and strengthened in two years of stimulating debate."

7. Cf. E. Cassirer, *The Philosophy of the Enlightenment*, tr. Fritz C. A. Koelln and James P. Pettegrove (Princeton, NJ: Princeton University Press, 1951; original: *Die Philosophie der Aufklärun* [Tübingen, 1932]).

8. On the now obvious limitations of Cassirer's research, see J. Kent Wright, "'A Bright Clear Mirror': Cassirer's *The Philosophy of the Enlightenment*," in ed. Baker and Reill, *What's Left of Enlightenment?*, 70ff.

9. Cassirer, *The Individual and the Cosmos in Renaissance Philosophy*, tr. Mario Domandi (Philadelphia: University of Pennsylvania Press, 1972; original: *Individuum und Kosmos in der Philosophie der Renaissance* [Leipzig, 1927]).

10. Cassirer, *Philosophy of the Enlightenment*, vi.

11. Ibid., 12.

12. Cf. Venturi, *Utopia and Reform in the Enlightenment* (Cambridge: Cambridge University Press, 1971), 1. Diaz too spoke out against "the various histories of the development of 'spirit,' from Cassirer to Dilthey to Meinecke, and maybe even, in his fashionable new structural-political guise, to Koselleck as well" ("Discorsi sulle 'Lumières.' Programmi politici e idea-forza della libertà," in *L'età dei Lumi. Studi storici sul Settecento europeo in onore di Franco Venturi*, ed. R. Ajello et al., 2 vols. [Naples: Jovene, 1985], vol. 1, 103).

13. Cf. B. Croce, *La storia come pensiero e come azione* (Bari, 1938), translated into English by Sylvia Sprigge as *History as the Story of Liberty* (London: Allen and Unwin, 1941). These two contrasting types were magisterially described in 1952 by one of the great Italian historians of the twentieth century: cf. F. Chabod, *Lezioni di metodo storico con saggi su Egidi, Croce, Meinecke* (Rome-Bari: Laterza, 1969), 179ff.

14. Venturi, *Utopia*, 3. Subsequent page references to this work are in parentheses within the text.

15. Cf. R. H. Popkin, *The History of Scepticism from Erasmus to Spinoza* (Berkeley: University of California Press, 1979).

16. Cf. C. Borghero, *La certezza e la storia. Cartesianesimo, pirronismo e conoscenza storica* (Milan: F. Angeli, 1983).

17. Cf. Momigliano, *Sui fondamenti*, 42.

18. Two useful texts for a preliminary investigation on this issue are H. V. White, *Metahistory: The Historical Imagination in Nineteenth-Century Europe* (Baltimore: Johns Hopkins University Press, 1973) and P. Novick, *That Noble Dream: The "Objectivity Question" and the American Historical Profession* (Cambridge: Cambridge University Press, 1988).

19. Cf. Nietzsche, "On Truth and Lies in a Nonmoral Sense," in *Philosophy and Truth*, tr. and ed. D. Breazeale (Atlantic Highlands, NJ: Humanities Press, 1979), 79ff., quoted in C. Ginzburg, *History, Rhetoric, and Proof* (Hanover and London: University Press of New England, 1999), 9.

20. On these issues, see Diego Marconi, *Per la verità. Relativismo e filosofia* (Turin: Einaudi, 2007).

21. Cf. Koselleck, *Futures Past*, ch. 7, "Representation, Event, and Structure," 105–114; Momigliano, *Sui fondamenti*, 454ff.

22. Momigliano, *Sui fondamenti*, 464. However, Momigliano's whole 1974 essay, "Storicismo rivisitato," deserves to be read in full.

23. Cf. G. Ricuperati, *Apologia di un mestiere difficile. Problemi, insegnamenti e responsabilità della storia* (Rome-Bari: Laterza, 2005), 144ff.

24. Chartier, *Au bord de la falaise*, 16. On these issues, see also the similar positions expressed in J. Appleby, L. Hunt, and M. C. Jacob, *Telling the Truth about History* (New York: Norton, 1994).

CHAPTER 9
THE *EPISTEMOLOGIA IMAGINABILIS* IN
EIGHTEENTH-CENTURY SCIENCE AND PHILOSOPHY

1. Cf. Paolo Rossi's uncompromising and justified polemics against the philosophers of science in his *I ragni e le formiche. Un'apologia della storia della scienza* (Bologna: Il Mulino, 1986).

2. "Different genres of truths, different orders of certainties, different degrees of probabilities." Cf. V. Ferrone, "Il dibattito su probabilità e scienze sociali nel secolo XVIII," *Physis* 22 (1980), 62.

3. On the debate that at the end of the century would lead to the theorization of a clear-cut separation between sciences of the spirit and sciences of nature, see A. Orsucci, *Dalla biologia cellulare alle scienze dello spirito. Aspetti del dibattito sull'individualità nell'Ottocento tedesco* (Bologna: Il Mulino, 1992). For a general historical overview of the subject, cf. P. Rossi, "Specializzazione del sapere e comunità scientifica," in Rossi, *La memoria del sapere* (Rome-Bari: Laterza, 1990), 315ff. It should be noted that Troeltsch attributed to Vico the historical merit of being the first to highlight the contrast between "naturalism and historicism," thus outlining the future opposition between sciences of the spirit and sciences of nature. Cf. E. Troeltsch, *Der Historismus und seine Probleme* (Tübingen: Mohr, 1922).

4. Cf. Rossi, *Lo storicismo tedesco contemporaneo* (Turin: Einaudi, 1956). On these issues, see also the extensive bibliography in F. Tessitore, *Introduzione a Lo storicismo* (Rome-Bari: Laterza, 1991).

5. J. G. Droysen, *Outline of the Principles of History* (*Grundriss der Historik*), tr. E. Benjamin Andrews (Boston: Ginn & Co., 1893), 12.

6. On Droysen's polemics against H. T. Buckle's *History of Civilisation in England*, which had been translated into German immediately after its publication in 1859, see his review of Buckle's book, "Die Erhebung der Geschichte zum Rang einer Wissenschaft," *Historische Zeitschrift* 9 (1863), 1–22.

7. For an illuminating description of the subjective turn in modern epistemology, which arose at precisely that moment, see Philipp Frank's classic work, *Modern Science and Its Philosophy* (Cambridge, MA: Harvard University Press, 1949). For an insightful discussion of the comprehensive effects caused by this radical change in every field, see C. A. Viano, "La ragione, l'abbondanza e la credenza," in *Crisi della ragione. Nuovi modelli nel rapporto tra sapere e attività umane*, ed. A. Gargani (Turin: Einaudi, 1979), 302ff.

8. M. Bloch, *Apologie pour l'histoire ou métier d'historien* (Paris: Colin, 1949). English ed.: *The Historian's Craft*, tr. Peter Putnam (Manchester : Manchester University Press, 1992).

9. Cf. B. Bensaude-Vincent, "Présences scientifiques aux semaine de synthèse (1929–1939)," in *Henri Berr et la culture du XXe siècle*, ed. A. Biard, D. Bourel, and E. Brian (Paris: Michel, 1997), 220ff. However, the whole volume deserves to be taken into account because it provides new insights into the historical context that launched the *Annales* school.

10. Bloch, *The Historian's Craft*, 14–15. Very similar considerations on the radical change in the image of science, and on the inevitable implications of that change for the way in which we think of historical knowledge can be found in Lucien Febvre's 1941

lecture at the École Normale Supérieure. Cf. L. Febvre, "Vivre l'histoire. Propos d'initiation", in Febvre, *Combats pour l'histoire* (Paris: Colin, 1953).

11. Bloch, *The Historian's Craft*, 70.

12. Ibid., 110.

13. Ibid., 46. One finds further confirmation of this view of history solely in terms of method (as opposed to the various "historicist" interpretations that were constantly in search of the "spirit" of events and of philosophies of history) in Bloch's polemical review of Friedrich Meinecke's 1939 study, *Die Entstehung des Historismus*. Cf. Bloch, *Histoire et historiens*, ed. É. Bloch (Paris: Colin, 1995).

14. Of course, it would have been interesting to see how Bloch would have addressed the question of prediction in history on the basis of the new conceptions of probable knowledge. However, even the latest critical edition of his papers fails to throw light on this issue. Cf. Bloch, *Apologie pour l'histoire ou métier d'historien*, ed. É. Bloch (Paris: Colin, 1993).

15. Cf. G. Bachelard, *The New Scientific Spirit*, tr. Arthur Goldhammer (Boston: Beacon, 1984).

16. This is how the views of the Vienna Circle were portrayed by Popper. In fact, the position of figures such as Neurath, Carnap, and Hempel was much more nuanced and open to an understanding of the social and psychological dimension of science, as is demonstrated in P. Parrini, *Una filosofia senza dogmi: materiali per un bilancio dell'empirismo contemporaneo* (Bologna: Il Mulino, 1980).

17. See, for instance, the 1970 Italian edition of Popper's work, Popper, *Logica della scoperta scientifica. Il carattere autocorrettivo della scienza* (Turin: Einaudi, 1970), xiii.

18. Among Popper's numerous works on this subject, see, for instance, his three-volume series, *Postscript to The Logic of Scientific Discovery* (ed. W. W. Bartley, III, [Totowa, NJ: Rowman and Littlefield, 1983]). Aspects that deserve special attention include Popper's "propensity interpretation" of probability, which upheld the realist and objective character of reality against a purely statistical interpretation such as that of quantum mechanics in the first volume of the *Postscript* (*Realism and the Aim of Science*, vol. 1, pt. 2), and his conviction that the indeterminacy formula $\Delta x \cdot \Delta p_x \geq \hbar/2$ can be seen as a scatter relation and as such is objective and verifiable (in the final volume: *Quantum Theory and the Schism in Physics*, vol. 1, ch. 3).

19. Ludwik Fleck, *Genesis and Development of a Scientific Fact*, ed. (and adapted) by Thaddeus J. Trenn and Robert K. Merton, tr. Fred Bradley and Thaddeus J. Trenn (Chicago: University of Chicago Press, 1979), 42. Subsequent page references to this work are in parentheses within the text.

20. Cf. the opinions expressed by Paolo Rossi in "Ludwik Fleck e una rivoluzione immaginaria," which is the introduction to the Italian edition of Fleck's work, *Genesi e sviluppo di un fatto scientifico* (Bologna: Il Mulino, 1983). Here he quite rightly criticizes the position of those philosophers who do not take an interest in the great debates of the early twentieth century.

21. Cf. T. S. Kuhn, *The Structure of Scientific Revolutions* (Chicago: University of Chicago Press, 1962).

22. Cf. especially Kuhn, *The Essential Tension: Selected Studies in Scientific Tradition and Change* (Chicago: University of Chicago Press, 1977), where the author dedicates ample space to the idea of the "autonomy of historical understanding" in cognitive terms and underlines its importance in the definition of a new concept of science.

23. Kuhn, *Structure of Scientific Revolutions*, 85 (subsequent page references, which are all, as here, to the 50th anniversary reissue of the book in 2012, are given in the text).

24. Kuhn always set clear limits to interpretation, limits that were objective, natural, and rational, in opposition to the relativistic nihilism of those who denied the possibility of any form of truth. For a defense of Kuhn's positions, see Appleby, Hunt, and Jacob, *Telling the Truth about History*, 165. More generally, on the debate involving R. Hanson, S. Toulmin, I. Lakatos, and P. K. Feyerabend, among many others, cf. M. Hesse, *Revolutions and Reconstructions in Philosophy of Science* (Bloomington: Indiana University Press, 1980); Rossi, *I ragni e le formiche*, 117. An undoubtedly important work that originated from this debate is Y. Elkana's essay, "A Programmatic Attempt at an Anthropology of Knowledge," in *Sciences and Cultures: Anthropological and Historical Studies of the Sciences*, ed. E. Mendelsohn and Y. Elkana (Dordrecht: Reidel, 1981), 1–76.

25. See, for instance, Rossi's pioneering study of Francis Bacon and Baconian sciences, *Francis Bacon: From Magic to Science*, tr. Sacha Rabinovitch (Chicago: University of Chicago Press, 1968; original: *Francesco Bacone: dalla magia alla scienza* [Bari, 1957]).

26. Cf. M. C. Jacob, *The Newtonians and the English Revolutions* (New York: Gordon and Breach, 1976); V. Ferrone, *The Intellectual Roots of the Italian Enlightenment. Newtonian Science, Religion, and Politics in the Early Eighteenth Century*, tr. Sue Brotherton (Atlantic Heights, NJ: Humanities Press, 1995; original: *Scienza, natura, religione: mondo newtoniano e cultura italiana nel primo Settecento* [Naples, 1982]).

27. Cf. Ferrone and Rossi, *Lo scienziato nell'età moderna* (Rome-Bari: Laterza, 1994); R. Hahn, *The Anatomy of a Scientific Institution: The Paris Academy of Sciences, 1666–1803* (Berkeley: University of California Press, 1971).

28. Cf. C. C. Gillispie, *Science and Polity in France at the End of the Old Regime* (Princeton: Princeton University Press, 1980); G. S. Rousseau and R. Porter, eds., *The Ferment of Knowledge: Studies in the Historiography of Eighteenth-Century Science* (Cambridge: Cambridge University Press, 1980).

29. See our discussion of Robert Darnton's work on Mesmerism in chapter 13.

30. On the contrary, one should always remember that the image of science that was developed by the Enlightenment came under different forms. And in any case, it could not be entirely subsumed under the positivistic view of science, as some would have us believe. On this, see *L'Illuminismo. Dizionario storico*, s.v. *Scienza*, 332ff.

CHAPTER 10
THE ENLIGHTENMENT–FRENCH REVOLUTION PARADIGM

1. An especially useful starting point is offered by the debates caused by Wittgenstein's theory of language games. See L. Wittgenstein, *Philosophical Investigations* (New York: Macmillan, 1953), which remains a fundamental text for the historians' epistemological redefinition of the logic of context.

2. Cf. M. Bloch, *The Historian's Craft*, 29.

3. Droysen and Bloch offer here two different points of view, the former being linked to the historicist tradition and more concerned with *understanding* historical events, while the latter sought their *explanation*. However, they agree in their conclusions. In his *Outline of the Principles of History*, J. G. Droysen writes:

Beginnings are neither sought by criticism nor demanded by interpretation. In the moral world nothing is without medial antecedents. Yet historical investigation does not propose to explain, in the sense of deriving, as mere effects and developments, the latter from the earlier, or phenomena from laws. If the logical necessity of the later lay in the earlier, then, instead of the moral world, there would be something analogous to eternal matter and the changes of matter. [. . .] The essence of interpretation lies in seeing realities in past events, realities with that certain plenitude of conditions which they must have had in order that they might become realities. (§ 37, 26).

As for Bloch, see *The Historian's Craft*, 24ff., where he denounces "the obsession with origins," that is to say the fixation of certain historians who are always seeking to explain more recent phenomena in terms of those that are more remote in time. Bloch cites as an example of this attitude Hippolyte Taine and his *Origines de la France contemporaine*.

4. Cf. B. Baczko, "Enlightenment," in *A Critical Dictionary of the French Revolution*, ed. F. Furet and M. Ozouf, tr. Arthur Goldhammer (Cambridge, MA: Harvard University Press, 1989), 659–668 (original: *Dictionnaire critique de la Révolution française* [Paris, 1988]).

5. Cf. G. Benrekassa, J. Biou, M. Delon, J. M. Goulemot, J. Sgard, and E. Walter, "Le Premier Centenaire de la mort de Voltaire et de Rousseau: significations d'une commémoration," *Revue d'Histoire Littéraire de la France* 79 (1979), 265ff.

6. Cf. A. Compagnon, *La Troisième République des lettres. De Flaubert à Proust* (Paris: Seuil, 1983); M. Agulhon, *Marianne au pouvoir. L'imagerie et le symbolique républicaine de 1880 à 1914* (Paris: Flammarion, 1989).

7. Cf. G. Ricuperati, "Le categorie di periodizzazione e il Settecento. Per una introduzione storiografica," *Studi Settecenteschi* 14 (1994), 9–106.

8. These developments are traced in further detail in Ferrone and Roche, *L'Illuminismo nella cultura contemporanea*.

9. R. Chartier, *The Cultural Origins of the French Revolution*, tr. Lydia G. Cochrane (Durham, NC: Duke University Press, 1991), 7 (original: *Les Origines culturelles de la Révolution française* [Paris, 1990]).

10. Cf. R. Darnton, *The Forbidden Best-Sellers of Pre-Revolutionary France* (New York: Norton, 1996). See also *The Darnton Debate: Books and Revolution in the Eighteenth Century*, ed. H. T. Mason, volume 359 in *Studies on Voltaire and the Eighteenth Century* (Oxford: Voltaire Foundation, 1998).

11. Cf. E. Burke, *Reflections on the Revolution in France* (London: Dodsley, 1790), 165ff.

12. Cf. Ferrone and Roche, *L'Illuminismo nella cultura contemporanea*, 50ff. On this subject, see also Meinecke's *Historism: The Rise of a New Historical Outlook*, tr. J. E. Anderson, translation revised by H. D. Schmidt (London: Routledge & Kegan Paul, 1972; original: *Die Entstehung des Historismus* [Munich-Berlin, 1936]).

13. Cf. B. Croce, *Discorsi di varia filosofia* (Bari: Laterza, 1945) and, above all, his *La letteratura italiana del Settecento* (Bari: Laterza, 1949).

14. See the contributions by these two authors to *L'Illuminismo. Dizionario storico*, 478ff. and 498ff. For an overview of the debate, and for the opposing view, which argues against going back to a study of the Enlightenment in national terms, cf. J. Robertson, *The Case for the Enlightenment. Scotland and Naples, 1680–1760* (Cambridge: Cambridge University Press, 2005), 27ff.

15. Croce, *History: Its Theory and Practice*, tr. Douglas Ainslie (New York: Harcourt, Brace and Company, 1921), 263. Italian original: *Teoria e storia della storiografia* (2nd ed., Bari, 1920). In this Italian version Croce actually defines the Revolution as "the catastrophe and the catharsis" (rather than "the triumph and the catastrophe") of Enlightenment historiography (241).

16. Cf. Chartier, "'La Chimère de l'origine'. Foucault, les Lumières et la Révolution française", Chartier, *Au bord de la falaise*, 132ff.

17. Cf. D. K. Van Kley, *The Religious Origins of the French Revolution: From Calvin to the Civil Constitution, 1560–1791* (New Haven, CT: Yale University Press, 1996); L. Hunt, *Politics, Culture, and Class in the French Revolution* (Berkeley: University of California Press, 1984).

18. On the political consequences of historiographical paradigms, cf. F. Furet, *La Révolution en débat* (Paris: Gallimard, 1999).

19. Cf. Bloch, *The Historian's Craft*, 29. While its conclusions have been controversial, and are indeed rather questionable, Lucien Febvre's 1942 study, *Le Problème de l'incroyance au XVIe siècle* (Paris, 1942), remains a classic study of these issues, which seeks to define the mechanisms of discontinuity and peculiarity of human action in specific historical periods from the epistemological and psychological point of view. See *The Problem of Unbelief in the Sixteenth Century: The Religion of Rabelais*, tr. Beatrice Gottlieb (Cambridge, MA: Harvard University Press, 1982).

20. Despite some differences, this seems to me to be also the position expressed in A. Dupront, *Qu'est-ce que les Lumières?* (Paris: Gallimard, 1996), 19ff. According to Dupront, the Enlightenment and the Revolution should be viewed together not in terms of cause and effect but within a long-term historical context that had as its object a "true Revolution, which fundamentally represents the shift from a traditional form of myth (in terms of religion, of sacrality, of political and religious authority) to a new form of myth, or renewed common faith, whose strongest trait is that it does not see itself—or does not want to see itself—as mythical."

CHAPTER 11
THE TWENTIETH CENTURY AND THE ENLIGHTENMENT AS HISTORICAL PROBLEM

1. P. Hazard, *The European Mind (1680–1715)*, tr. J. Lewis May (London: Hollis & Carter, 1953), xv and xviii (original: *La Crise de la conscience européenne* [Paris, 1935]).

2. F. Venturi, "L'Illuminismo nel Settecento europeo", in *Rapports du XIe Congrès international des sciences historiques* (1960; Stockholm: Almqvist und Wiksell, 1962), 106.

3. Among the many essays that were moving in this direction, see for instance, J. P. Belin, *Le Mouvement philosophique de 1748 à 1789: étude sur la diffusion des idées des philosophes à Paris d'après les documents concernant l'histoire de la librairie* (Paris: Burt Franklin, 1913).

4. Venturi, *Utopia and Reform*, 14 (emphasis added).

5. R. Darnton, "George Washington's False Teeth," *New York Review of Books*, March 27, 1997, 34–38. For similar considerations, see also M. C. Jacob, *The Enlightenment: A Brief History with Documents* (Boston-New York: Bedford/St Martins, 2001) and, especially, J. Robertson, *The Case for the Enlightenment*, 28ff.

6. For an introduction to Venturi's work, see *Il coraggio della ragione. Franco Venturi intellettuale e storico cosmopolita*, ed. L. Guerci and G. Ricuperati (Turin: Fondazione Luigi Einaudi, 1998). See also F. Venturi, *La lotta per la libertà. Scritti politici*, ed. L. Casalino (Turin: Einaudi, 1996).

7. E. Garin, *Cronache di filosofia italiana, 1900–1943* (Bari: Laterza, 1966), vol. 1, 23.

8. Cf. Venturi, *Jeunesse de Diderot, 1713–1753*, tr. Juliette Bertrand (Paris: Skira, 1939), 10. In reviewing this work, Lucien Febvre understood clearly the originality of this new interpretation of the Enlightenment, and wrote that Venturi had assigned "a political meaning to the French philosophy of the Enlightenment [. . .] a new politics, that was dynamic and full of possibilities, at a time when traditional politics seemed sterile" (*Annales d'histoires sociale* 2, [1940], 44).

9. Despite being against any form of philosophical providentialism, Venturi always held in high esteem Croce's 1924 study of the *History of the Kingdom of Naples*, which represents a classic example of ethico-political history, as well as his two volumes on methodology, *Theory and History of Historiography* (1917) and *History as the Story of Liberty* (1938).

10. See the preface to the second edition of Venturi, *Il populismo russo* (Turin: Einaudi, 1972), vol. 1, ixff.

11. Venturi, *Utopia and Reform*, 2. As an example of this new political historiography of the Enlightenment, Venturi would point to F. Diaz's important study, *Filosofia e politica nel Settecento francese* (Turin: Einaudi, 1962).

12. Venturi, *Utopia and Reform*, 11.

13. Cf. Venturi, "La circolazione delle idee," *Rassegna storica del Risorgimento* 41 (1954), 203–222.

14. Venturi, *Settecento riformatore*, vol. 1, *Da Muratori a Beccaria* (Turin: Einaudi, 1969), xiii. The series was completed by Venturi in 1990. Volume 3 was translated into English by R. Burr Litchfield as *The End of the Old Regime in Europe, 1768–1776: The First Crisis* (Princeton, NJ: Princeton University Press, 1989). Volume 4 of Venturi's work appeared in two volumes as *The End of the Old Regime in Europe (1776–1789), Part I: The Great States of the West* and *Part II: Republican Patriotism and the Empires of the East*, both edited by Litchfield (Princeton, NJ: Princeton University Press, 1991).

15. Venturi constantly reasserted his dislike for a reductionist and deterministic history of the Enlightenment, such as that practiced in France, which he accused of being Marxist. In 1984, at a seminar organized by the Fondazione Luigi Einaudi in Turin, he again brusquely asserted:

> The concept of "mentality" as it is used by French historians and their followers is hopelessly static. An atom, a germ of a nascent political consciousness, is far more revealing and indispensable for a historian. A consciousness that is always single, individual, often original and maybe a little weird. Living in an era of revolution is hard. One is strongly tempted to take refuge in the half-shadow of collective mentality, of ideologies, of the various Churches and religions. But what counts are the innovators, as I tried to show by following the progress of men like Linguet, Brissot, Del Turco, Radishchev and many others (*Annali della Fondazione Luigi Einaudi* 19 [1985], 453).

See the account of these issues in D. Roche, "Histoire des idées, histoire de la culture, expériences françaises et expériences italiennes," in *Il coraggio della ragione*, 151ff.

16. See the publication of *Livre et société* (Paris, 1970). For similar developments in the United States, see Darnton, "In Search of the Enlightenment: Recent Attempts to Create a Social History of Ideas," *Journal of Modern History* 43 (1971), 113ff.

17. See the account of the "primauté tyrannique du découpage social" in the 1960s and 1970s in R. Chartier, "Intellectual History or Sociocultural History? The French Trajectories," in *Modern European Intellectual History: Reappraisals and New Perspectives*, ed. D. LaCapra and S. L. Kaplan (Ithaca: Cornell University Press, 1982), 13–46.

18. As we know, Cochin's 1921 *Les sociétés de pensée et la démocratie* was reprised within the historiographical debate as an example of a possible sociological interpretation of the Revolution by F. Furet in his *Penser la Révolution française* (Paris, 1978) (English version: *Interpreting the French revolution*, tr. Elborg Forster [Cambridge: Cambridge University Press, 1981]).

19. On the issue of these appropriations and of cultural consumption as a creative fact, at both the individual and the collective level, cf. M. de Certeau, *The Practice of Everyday Life*, tr. Steven Rendall, Berkeley: University of California Press, 1984 (original: *L'Invention du quotidien*, vol. 1, *Arts de faire* [Paris, 1990]). On the various theoretical foundations of the new cultural history, see *The New Cultural History*, ed. L. Hunt (Berkeley: University of California Press, 1989); *Beyond the Cultural Turn*, ed. V. E. Bonnell and L. Hunt (Berkeley: University of California Press, 1999).

20. On acculturation as historical process, dynamic concept, or act of creation, as opposed to a static cultural system used by anthropologists and sociologists to find structural laws, see A. Dupront's pioneering essay "De l'acculturation," in *XIIe Congrès international des sciences historiques*, vol. 1, *Grands thèmes* (Horn-Vienna: Ferdinand Berger & Söhne, 1965), 7–36.

21. See the way in which Clifford Geertz's theories are applied in Darnton, *The Great Cat Massacre and Other Episodes in French Cultural History* (New York: Basic Books, 1984). Among various other research strategies available to historians, we should also mention the theory of "negotiation" applied by the New Historicists. Cf. B. Thomas, *The New Historicism and Other Old-Fashioned Topics* (Princeton: Princeton University Press, 1991).

22. Cf. R. Barthes, "Histoire et sociologie du vêtement," in *Annales E.S.C.* 21 (1957), 441 (phrase as translated in P. Calefato, *The Clothed Body* [Oxford: Berg, 2004], 7). For a fundamental theoretical discussion of these issues, see P. Bourdieu's *Outline of a Theory of Practice*, tr. Richard Nice (Cambridge: Cambridge University Press, 1977; original: *Esquisse d'une théorie de la pratique* [Geneva, 1972]) and *Distinction: A Social Critique of the Judgement of Taste*, tr. Richard Nice (Cambridge, MA: Harvard University Press, 1984; original: *La Distinction. Critique sociale du jugement* [Paris, 1979]). Bourdieu's concepts of "intellectual field" and of *habitus* are useful aids for an understanding of the link between practices and representations.

23. In this connection, see Roche, *The Culture of Clothing: Dress and Fashion in the Ancien Régime*, tr. Jean Birrell (Cambridge: Cambridge University Press, 1994; original: *La Culture des apparences* [Paris, 1989]); Ferrone, "The Accademia Reale delle Scienze: Cultural Sociability and Men of Letters in the Turin of the Enlightenment under Vittorio Amedeo III," *Journal of Modern History* 70 (1998), 519–560. The project that led to the production of the volume *L'Illuminismo. Dizionario storico* was also built on these theoretical premises, which aimed at rethinking the world of the Enlightenment in a unified way and on the basis of new historical and cultural foundations, according to a definition of culture as "the set of linked and inseparable practices and representations that are common to a society as a whole." On these issues in general, see also A. Torre's polemical contribution to the debate, "Percorsi della pratica, 1966–1995," *Quaderni storici* 30, n. 89 (1995), 191ff.; and the equally polemical reply from Chartier, "Rappresentazione della pratica, pratica della

rappresentazione," ibid. 30, n. 92 (1996), 487ff., which highlights various interpretations that are possible within the new cultural history. An insightful and sophisticated example of cultural history that takes into account the interactive dynamic of representations and practices can be found in S. Cerutti, *Giustizia sommaria. Pratiche e ideali di giustizia in una società di Ancien Régime (Torino XVIII secolo)* (Milan: Feltrinelli, 2003).

CHAPTER 12
WHAT WAS THE ENLIGHTENMENT?

1. For an interesting example of how the new cultural history has tackled these specific issues, see chapter 4, "The Formality of Practices: From Religious Systems to the Ethics of the Enlightenment (the Seventeenth and Eighteenth Centuries)" in Michel de Certeau, *The Writing of History*, tr. Tom Conley (New York and Guildford: Columbia University Press, 1988; original: *L'Écriture de l'histoire* [Paris, 1975]).

2. It will be worth remembering here T. Kuhn's definition of a paradigm: "These I take to be universally recognized scientific achievements that for a time provide model problems and solutions to a community of practitioners." (*The Structure of Scientific Revolutions*, x.)

3. M. Foucault, *The Order of Things*, 309 (subsequent page references to this work are in parentheses within the text).

4. D. Cantimori, "Valore dell'umanesimo," in Cantimori, *Studi di storia* (Turin: Einaudi, 1976), vol. 2, 381. For what is still a fundamental study of these issues, see E. Garin, *Italian Humanism: Philosophy and Civic Life in the Renaissance*, tr. Peter Munz (New York: Harper & Row, 1965; original: *L'umanesimo italiano. Filosofia e vita civile nel Rinascimento* [Bari, 1952]).

5. Cf. M. Jacob, *Strangers Nowhere in the World: The Rise of Cosmopolitanism in Early Modern Europe* (Philadelphia: University of Pennsylvania Press, 2006).

6. See P. Rossi's comments on this passage in *Immagini della scienza* (Rome: Editori Riuniti, 1977), 93.

7. Cf. L. Guerci, *Libertà degli antichi e libertà dei moderni. Sparta, Atene e i "philosophes" nella Francia del '700* (Naples: Guida, 1979).

8. Cf. the entry for "Wicked" in Voltaire's *Philosophical Dictionary* (tr. William F. Fleming).

9. P. Gay, *The Enlightenment*, vol. 1, 8.

10. One of the first authors who unequivocally linked the Enlightenment secularization process and the wars of religion was E. Troeltsch, in his 1897 essay on the Enlightenment (cf. the entry for "Enlightenment" in *The New Schaff-Herzog Encyclopedia of Religious Knowledge*, vol. 4 *Draeseke-Goa*, ed. Samuel Macauley Jackson [New York: Funk and Wagnalls, 1909], 141–47).

11. The tone and the arguments of this polemic are well summarized in Diderot's letter to Voltaire of September 1762 (quoted in Gay, *The Enlightenment*, 206):

> Notre devise est: Sans quartier pour les superstitieux, pour les fanatiques, pour les ignorants, pour les fous, pour les méchants et pour les tyrans [. . .]. Est-ce qu'on s'appelle philosophes pour rien? Quoi! Le mensonge aura ses martyrs, et la vérité ne sera prêchée que par les lâches? Ce qui me plaît des frères, c'est de les voir presque tous moins unis par la haine et le mépris de celle que vous appelée l'infâme que par l'amour de la vertu, par le sentiment de la bienfaisance

et par le goût du vrai, du bon, et du beau, espèce de trinité qui vaut un peu mieux que la leur. Ce n'est pas assez que d'en savoir plus qu'eux; il faut leur montrer que nous sommes meilleurs, et que la philosophie fait plus de gens de bien que la grâce suffisante ou efficace.

12. On this, see F. Venturi's fundamental work, *L'antichità svelata e l'idea del progresso in N. A. Boulanger (1722–1759)* (Bari: Laterza, 1947).

13. On these issues, see V. Ferrone, *I profeti dell'Illuminismo. Le metamorfosi della ragione nel tardo Settecento italiano* (Rome-Bari: Laterza, 1989), 338ff.

14. Venturi, *Jeunesse de Diderot*, 24.

15. Cf. the entry for "Atheism" in Voltaire's *Philosophical Dictionary*.

16. Ibid.

17. Cf. Jacob, *The Newtonians*; Ferrone, *Intellectual Roots*.

18. Cf. the entry for "Toleration" in Voltaire's *Philosophical Dictionary*.

19. Cf. the entries for "Councils," "Faith," and "Toleration" in Voltaire's *Philosophical Dictionary*.

20. Cf. V. Ferrone, "Le radici illuministiche della libertà religiosa," in *Le ragioni dei laici*, 57ff., on the importance of Voltaire's position in the lay history of the West, and on the tendentious use of Gospel pronouncements by today's Catholic historians to claim that it was Christianity that first brought freedom to the Western world.

21. Cf. the interesting book by B. Baczko, *Job, mon ami. Promesses du bonheur et fatalité du mal* (Paris: Gallimard, 1997), 382ff.

22. It is only in the past few years that a more complex picture has begun to emerge and that more attention has been paid also to issues like progress, reason, and morality in the light of questions such as the reflection on evil and the *Angst* of eighteenth-century man. On this, see J. Deprun, *La Philosophie de l'inquiétude en France au XVIIIe siècle* (Paris: Vrin, 1979); Ferrone, *I profeti dell'Illuminismo*.

23. Cf. G. Paganini, "Scetticismo e certezza," in *Illuminismo. Un vademecum*, ed. G. Paganini and E. Tortarolo (Turin: Bollati Boringhieri, 2008), 252ff.

24. Cf. the entry for "Soul" in Voltaire's *Philosophical Dictionary*.

25. Cf. Ferrone, *I profeti dell'Illuminismo*, 260ff.

26. Cf. the entry for "Miracles" in Voltaire's *Philosophical Dictionary*.

27. Cf. especially Voltaire's pronouncements in his *Treatise on Toleration*.

28. The quotations in these pages are from Voltaire, *Letters Concerning the English Nation: "The second edition, with large additions"* (London: C. Davis, 1741), Letter 25, "On Pascal's Thoughts concerning Religion, & c.," 197–255 (paragraph and page number are given within the text).

29. Cf. R. Darnton, "Philosophers Trim the Tree of Knowledge: The Epistemological Strategy of the *Encyclopédie*," in Darnton, *The Great Cat Massacre*, 191–213.

30. It is important to remember that it was the Enlightenment itself that first developed the very idea of a scientific revolution. On this, cf. V. Ferrone, "Clio e Prometeo. La storia della scienza tra illuministi e positivisti," *Studi storici* 30 (1989), 339ff.

31. Denis Diderot, "Encyclopedia," in *The Encyclopedia of Diderot & d'Alembert Collaborative Translation Project*, tr. Philip Stewart (Ann Arbor: MPublishing, University of Michigan Library, 2002). http://hdl.handle.net/2027/spo.did2222.0000.004 (accessed March 3, 2014).

32. On these issues in general, cf. G. Gusdorf, *Introduction aux sciences humaines. Essai critique sur leurs origines et leur développement* (Paris: Les Belles Lettres, 1960); S. Moravia, *La scienza dell'uomo nel Settecento* (Bari: Laterza, 1978).

33. Cf. L. Febvre, "*Civilisation*. Évolution d'un mot et d'un groupe d'idées," in Lucien Febvre et al., *Civilisation: le mot et l'idée* (Paris: Renaissance du Livre, 1930); see also the entry "Civilizzazione" by H.-J. Lüsebrink, in *L'Illuminismo. Dizionario storico*, 68ff.

34. On the connection between civilization and the rise of modern civil society on the basis of the eighteenth-century concept of "sociability," see D. Gordon, *Citizens without Sovereignty: Equality and Sociability in French Thought, 1670–1789* (Princeton: Princeton University Press, 1994); C. Gautier, *L'Invention de la société civile. Lecture anglo-écossaise. Mandeville, Smith, Ferguson* (Paris: Presses universitaires de France, 1993).

35. Cf. Venturi, *L'antichità svelata*, 72ff.

36. Cf. P. Bénichou, *The Consecration of the Writer, 1750–1830*, tr. Mark K. Jensen (Lincoln: University of Nebraska Press, 1999; original: *Le Sacre de l'écrivain (1750–1830). Essai sur l'avènement d'un pouvoir spirituel laïque dans la France Moderne* [Paris, 1973]).

37. The most important study on these matters is still R. Darnton, *The Business of Enlightenment: A Publishing History of the Encyclopédie, 1775–1800* (Cambridge, MA: Belknap Press, 1979).

38. Cf. E. L. Eisenstein, *The Printing Revolution in Early Modern Europe* (Cambridge: Cambridge University Press, 1983).

39. Cf. Chartier, "Libri e lettori," in *L'Illuminismo. Dizionario storico*, 295ff.

40. Cf. *L'Europe et le livre. Réseaux et pratiques du négoce de librairie, XVIe–XIXe siècles*, ed. F. Barbier, S. Juratic, D. Varry (Paris: Klincksieck, 1996).

41. Cf. R. Darnton, *Édition et sédition. L'univers de la littérature clandestine au XVIIIe siècle* (Paris: Gallimard, 1991).

42. Cf. the entry "Romanzo" by Y. Séité, in *L'Illuminismo. Dizionario storico*, 309ff.

43. Cf. M. Reinhart, "Élite et noblesse dans la seconde moitié du XVIIIe siècle," *Revue d'Histoire moderne et contemporaine* 3 (1956), 21ff. See also, more generally, D. Richet, *La France moderne: l'esprit des institutions* (Paris: Flammarion, 1980).

44. Cf. H. Bots and F. Waquet, *La République des Lettres* (Paris: Belin, 1997).

45. Pierre Bayle, *A General Dictionary, Historical and Critical*, tr. J. P. Bernard et al., vol. 4 (London: James Bettenham, 1736), 207.

46. Cf. Bots and Waquet, *La République des Lettres*. For a still extremely useful account, see also M. Pellisson, *Les Hommes de lettres au XVIIIe siècle* (Paris: A. Colin, 1911), as well as D. Masseau, *L'Invention de l'intellectuel dans l'Europe du XVIIIe siècle* (Paris: Presses Universitaires de France, 1994), 16ff. Also, in support of Duclos's conclusions, cf. L. Brockliss, *Calvet's Web: Enlightenment and the Republic of Letters in Eighteenth-Century France* (Oxford: Oxford University Press, 2002).

47. Voltaire, "Men of Letters," in *The Encyclopedia of Diderot & d'Alembert Collaborative Translation Project*, tr. Dena Goodman (Ann Arbor: MPublishing, University of Michigan Library, 2002). http:// http://hdl.handle.net/2027/spo.did2222.0000.052 (accessed March 11, 2014).

48. Immanuel Kant, preface to the first edition, *The Critique of Pure Reason*, tr. J.M.D. Meiklejohn, ed. Vasilis Politis (Rutland, VT: E. Tuttle, 1993), quoted here from Chartier, "The Man of Letters," in *Enlightenment Portraits*, ed. Michel Vovelle, tr. Lydia G. Cochrane (Chicago: University of Chicago Press, 1997), 142–189 (144). This work was originally published as *L'uomo dell'Illuminismo* (Rome-Bari, 1992). Chartier's essay contains an important discussion both of this quotation and of the passage by Voltaire quoted above. Cf. also Koselleck, *Critique and Crisis*.

49. Cf. J. Brewer, *The Pleasures of the Imagination: English Culture in the Eighteenth Century* (London: HarperCollins, 1997). On the rise of consumer society in general, see

Roche, *A History of Everyday Things: The Birth of Consumption in France, 1600–1800*, tr. Brian Pearce (Cambridge: Cambridge University Press, 2000; original: *Histoire des choses banales. Naissance de la consommation, XVIIe–XIXe siècle* [Paris, 1997]).

50. Voltaire, *Letters Concerning the English Nation*, Letter 12, "On the Lord Bacon," 68–76 (69).

51. On these issues in general, cf. J. Van Horn Melton, *The Rise of the Public in Enlightenment Europe* (Cambridge: Cambridge University Press, 2001); D. Goodman, *The Republic of Letters: A Cultural History of the French Enlightenment* (Ithaca, NY: Cornell University Press, 1994).

52. Cf. Keith M. Baker, *Inventing the French Revolution: Essays on French Political Culture in the Eighteenth Century* (Cambridge: Cambridge University Press, 1990), 193. For a general survey of this issue, see E. Tortarolo, "Opinione pubblica," in *L'Illuminismo. Dizionario storico*, 283ff.

53. For an attempt to trace the history of these phenomena, cf. V. Ferrone, "The Accademia reale delle Scienze."

54. Cf. Darnton, *Gens de lettres, gens du livre* (Paris: O. Jacob, 1992), 267.

55. Cf. Chartier, "The Man of Letters," 183.

56. See W. Doyle, *The Ancien Regime* (Atlantic Highlands, NJ: Humanities Press International, 1986), 36: "The Enlightenment was an Ancien Regime phenomenon. The Revolution transformed it by wrenching it, like so much else, into a new and different shape."

57. Cf. Koselleck, *Critique and Crisis*.

CHAPTER 13
CHRONOLOGY AND GEOGRAPHY OF THE ENLIGHTENMENT

1. Cf. É. Lousse, *La Société d'Ancien Régime. Organisation et représentation corporatives* (Louvain: Éditions Universitas, 1952[2]), 133; J. Revel, "Les Corps et communautés," in *The Political Culture of the Old Regime*, ed. K. M. Baker (Oxford: Pergamon, 1990), 227.

2. Alexis de Tocqueville, *The Old Regime and the Revolution* (New York: Harper & Brothers, 1856), 30–31.

3. Ibid., 29.

4. Cf. D. Venturino, "La Naissance de l'Ancien Régime," in *The Political Culture of the French Revolution*, ed. C. Lucas (Oxford: Pergamon, 1988), 11ff.

5. Cf. W. Doyle, *The Ancien Regime*, 3.

6. See, for instance, in the English context, the controversial book by J.C.D. Clark, *English Society, 1688–1832: Ideology, Social Structure and Political Practice during the Ancien Régime* (Cambridge: Cambridge University Press, 1985). On these issues, see also J.-Y. Grenier, *L'Économie d'Ancien Régime* (Paris: A. Michel, 1997). On the persistence in time of a long European *Ancien Régime*, see A. Mayer, *The Persistence of the Old Regime: Europe to the Great War* (New York: Pantheon, 1981).

7. Cf. P. Goubert and D. Roche, *Les Français et l'Ancien Régime*, 2 vols. (Paris: A. Colin, 1991), vol. 1, *La Société et l'Etat*, 24.

8. Cf. C. Mozzarelli's introduction to the Italian version of W. Doyle's book, *L'Ancien Régime* (Florence: Sansoni, 1988), xxff.; R. Mousnier, *Les Institutions de la France sous la monarchie absolue, 1598–1789*, vol. 1 (Paris: Presses Universitaires de

France, 1974); M. Fumaroli, *L'Âge de l'éloquence. Rhétorique et "res literaria," de la Re-naissance au seuil de l'époque classique* (Geneva: Droz, 1980).

9. The following is based on data and other indications provided in L. Guerci, *L'Europa del Settecento. Permanenze e mutamenti* (Turin: UTET, 1988), which is still the best synthesis on these topics in international terms.

10. On these issues in general, see E. P. Thompson, *The Making of the English Working Class* (New York: Vintage, 1966); K. Polanyi, *The Great Transformation* (Boston, MA: Beacon, 1944). For more specific discussions of individual aspects, cf. W. H. Sewell, *Work and Revolution in France: The Language of Labor from the Old Regime to 1848* (Cambridge: Cambridge University Press, 1980); S. Cerutti, *Mestieri e privilegi. Nascita delle corporazioni a Torino, secoli XVII-XVIII* (Turin: Einaudi, 1992).

11. Cf. *Le Problème de l'altérité dans la culture européenne. Anthropologie, politique et religion aux XVIIIe et XIXe siècles*, ed. G. Abbatista and R. Minuti (Naples: Bibliopolis, 2006).

12. Cf. J. Habermas, *The Structural Transformation of the Public Sphere: An Enquiry into a Category of Bourgeois Society*, tr. Thomas Burger with the assistance of Frederick Lawrence (Oxford: Polity, 1999; original: *Strukturwandel der Öffentlichkeit* [Neuwied, 1962]). Among the numerous critiques related to this issue, see R. Darnton, *The Darnton Debate: Books and Revolution in the Eighteenth Century*, 277ff.; and R. Chartier, *The Cultural Origins*.

13. Cf. A. Lilti, *Le Monde des salons. Sociabilité et mondanité à Paris au XVIIIe siècle* (Paris: Fayard, 2005).

14. Cf. D. Roche, *Les Républicains des Lettres. Gens de culture et Lumières au XVIIIe siècle* (Paris: Fayard, 1988).

15. Cf. V. Ferrone, *La società giusta ed equa. Repubblicanesimo e diritti dell'uomo in Gaetano Filangieri* (Rome-Bari: Laterza, 2003), 21ff.

16. F. Venturi, *Utopia and Reform*, 118. Subsequent page references to this work are in parentheses within the text.

17. Robertson's case is different, though no less ambitious. His intellectual history, however, pays closer attention to the context and to the opportunities afforded by comparative history. On the one hand, Robertson's 2005 volume, *The Case for Enlightenment*, published in Cambridge under the general editorship of Quentin Skinner, directly opposed Israel's views, as it played down the historical importance of antireligious polemics in favor of a "convergence between Augustinian and Epicurean currents of thinking about the nature of man and the possibility of society which occurred after 1680" (8). Within this framework, the intellectual originality of the Enlightenment is all generically to be found in its "commitment to the study of human betterment" (32). On the other hand, Robertson's work launches a renewed attack against recent forms of social and cultural history of the Enlightenment, which were guilty mainly of having weakened the prospects of arriving at a unified view of that movement.

18. Cf. Darnton, "Two Paths through the Social History of Ideas," in Darnton, *The Darnton Debate: Books and Revolution in the Eighteenth Century*, 280.

19. Now in Darnton, *The Literary Underground of the Old Regime* (Cambridge, MA: Harvard University Press, 1982), 1–40.

20. Cf. Darnton's *Édition et sédition* and *The Forbidden Best-Sellers*.

21. Cf. Darnton, "The High Enlightenment and the Low-life of Literature," in his *The Literary Underground*, 40.

22. For a preliminary attempt at giving an overall definition of the original traits of this late Enlightenment, see Ferrone, *I profeti dell'Illuminismo*.

23. "Le règne des lettres est passé; les physiciens remplacent les poètes et les romanciers; la machine électrique tient lieu d'une pièce de théâtre." Quoted in Darnton, *Mesmerism and the End of the Enlightenment in France* (New York: Schocken, 1976[2]), 26, nt. 13.

24. Ibid., 39. Nt. 19 on this page translates the epigram thus: "Formerly Molinist/ Later Jansenist/Then Encyclopedist/And then Economist/At present Mesmerist. . . ."

25. Ibid., 165.

26. This is obviously a polemical reference to the famous inquisitorial expression *extra ecclesiam nulla salus*. These expressions, including the definition "*prophètes philosophes*," first appeared in J.-L. Carra, *Système de la raison ou les prophètes philosophes* (London, 1773), 96ff.

27. On the resounding and unexpected success of these "popular" sciences, see Ferrone, *I profeti dell'Illuminismo*, 62ff.

28. For a general picture, cf. R. Lenoble, *Esquisse d'une histoire de l'idée de Nature* (Paris: A. Michel, 1969); J. Ehrard, *L'Idée de nature en France dans la première moitié du XVIIIe siècle* (Paris: S.E.V.P.E.N, 1963).

29. Cf. D. Diderot, *De l'interprétation de la nature*, in *Oeuvres philosophiques*, ed. P. Vernière (Paris: Garnier Frères, 1967), 229ff.

30. Cf. Ferrone, *I profeti dell'Illuminismo*, 98ff.

CHAPTER 14
POLITICIZATION AND *NATURA NATURANS*

1. In 1916, the *philosophes'* emancipation project was indeed called "a magnificent revolution" by Antonio Gramsci, a writer and political theorist who had a specific interest in the process of ideological construction of cultural hegemonies in the modern world. In January 1916 he wrote an article for a socialist newspaper in Turin, *Il Grido del Popolo*, in which he advocated creating a socialist cultural hegemony:

> The latest example, the closest to us in time and thus the least alien to us, is the French Revolution. The preceding period in culture, known as the Enlightenment, a period which has been so slandered by facile critics of theoretical reason, was in fact not—or at least not entirely—a featherweight gathering of superficial, dilettante intellectuals, discoursing about anything and everything with complacent indifference, believing themselves to be men of their time only when they had read D'Alembert and Diderot's *Encyclopédie*. It was not, that is to say, simply a phenomenon of pedantic, arid intellectualism, like the one we see before our eyes now, exhibited in its full glory in the low-grade popular Universities. The Enlightenment was a magnificent revolution in itself; and, as De Sanctis acutely observed in his *History of Italian Literature*, it created a kind of pan-European unified consciousness, a bourgeois International of the spirit, with each part sensitive to the tribulations and misfortunes of the whole (A. Gramsci, "Socialism and culture," in Gramsci, *Pre-Prison Writings*, ed. Richard Bellamy, tr. Virginia Cox [Cambridge: Cambridge University Press, 1994], 10–11).

On the concept of identity as cultural fact and historical construct and process, rather than as something based on ethnical identity, like a community's fixed "essence," cf. F. Remotti, *Contro l'identità* (Rome-Bari: Laterza, 1996).

2. Cf. Michel de Certeau, "The Formality of Practices: From Religious Systems to the Ethics of the Enlightenment (the Seventeenth and Eighteenth Centuries)," ch. 4 in de Certeau, *The Writing of History*, tr. Tom Conley (New York: Columbia University Press, 1988).

3. Cf. P. Delpiano, *Il governo della lettura. Chiesa e libri nell'Italia del Settecento* (Bologna: Il Mulino, 2007); M. Caffiero, *La politica della santità. Nascita di un culto nell'età dei Lumi* (Rome-Bari: Laterza, 1996); D. Menozzi, "La Chiesa e la modernità," in *Storia e problemi contemporanei* 26 (2000), 19ff.

4. J. A. Bénard, *The French Stage and the French People, as Illustrated in the Memoirs of M. Fleury*, ed. T. Hook (London: Henry Colburn, 1841), 97. On Voltaire's triumph, see also T. Besterman, *Voltaire* (London: Longmans, 1969). Voltaire's reception at the lodge of the *Neuf-Soeures* was equally rapturous and well publicized thanks to the European gazettes: cf. L. Amiable, *Une Loge maçonnique d'avant 1789. La loge des neuf soeurs* (Paris, 1989), 46ff.

5. Bénard, *The French Stage*, 99–100. Theodore Hook's 1841 version (which is the only available English translation of this text) at times significantly alters Fleury's account [translator's note]. Cf. the French original in J.-A. Bénard dit Fleury, *Mémoires* (Paris: J. B. Lafitte, 1847), 137ff.:

> Entre les deux pièces, son buste, placé sur le théâtre, fut couronné par tous les acteurs avec des transports et un délire universel, qui dura plus de vingt minutes. Tout à coup, et d'un mouvement spontané, par l'accord d'une pensée unanime de respect, les femmes se levèrent, et se tirent ainsi debout, agitant leurs mouchoirs. On ne peut peindre l'effet de ce mouvement! Rien n'avait été préparé d'avance, et cette inspiration avait gagné tout le monde.

6. Bénard, *The French Stage*, 100–101. [Translator's note: This is an even more obvious example of how Hook "transformed" Fleury's text, in this case for obvious ideological reasons.] Cf. the original French:

> Comme la voiture tournait devant la rue du Bac, une foule d'ouvriers, bras nus, étaient sortis de leur atelier pour voir le cortège; je l'avouerai, ils ne paraissaient pas bien comprendre toute la valeur du cri littéraire. Voltaire était pour eux un philosophe, c'est-à-dire, dans leur pensée, un ennemi des prêtres [. . .]. Ils partent, se ruent sur la voiture, jettent en l'air leur bonnet, en s'écriant au milieu des autres cris: "Vive le défenseur de Calas! Vive le défenseur de Sirven!" [. . .] Le fanatisme et l'intolérance n'osèrent rugir qu'en secret, et pour le première fois peut-être, on vit l'opinion publique en France jouir avec éclat de tout son empire.

7. Cf. Ferrone, *I profeti dell'Illuminismo*, 262ff.

8. Cf. G. Baioni, *Il giovane Goethe* (Turin: Einaudi, 1996), 99ff.

9. A particularly useful discussion of this topic is found in D. Arasse, "L'Artiste," in D. Arasse et al., *L'Homme des Lumières*, ed. M. Vovelle (Paris: Seuil, 1996).

10. On this, see the pioneering study by G. Tocchini, *I fratelli d'Orfeo. Gluck e il teatro musicale massonico tra Vienna e Parigi* (Florence: Olschki, 1998) and, more general, the entry for "Musica" by W. Weber in *L'Illuminismo. Dizionario storico*, 217ff.

11. Cf. M. Delon, *L'Idée d'énergie au tournant des lumières (1770–1820)* (Paris: Presses universitaires de France, 1988).

12. Cf. J. Starobinski, *The Invention of Liberty, 1700–1789*, tr. Bernard C. Swift (Geneva: Skira, 1964; original: *L'Invention de la liberté, 1700–1789*, same publisher and date). See also and especially the entry for "Libertà" by F. Diaz in *L'Illuminismo. Dizionario storico*, 49ff., which discusses Diderot's famous defense of Raynal and *libertas philosophandi* in his

letter to Grimm of March 1781: "The common people say 'live first, then philosophize'. But he who has donned the mantle of Socrates and loves truth and virtue more than life will rather say: 'Philosophize first, and then live'."

13. Jean-Jacques Rousseau, *The Social Contract*, tr. G.D.H. Cole, book 1, chapter 4, www.marxists.org/reference/subject/economics/rousseau/social-contract/ch01.htm#004 (accessed April 5, 2014).

14. Important studies on this topic include *The Transformation of Political Culture: England and Germany in the Late Eighteenth Century*, ed. E. Hellmuth (Oxford: Oxford University Press, 1990); *Aufklärung als Politisierung-Politisierung der Aufklärung*, ed. H. E. Bödeker und U. Herrmann (Hamburg: Meiner, 1987).

15. This historical period and these events are admirably studied in F. Venturi, *Settecento riformatore*, vol. 3, *La prima crisi dell'Antico Regime (1768–1776)*; vol. 4(2), *La caduta dell'Antico Regime (1776–1789)* (Turin: Einaudi, 1979). English translation of vol. 3: *The End of the Old Regime in Europe* (see p. 190, n. 14).

16. Cf. *Analysis of the science of legislation, from the Italian of the Chevalier Filangieri*, tr. W. Kendall (London: G.G.J. and J. Robinson, [1791]), 1.

17. For an important discussion of these issues, see Venturi, *Settecento riformatore*, vol. 2, *La chiesa e la repubblica dentro i loro limiti* (Turin: Einaudi, 1976).

18. This issue was still being addressed in their contributions by the eminent scholars who were called upon by the Fondazione Einaudi in Turin to discuss the publication of the final volumes of Venturi's work. Cf. the collective volume *Settecento riformatore*, in *Annali della Fondazione Luigi Einaudi* 19 (1985), 403–454.

19. *Analysis of the science of legislation*, 64–66.

20. ". . . formée à l'ombre d'un ouvrage dont l'exécution pouvait illustrer le siècle, exerçait un dispotisme rigoureux sur les sciences, les lettres, les arts, les moeurs. Armée du flambeau de la Philosophie, elle avait porté l'incendie dans les esprits, au lieu d'y répandre la lumière: elle attaquait la Religion, les lois, la morale: elle prêchait le Pyrrhonisme, l'indépendance; et dans le temps quelle détruisait tout autorité, elle usurpait une tyrannie universelle." Cf. Diaz, *Filosofia e politica nel Settecento francese*, 187.

21. Ibid., 138.

22. Cf. A. Trampus's important study, *Il diritto alla felicità. Storia di un'idea* (Rome-Bari: Laterza, 2008).

AFTERWORD

1. Recent studies by the present author to be published in English translation include: *The Intellectual Roots of the Italian Enlightenment: Newtonian Science, Religion and Politics in the Early Eighteenth Century*, tr. Sue Brotherton, with a preface by Margaret C. Jacob (Atlantic Heights, NJ: Humanities Press, 1995); *The Politics of Enlightenment: Republicanism, Constitutionalism, and the Rights of Man in Gaetano Filangieri*, tr. with a preface by Sophus A. Reinert (London: Anthem, 2012); "The Man of Science" in *Enlightenment Portraits*, ed. M. Vovelle, tr. Lydia Cochrane (Chicago: University of Chicago Press, 1997, 190–225); "The Accademia Reale delle Scienze: Cultural Sociability and Men of Letters in the Turin of the Enlightenment under Vittorio Amedeo III," *Journal of Modern History* 70 (September 1998), 519–560.

2. An important milestone in Italian historiography is A. Momigliano, *Sui fondamenti*.

3. Cf. *L'Illuminismo. Dizionario storico*; Spanish edition: *Dictionario historico de la Ilustración* (Madrid: Alianza Editorial, 1998). French edition: *Le monde des lumières* (Paris: Fayard, 1999); Russian edition: *Мир Просвещения Исторический словарь* (Moscow: Памятники исторической мысли, 2003). This collaborative research effort also resulted in seminars and conferences that took place in Paris and Venice. Contributors included, among others, G. Klingestein, M. C. Jacob, J. Pocock, R. Chartier, J. Starobinski, G. Benrekassa, L. Hunt, D. Goodman, W. Weber, R. Birn, F. Diaz, M. Delon, E. Tortarolo, and G. Ricuperati.

4. Venturi, *Utopia*, 2–3. On Venturi's debate with Italian historians of philosophy and especially with E. Garin, for whom the Enlightenment originated from the guiding principles of the Renaissance, cf. V. Ferrone, "Eugenio Garin: il lungo illuminismo 'da Petrarca a Rousseau'" in *Eugenio Garin. Dal Rinascimento all'Illuminismo*, ed. Olivia Catanorchi and Valentina Lepri (Rome-Florence: Edizioni di storia e letteratura, 2011), 269–279.

5. Venturi, *Utopia*, 14.

6. The results of Venturi's monumental research activity on these lines of enquiry can be read in his seven-volume *Settecento riformatore*. See above, p. 189, no. 4.

7. Venturi, *Utopia*, 17.

8. J. Israel, "How to Write the Intellectual History of the Enlightenment—and the Revolution: A Critical Foray," in *Rivista Storica Italiana* 124 (2012), 1076.

9. Hence probably the joking title—"Spinoza Got It"—of Jacob's review of Israel's *A Revolution of the Mind*, which attributes the creation of the Enlightenment to ideas formulated once and for all by Spinoza (*London Review of Books*, November 8, 2012, 26–27).

10. Much of this follows on the work of Gilles Deleuze and Antonio Negri. On the political import of this surge in Spinoza studies, see Negri, *Spinoza for Our Time* (New York: Columbia University Press, 2013; original edition, Paris 2010). Negri's book constitutes the ideological manifesto of a new revolutionary Left that draws on the "subversive" character and the theoretical premiss of the "democracy of the multitude" found in Spinoza. In his study, Negri discusses Israel's contribution alongside other recent studies on the subject.

11. Indeed especially harsh criticism has been voiced by intellectual historians and historians of philosophy, including Jacob, P. Casini, S. Berti, T. Verbeek, A. La Vopa, S. Moyn, D. Edelstein, S. Stuurman. A strongly negative reaction to Israel's critique of a sociocultural history of the Enlightenment is found in A. Lilti, "Comment écrit-on l'histoire intellectuelle des lumières? Spinozisme, radicalisme et philosophie," *Annales HSS* 1 (2009), 171–206, to which Israel replied in his third volume and then in the article in *Rivista Storica Italiana* mentioned in nt. 8.

12. For a different and more cogent use of these sources, see D. M. McMahon, *Enemies of the Enlightenment. The French Counter-Enlightenment and the Making of Modernity* (New York: Oxford University Press, 2001).

13. In fact, we have known for a long time that there were profound divisions and contrasting positions within the Enlightenment, without the need for such a rigid opposition of two Enlightenments. In this respect, Israel would probably have benefited from reading an important work by one of the great historians of the Enlightenment, F. Diaz's *Filosofia e politica nel Settecento francese*, which examined for the first time in detail the clash between materialists such as d'Holbach and Diderot and deists such as Voltaire and

d'Alembert from a philosophical and historical point of view, but without calling into question the fundamental unity of the Enlightenment as a movement.

14. Israel seems entirely oblivious of the controversies caused in Italy by the way in which Catholic historians have been increasingly referring to a "Catholic Enlightenment," using a term first created in Germany at the beginning of the twentieth century by the historian of the Church Sebastian Merkle. On this, see V. Ferrone, *Lo strano Illuminismo di Joseph Ratzinger. Chiesa, modernità e diritti dell'uomo* (Rome-Bari: Laterza, 2013).

15. An interesting recent discussion of this point is found in D. Edelstein, *The Enlightenment: A Genealogy* (Chicago: University of Chicago Press, 2010).

16. It is always useful to reread carefully the definition of *Philosophe* in the *Encyclopédie*. Cf. G. Ricuperati's remarks in this respect in *L'Illuminismo. Dizionario storico*, 7ff.

17. Cassirer was no doubt right on many counts concerning the central role played by science in the form of rationality typical of the Enlightenment. However, he was wrong in his enquiry into the character and different images of eighteenth-century science, which he linked exclusively to what he saw as the prevalence of Newton's physical and mathematical paradigm and of mechanistic reductionism. On the clash between contrasting images of science within the Enlightenment, cf. V. Ferrone, *Una scienza per l'uomo. Illuminismo e Rivoluzione scientifica nell'Europa del Settecento* (Turin: UTET, 2007) and especially *I profeti dell'Illuminismo*.

18. On these issues, cf. V. Ferrone, "The Man of Science."

19. The same pronouncement is repeated without being expanded further in Israel, "Philosophy, Religion and the Controversy about Basic Human Rights in 1789," in *Self-Evident Truths? Human Rights and the Enlightenment*, ed. Kate E. Tunstall (New York: Continuum, 2012), 111ff.

20. Cf. B. Tierney, *The Idea of Natural Rights: Studies on Natural Rights, Natural Law and Church Law, 1150–1625* (Atlanta: Eerdmans, 1997), 22.

21. It is well known that none of these thinkers were in any way close to Spinoza's material monism, rather tending towards deism and the belief in a natural religion. On the importance of Rousseau and especially of his novels, which created the conditions within public opinion for empathetic and emotional acceptance of human rights, see, for instance, an important work by L. Hunt, *Inventing Human Rights: A History* (New York: Norton, 2007). Also on Rousseau, but from a different perspective, based more on the history of political ideas, see Ferrone, "Il problema Rousseau e i diritti dell'uomo. La pratica politica dei diritti tra natura e cultura, individuo e comunità, 'stato di pura natura' e società civile," in *Studi Francesi* 56 (2012), 221–256, now also a chapter in a new book based on years of research into the history of the rights of man as a modern political discourse created by the culture of the Enlightenment (Ferrone, *Storia dei diritti dell'uomo*).

22. On this, and on the positive reactions towards this perspective on the part of French historians, see T. Ménissier's preface to Ferrone, *La Politique des Lumières. Constitutionnalisme, républicanisme, Droits de l'homme, le cas Filangieri*, tr. S. Pipari (Paris: L'Harmattan, 2009).

INDEX

||||||||||||||||||||||||||

rationalism, 38, 41, 61; classical rationalism, 96–97; Kant's "great undertaking" in the modern development of, 38; Newtonian and Lockian rationalism, 164; and power, 40; scientific rationalization, 139
rationality (Western), 39; dialogue between "lay rationality" and Christianity, 48; and domination, 26
Ratzinger, Joseph, 48, 166, 180n13, 182–183n29; on the conflict between the Church and the Enlightenment. 182n27; and the "second Enlightenment," 53–54. *See also* Benedict XVI (pope)
Rawls, John, 42
Raynal, Guillaume-Thomas-François, x, 124, 139, 153
realism: Italian realism, 102; "naïve realism," 6
reason, 48; autonomy of in respect to reality, 14; "communicative reason," 26; "crisis" of, 69; deployment of instrumental reason in the Enlightenment, 37; despotism of, 36; differentiation between reason and nonreason, 36; private use of, 9; public use of, 9, 10, 116; "purposiveness" of reflexive reason, 15; scientific reason, 61; as the sole criterion of truth, 161
Reflections on the Revolution in France (Burke), 81, 145
Reformation, the. *See* Protestant Reformation, the
regalism, 128
Reign of Terror. *See* Jacobean Terror, the (Reign of Terror)
relativism, 42, 65; Christian relativism, 180n15; danger of, 66; of modern historicism, 174n11; programmatic relativism, 65
religion, 108–109, 180n13; and Enlightenment philosophy, 99–101; lasting effects of religious wars on Western society, 100; natural religion, xii, 108; "religious cleansing," 100; as the savior of the Enlightenment, 52; separation of religion and politics, 47
Renaissance, the, 35–36, 171; Hermetic tradition of, 143; mechanism of patronage in, 118; rejection of the Hermetic knowledge of the Renaissance magi, 98
Republic of Letters, the, 63, 82, 92, 97, 114, 136, 141, 49; and artists, 143; constitution of, 115; culture of the Enlightenment in, 132; Kant's opposition to the myth of, 126; meaning/definition of, 119; politicization of, 145; radicals within, 153

"republican spirit," 118
republicanism, 125, 161, 165
research hypotheses: teleological nature of, 79–80; validity of, 79
respublica christiana, collapse of in the sixteenth century, xii
respublica literaria and *respublica literaria christiana*, 114–115
Restoration, the, 60; historians of, 83
Rêve de d'Alembert (Diderot), 137
Revolution of the Mind, A (Israel), 160
Rey, Abel, 69
rhabdomancy, 136
rhetoric, 65; Aristotelian view of, 65
Ricoeur, Paul, 66
Richelieu, Cardinal, 118
Rickert, Heinrich, 68
rights of man, 111, 125, 169; language of, 151–152; natural rights, 170; principles of, xi–xii
Robertson, John, 130, 196n17
Robertson, William, 111
Robespierre, Maximilien de, 24, 81
Robinet, Jean-Baptiste-René, 137
Roche, Daniel, 62
Romanticism, 21, 27, 60
Rome (imperial), 99
Rorty, Richard, 43
Rosa, Mario, 182n27
Rosselli, Carlo, 89
Rossi, Paolo, 156, 186n20
Rousseau, Jean-Jacques, xiii, 11, 22, 28, 77, 81, 82, 91, 111, 118, 129, 153, 165; opposition of to the *Ancien Régime*, 166; *panthéonisation* of, 80; political theology of, 103; political theories of, 17; on public happiness, 122–123
Russia, 123, 129, 148
Rutherford, Ernest, 69

Saint Petersburg, 82, 134, 137
Sainte-Beuve, Charles Augustin, 81
Sallust, 99
Salons (Diderot), 144
Salvemini, Gaetano, 89
Saulchoir: Una scuola di teologia, Le (Chenu), 181n21
Schmitt, Carl, 59
science, 26, 168, 193n39, 201n17; corporative structure of the scientific community, 169; crucial transformations in during the eighteenth century, 76–77; debates concerning scientific fact, 73–74; debates concerning